SO-AWH-408

Oscar Israelowitz's

ISRAEL
TRAVEL GUIDE

5th Edition

Celebrating Israel 60th Anniversary

ISRAELOWITZ PUBLISHING

P.O.Box 228 Brooklyn, NY 11229
Tel. (718) 951-7072
e-mail: oscari477@aol.com
website: www.israelowitzpublishing.com

Copyright © 2008 by Oscar Israelowitz

All rights reserved under Pan American and International Copyright Conventions. Reproduction in whole or part without permission is prohibited. The use of a scanner or the copying of any part of this book on a personal website without permission is an international offense and will be prosecuted to the fullest extent of the law.

International Standard Book Number: 1-878741-76-4

Contents

4 CONTENTS

Welcome to Israel's Ben-Gurion Airport Terminal 3, which was designed by Moshe Safdie.

Introduction

The 2008 Edition of the *Israel Travel Guide* contains all of the information a first-time and seasoned traveler will need while staying in Israel. The guide contains detailed do-it-yourself walking and driving tours to all parts of the country, including the Old City of Jerusalem, the new city of Jerusalem, Tel Aviv, Haifa, Tiberius, Safed, Be'er Sheva, and Eilat.

The guide contains lists of restaurants, pizza shops, fast -food eateries, etc. There are lists of hundreds of hotels for all budgets (from economy to luxury), kibbutz guest houses, holiday villages, youth hostels, and bed & breakfasts.

For those interested in sport activities, Israel is the place for you. This guide contains information about horseback riding, rafting, kayaking, skiing, Israeli folk dancing, snorkeling, swimming pools, water parks, and dozens of hiking trails.

The Israel Travel Guide is divided into fourteen tours: Jerusalem–Old City Tour and New City Tour, the Judean Hills, the Dead Sea, Central Israel, Tel Aviv, South of Tel Aviv, the Negev, Eilat, North of Tel Aviv, Haifa, North of Haifa, the Galilee, and the Golan Heights. Each section contains detailed driving instructions and hundreds of exciting stops along the way. There are breathtaking views, kibbutzim, museums, water parks, historic fortresses, nature reserves, ancient synagogues, and lots of surprises.

The northern part of the country includes the Galilee, Golan Heights and the Jezreel and Hula Valleys. Some of the stops include the major cities of Haifa, Tiberius and Safed. There are stops at a museum devoted to the children who perished in the Holocaust, a hike that takes you to a beautiful spring surrounded by black basalt fluted columns, alligator and ostrich farms, thermal hot springs which were in use as far back as the Roman period, beautiful mosaic tiles on the floors of third century synagogues, boat rides on the Sea of Galilee, and skiing atop Mount Hermon.

The central part of the country might be where you will spend most of your visit to Israel. It includes Israel's largest cities, Jerusalem and Tel Aviv. There are detailed walking tours of Jerusalem's Old City with visits to the Western Wall, an archaeological dig, the Tunnel Tour, synagogues dating from the Middle Ages, the great churches and mosques, an ancient shopping mall–the Cardo, which was in use during Roman times and recently restored with exquisite boutiques, and a walk along the walls surrounding the Old City of Jerusalem. The tour of Jerusalem's new city includes stops at the Knesset, Israel Museum, Jerusalem Supreme Court, the Biblical Zoo, the new Menachem Begin Heritage Museum, the Great Synagogue and Heichal Shlomo, Museum of Islamic Art, Chagall Windows, Mount Herzl, and Yad Vashem.

The Central Israel section includes stops in and around Tel Aviv with its exciting night life. Stops include the Tel Aviv Museum of Art, Beit Hatefutsoth, the Haganah Museum, Ben-Gurion's House, the Palmach Museum, Ha'aretz Museum, Safari Park, and the Harry Oppenheimer Diamond Museum.

There are many stops along the way between Jerusalem and Tel Aviv including the Rishon Le'Zion wine cellars, the Weizmann Institute and the Atomic Reactor in Rehovot, the Stalactite Caves at Sorek, the Tombs of the Maccabees at Modi'in, and Mini Israel at Latrun.

The Dead Sea tour will take the visitor to the lowest point on the planet–1,292 feet high concentrations of salt and other minerals. The tour continues to the Qumran below sea level! You can float in its waters. Actually, it's impossible to sink due to the high concentrations of salt and other minerals. The tour continues to the Qumran Caves, site of the discovery of the Dead Sea Scrolls, to the beautiful nature reserve at Ein Gedi, with its beautiful waterfalls and hiking trails, and finally to the mountain fortress at Masada, where a group of Jewish zealots withstood the onslaught of the Roman Legions for three years.

Another section of the Israel Travel Guide contains points of interest in the southern part of the country. Stops include visits to the capital of the Negev in Be'er Sheva, the Air Force Museum, a museum devoted to bedouin culture, jeep tours in the great craters in the Negev, Ben-Gurion's kibbutz and gravesite in Kibbutz Sde Boker, the Hai Bar Nature Reserve, and the archaeological remains of two Nabatean cities.

The tour continues to Israel's southernmost city, Eilat. Stops include visits to the Coral World Underwater Observatory and underwater restaurant, where one can go underwater in a glass-enclosed bubble and see the gorgeous coral reefs and its rainbow-hued tropical fish. There are detailed hiking trails to the canyons, Timna Valley, and Solomon and Amram's Pillars–spectacular Nubian sandstone rock formations.

There's so much to see and do in Israel, so let's begin...

Travel Tips

PASSPORTS & VISAS

Every visitor to Israel must hold a valid passport. Visitors may remain in Israel for up to three months from date of arrival, subject to the visa issued. Visitors from the United States, Canada, and most Western European countries will be issued visitors' visas free of charge at the port of entry in Israel. Visas may be extended at Ministry of the Interior offices throughout Israel.

Upon arrival in Israel, visitors will present their passports and entry forms to be stamped by the Passport Control official. Persons who do not wish their passports stamped should inform the official accordingly before submitting their documents.

Note: Animals, plants, firearms, fresh meat, and raw materials may not be brought into Israel unless a permit has been secured in advance.

TRANSPORTATION FROM AIRPORT

United Tours operates a shuttle bus (No. 222) between Ben-Gurion Airport and Tel Aviv, stopping at the El Al Terminal on Arlozorov Street and the Palace Hotel on Hayarkon Street (a 20-minute ride).

The service operates every hour on the hour, from 4:00am until midnight. A similar shuttle bus service (No. 111) is available at major hotels in Jerusalem (a 45-minute ride).

Buses operated by the Egged Cooperative leave Ben-Gurion Airport every 20 minutes from the Central Bus Terminal in Tel Aviv (5:00am to 10:00pm), Jerusalem (6:30am to 8:00pm), and Haifa (7:00am to 8:00pm).

• Nesher Taxis operates a shared mini bus (called a *Shayrut*) between Ben-Gurion Airport and Jerusalem. Each person is charged a fixed rate and is taken to any location in Jerusalem. The good thing about this service is that is very reasonable. But the bad thing about this service is that the *Shayrut* holds about twelve people. You might be the last stop of the ride. It can take as long as one and a half hours until every one is dropped off before you. This can be very exhausting especially after a ten-hour flight from New York.

• There are regular taxis at the airport. They can take a passenger anywhere in the country. Fares are government-regulated. Passengers are entitled to be shown the official price list. A receipt is available if the meter is in operation. But you can always "handle" a price in advance of tho trip.

• Most car rental agencies have offices at Ben-Gurion Airport.

• There is a new station of Israel Railways right at the new terminal (Terminal 3) in Ben-Gurion Airport. There are connections to Tel Aviv, Beit Shemesh, Kfar Saba, Be'er Sheva, Ashdod, Nahariya and Jerusalem. You can take the "train to the plane." Israel Railways is constructing a new line which will run to Jerusalem via Modi'in. There will a tunnel under Canada Park and then the train will follow Route 1 to Jerusalem, below the Central Bus Station.

CURRENCY
The currency of Israel is the Shekel (IS), also called the New Israeli Shekel (NIS). Each Shekel is divided into 100 agorot. Banknotes circulate in denominations of NIS 100, 50, 20, 10 and 5 Shekalim (or Shekels). Coins are in denominations of 5 Shekels, one Shekel and 50, 10 and 5 agorot.

HEALTH REGULATIONS
There are no vaccination requirements for visitors entering Israel.

FACILITIES FOR THE HANDICAPPED
Many hotels and public institutions in Israel (including Ben-Gurion Airport)   provide ramps, specially-equipped lavoratories, telephones and other conveniences for the handicapped. The Yad Sarah Organization, with branches located throughout Israel,

provides wheelchairs, crutches, and other medical appliances on loan, free of charge.

HEALTH REGULATIONS
There are no vaccination requirements for visitors entering Israel.

FACILITIES FOR THE HANDICAPPED
Many hotels and public institutions in Israel (including Ben-Gurion Airport)   provide ramps, specially-equipped lavoratories, telephones and other conveniences for the handicapped. Tho Yad Sarah Organization, with branches located throughout Israel, provides wheelchairs, crutches, and other medical appliances on loan, free of charge.

ELECTRICAL APPLIANCES
The electric current in Israel is 220 Volts AC, single phase, 50 Hertz. Most Israeli sockets are of the three-pronged variety, but many accommodate some European two-pronged plugs as well. Electric shavers, traveling irons, and other small appliances may require adapters and/or transformers, which can be purchased in Israel.

WHAT TO PACK
Summer (April-October): Lightweight suit, slacks, shorts and open-neck shirts for men; several light cotton daytime dresses and a more formal evening dress for women. Light shoes, sandals and walking shoes or sneakers, sunglasses, light hat or cap, swimsuit and beachwear, a light coat, jacket, or sweater for cool evenings in the hills.

Winter (November-March): Warm coat, sweaters, raincoat, hat, walking shoes, overshoes, shirts, slacks, sports jacket, and suit for men; warm suit, blouses, skirts and slacks, long dress or evening skirt for women. Lighter clothing and swimsuits for Eilat and the Dead Sea.

Don't forget a small umbrella!

Additional Travel Tips

• It is best to go on an organized bus tour or with a licensed Israeli tour guide while visiting remote sections of the country.

• Always listen to the radio news reports or inquire at your hotel if there are any "trouble" spots in the vicinity of your travel itinerary. Some roads may have been closed due to security.

• If you see an abandoned package or knapsack on a bus, in a bus station, airport lounge, or even on the street, do not touch it. Call police or tell someone about it immediately. It may be a bomb!

• Be extremely careful while crossing or walking on the street or road. Israelis are noted to be terrible drivers. They will not stop their cars if a pedestrian is crossing the road. There have been more traffic fatalities on Israeli roads than fatalities in all of Israel's wars.

• There are security checks everyhere in Israel—bus stations, shopping malls, restaurants, movies, train stations, etc.

• If you are in a car, do not pick up hitchhikers. Never hitchhike.

• Do not take photographs at or near the airport, military installations, railways, or along border roads—this is for security reasons.

• Women should dress modestly in synagogues and in certain neighborhoods such as Me'a Shearim in Jerusalem or in B'nei Brak. There are usually signs in English warning women of this before entering the neighborhoods.

• If you are planning on taking city buses, you can get a bus pass or *cartisia* directly on the bus. It comes out much cheaper per ride. You can purchase a 10-ride or 30-ride ticket.

• Hold onto your bus ticket (whether you're buying one ride or multiple rides). On occasion, inspectors board the buses unexpectedly, and demand proof of payment. If you don't have a receipt, you may be fined on the spot.

• You must hold onto your railroad ticket until you reach your final station. There is a machine through which you must feed your ticket when entering and another machine as exit at your last stop. After you leave the railroad station, you may discard that used ticket.

• When traveling north of Tel Aviv by train, be aware of the only express line on the entire railroad system. It goes from the Tel Aviv University station to Binyamina (Caesarea) non-stop. So, if you are planning on going from Tel Aviv to Herzliya, Beit Yehoshua, Netanya or Pardes Channah—be sure to take a local train. Ask someone in the station if the train is express or local and take the correct train to your destination.

• Students can use the International Student Card for discounts on tours, concerts, museums, national parks, etc. Students should inquire about this card from his/her school or college back home.

• If you wish to meet the "real" Israelis, you should check out some of the Israeli folk dance sessions listed later on in this guide. Israeli folk dancing was started by the early *halutzim* or pioneers. After working long and hard hours in the fields, the kibbutzniks would entertain themselves by doing Israeli folk dancing. Today's sessions are very popular with the "locals." The sessions are designed for the intermediate to advanced Israeli folk dancer. But you don't have to know the dances to be entertained and watch the fun. The music is also wonderful—ranging from classic Israeli folk songs to Oriental Yemenite melodies. There are dance instructions (in Hebrew) usually given in the beginning of the session. Some sessions are relatively small (about 150 people) while others such as the one in Tel Aviv University on Sunday night have as many as 1,000 Israeli folk dancers of all

ages.
• When hiking throughout Israel, always carry a generous supply of fresh water. Fresh-water springs, which you are not familiar with, can be extremely dangerous. You can purify the water by using water purification tablets.
• Always wear a head covering in the sun during the summer. The sun can be hazardous. Always use a sun screen blocking lotion (#30 or higher).
• While camping or hiking look out for scorpions and snakes before sitting down, reaching up on a ledge of rocks or before putting on your shoes in the morning if they were left outdoors. If bitten by a snake or scorpion seek medical attention immediately.
• There are leopards and coyotes living in Israel's deserts. Do not try to approach these wild animals.
• There are live minefields in the Golan Heights and along the Egyptian border (near Eilat). The minefields are fenced-in and are posted with small yellow signs with red triangles. Do not attempt to cross over these protective fences!
• Do not enter a military zone without official permission. The Israeli army conducts maneuvers and training exercises along its borders, often using live ammunition!

Accommodations

HOTELS
Israel has over three hundred hotels, offering a wide choice of accommodations to suit all tastes, purposes, and budgets, ranging from small simple facilities to five-star luxury establishments, with prices varying according to grade and season.

KIBBUTZ HOTELS
The kibbutz (collective village) is a uniquely Israeli social experience, in which all property is collectively-owned and members receive no salaries, but are provided with housing, education for their children, medical services, social amenities, and other necessities. Most kibbutzim are essentially agricultural settlements, but many are shifting to a more industrially-oriented economy. There are about 250 kibbutzim throughout Israel.
Several kibbutzim, mostly in northern and central Israel, have established hotels on the premises, providing visitors with a close view of this world-renowned lifestyle. Kibbutz hotels are graded as three- or four-star establishments. They offer guests the opportunity for a relaxed, informal holiday in delightful rural surroundings. Some present special evening programs about the kibbutz experience.

HOLIDAY VILLAGES
Excellent accommodation is available at Israel's holiday resort villages. They offer a wide variety of water sports, including swimming, water-skiing, skin-diving, and sailing, as well as horseback riding, tennis, a full touring program, and evening entertainment. Predominantly geared to the younger set, with emphasis on open-air life and informality, most holiday villages are open during the summer months only.

YOUTH HOSTELS
The Israeli Youth Hostels Association, affiliated with the International Youth Hostels Association (IYHA), operates some thirty youth hostels throughout the country for guests of all ages. All offer dormitory accommodations and most also provide meals and self-service kitchen facilities. Some hostels also provide family accommodation for parents accompanied by at least

one child. Individual reservations should be booked directly at specific hostels and group reservations with the IYHA.

The IYHA also arranges individual package tours, called "Israel on the Youth Hostel Trail," for 14, 21 or 28 days. These include nights in any of 25 youth hostels, with breakfast and dinner, unlimited bus travel, a half-day guided tour, free admission to National Parks, a map, and other informative material.

FIELD SCHOOLS

The Society for the Protection of Nature in Israel (SPNI) operates a system of 26 field schools throughout Israel, each specializing in the natural history and ecology of its environment. Most also have overnight accommodations for visitors, including a dining room and other services. The field schools, generally located far from densely-populated regions, also offer a wide variety of unconventional, enlightening, and scenic desert and mountain tours. For information call (03) 537-4425.

HEALTH RESORTS & SPAS

A rare combination of unique therapeutic factors–the mineral-rich Dead Sea, therapeutic mud, sulphur, thermal mineral springs, and a mild, sunny and extremely dry climate–have made certain areas of Israel excellent year-round health resorts, internationally renowned since ancient times.

Most health resorts are centered in two main areas: the Sea of Galilee (655 below sea level) and the Dead Sea (1,286 feet below sea level). Offering a wide range of accom -

modations and equipped with modern facilities, they provide a choice of treatments for a variety of ailments and conditions.

The *Tiberias Hot Springs*, on the Sea of Galilee, provides treatment for muscular and joint diseases, traumatic disturbances and sinusitis.

Zohar Hot Springs, on the Dead Sea, provides reatment for muscular and joint diseases, traumatic disturbances, allergies, and skin diseases.

Yesha Hot Springs, on the Dead Sea, south of Kibbutz Ein Gedi, provides treatment for muscular and joint diseases.

Arad - This desert town in the Judean Hills (2,034 feet above sea level) is about a half hour from the Dead Sea. Its cool, dry, and pollen-free air makes it an ideal resort for people suffering from asthma, allergies, and breathing difficulties.

Hamei Yoav Thermal Mineral Baths is a recently-opened health spa at Kibbutz Sde Yoav, near Ashkelon. A constant stream of water rich in health-promoting minerals flows into a series of shallow pools, providing comfortable bathing facilities at varying temperatures.

NOTE: It is best to purchase a set of detailed city road maps published by Carta Maps (in English) or Atlas Zahav (in Hebrew). They are the best road maps available. They provide information about all streets in town, synagogues, museums, public buildings, bus stations, parks and gardens, shopping malls, swimming pools and sports facilities.

Acknowledgements

The Publishers wish to thank the following organizations in providing information and material used in the production of this book...

The Israel Government Tourist Office, Ministry of Defense, Jewish National Fund, The Israel Museum, Beth Hatefutsoth–Museum of the Diaspora, Yad Vashem, Museum of Printing Art, Museum of Rishon Le-Zion, Reuben and Edith Hecht Museum, L.A. Mayer Museum for Islamic Art, Haganah Museum, Archaeological Museum of Grain Handling in Israel, Tel Aviv Museum of Art, Joe Alon Center–Museum of Bedouin Culture, Museum of the Underground Pioneers–Acre, Jewish Legions Museum, Clandestine Immigration and Naval Museum, The Collection Houses, The Etzel Museum, Museum of the Underground Prisoners (Russian Compound), Beit Hashomer Museum, The Babylonian Jewry Heritage Center, Museum of Taxation, Golan Archaeological Museum, and the Ghetto Fighters' House.

We wish to thank the following people in assisting us in the production of this book:

Mark Goldberg, Batsheva Sobleman, Estee Yaari, Adi and Shlomit (Israel Museum), Shira Shein, Ofra Rimon, Rachel Hasson, Zeev Lachlish, Ronit Holzman, Shlomin Nemlich, Annemick Gringold, Dr. Zvi Yehuda, Mira Dror, Wendy Kansky, Yitzchack Dobo, Aliza Vardi, Gloria Golan, A. Coval, Israel Nisman and Brenda Guttman.

We also wish to thank the following websites for their most useful information:
www.eLuna.com   www.ilmuseums.com   www.israelhotels.org.il   www.telavivinf.com
www.aish.com www.israrail.org   www.rokdim.co.il   www.interart.co.il

Emergency Phone Numbers: Police................100
                             Medical..............101
                             Fire...................102

Historical & Archaeological Periods

3000-1200 B.C.E. Canaanite Period (Bronze Age)
1700-445 B.C.E. Biblical Period (Abraham, Isaac, Jacob)
1500-1200 B.C.E. Exodus from Egypt - Settlement of the Land of Israel
1200-300 B.C.E. Israelite Period (Iron Age)
950-922 B.C.E. First Temple built by Solomon in Jerusalem.
586 B.C.E. Destruction of First Temple (Babylonian Exile)
586-332 B.C.E. Persian Period
520 B.C.E. Second Temple in Jerusalem built.
350-167 B.C.E. Hellenistic Period
332 B.C.E. Alexander the Great conquers Israel.
167 B.C.E. Antiochus desecrates the Holy Temple.
167-37 B.C.E. Hashmonean (Maccabean) Period
165 B.C.E. Judah Maccabee recaptures Jerusalem (Chanukah).
63 B.C.E.-324 C.E. Roman Period
70 C.E. Titus destroys Temple and Jerusalem.
72 Masada falls.
132-135 Second Revolt (Bar Kochba)
135 Hadrian rebuilds Jerusalem as Aelia Capitolina and all Jews are forbidden to enter city.
200 Mishnah completed.
395-638 Byzantine Period
500 Jerusalem Talmud completed.
638-1099 Early Arab Period
1099-1291 Crusader Period
1291-1517 Mameluke Period
1516-1917 Ottoman (Turkish) Period
1538 Suleiman the Magnificent restores walls of Jerusalem.
1799 Napoleon invades the Holy Land.
1878 First modern Jewish Agricultural Settlement established in Petach Tikvah.
1888 Aliya Aleph (Bilu immigrants)
1904 Aliya Bet
1909 Establishment of Tel Aviv.
1917-1948 British Mandate Period
1920 Aliya Gimmel
May 14, 1948 State of Israel established.
1948-1949 War of Independence
1956 Sinai Campaign
1967 Six Day War
1973 Yom Kippur War
1979 Israel-Egypt Peace Treaty
1995 Israel-Jordan Peace Treaty

Tour # 1 Jerusalem
Old City Tour

Jerusalem

THE KOTEL - WESTERN WALL

This is Jewry's most sacred site and premier place of pilgrimage throughout the Exile. From the times of King Solomon to the return from the Babylonian exile and the Hashmonean period (10th to 1st centuries B.C.E.), the Temple Mount in Jerusalem was a relatively small platform built on top of Mount Moriah and its highest point was the site of the Holy Temple.

King Herod's greatest building project was to double the area of the Temple Mount by incorporating part of the hill to the northwest (which had to be levelled and on which he built the Antonia Fortress) and by filling up parts of the surrounding valleys. Herod transformed the Second Temple into an edifice of splendor and surrounded the Temple Mount on its four sides with massive retaining walls. The walls, founded on bedrock, were built of large ashlar stones with beautifully dressed margins. Each course was set back about 2-3cm from the course below it; the stones weigh some five tons each, the corner blocks tens of tons.

During the British Mandate period (1917-1948) Jews were permitted to pray at the Kotel only during a few specified hours per week. The Jordanians ruled the Old City of Jerusalem from 1948 to 1967 and did not allow any Jew to pray at the Kotel. Following the Six Day War in 1967, all houses built up to the edge of the Kotel were demolished. A new expansive plaza for prayers was created.

Moshe Safdie's plan for the Western Wall plaza called for exposing all 26 courses of massive stone blocks dating from Herodian times. At present only seven are exposed to view above ground level. As is stands today, the plaza resembles a large parking lot. Safdie's plan called for several terraces descending at nine meter intervals until the bottom course was reached. This way, a person standing on any terrace would feel close to the Kotel. Those plans were never carried out.

JERUSALEM ARCHAEOLOGICAL PARK

Excavations at the southern end of the Temple Mount have been underway since 1968. The excavations have cut through more than 3,000 years of history and include 25 layers. The Second Temple finds are the most impressive, and include the remains of an ancient staircase and the Hulda Gate through which Jewish pilgrims entered the Temple compound. Other finds include paved streets, complex water systems, synagogues, shops, and ritual baths dating from the Herodian and Byzantine periods.

The newly constructed Davidson Exhibition and Virtual Reconstruction Center is located at the entrance of the Jerusalem Archaeological Park. It is about 100 meters south of the Temple Mount complex, in the recently excavated and restored underground storage complex belonging to a 7th century C.E. Umayyad Palace.

The new center offers the visitor an in-depth archaeological and historical intro-duction to the Jerusalem Archaeological Park by means of an exhibition of archaeological objects, augmented by visual, textual and audio information. One of the highlights of this modern facility is a real-time virtual reality reconstruction of the Herodian Temple Mount as it stood prior to its destruction by Roman troops in 70 C.E. Real-time technology allows users to interact with the computer environment, enjoying freedom of movement as in the physical world.

The center uses cutting-edge visualization tools, including a powerful Silicon Graphics

Judaism's holiest site, the Western Wall or Kotel. Note the scraps of paper inscribed with private prayers lovingly placed in the crevices.

Onyx2 InfiniteReality3 computer, a high-resolution display and integration technology. This provides the audience with breathtaking three-dimensional images that are at the same time scientifically accurate.

Hours for the Jerusalem Archaeological Park are Sunday-Thursday 8:30-5:00, Friday 8:30-2:00. Hours for the Virtual Tour in the Davidson Center are Sunday-Thursday 9:00-4:00, Friday 9:00-1:00. For further information Tel. (02) 627-7550.

ANCIENT ENTRANCES
TO THE TEMPLE MOUNT

There were several entrances along the western retaining wall to the Temple Mount in ancient times. At the southern edge are the remains of Robinson's Arch. To the left of Robinson's Arch is another entrance called Barclay's Gate. It is located on the right side of today's women's section at the Kotel (just to the right of the vegetation growing on the Kotel in the women's section). The hill on the right, which leads up to the Temple Mount today, is in danger of becoming a mudslide. Plans are now underway to remove this hill and investigate what archaeological items are contained therein and construct a new metal bridge instead. Just to the left of Barclay's Gate is the Western Wall or Kotel. As you proceed to the left, there is an enclosed area along the Kotel, you will see

Above this interior space, which is used for prayer and learning, is an area known as Wilson's Arch. It served as the supporting arch for the upper main road and/or entrance to the Holy Temple. Robinson and Wilson were English supporting arch for the upper main road and/or entrance to the Holy Temple. Robinson and Wilson were English archaeologists who did extensive excavations around the Temple Mount in the 19th century.

TUNNEL TOUR

Immediately after the Six Day War, the Ministry of Religious Affairs began a project of exposing the entire length of the Western Wall. It was a difficult operation, which involved digging beneath residential neighborhoods that had been constructed on ancient structures from the Second Temple period and were built up against the Western Wall. Some residents used underground spaces as water holes or for sewage collection. The excavations required close supervision by experts in the fields of structural engineering, securing subterranean tunnels, archaeology, and of course, Jewish law.

When the Second Temple was still standing, a huge bridge connected the upper city of Jerusalem with the Temple Mount. This bridge also supported an aqueduct that brought water to the temple for use in the daily services. Wilson's Arch, which is connected to the Western Wall, has a distinctive Herodian style, is believed to be the remains of the original bridge.

The tour features an electronic three-dimensional model of the entire length of the retaining Western Wall. It features various entranceways, bridges, and arches linking the old city with the Temple Mount. What is believed to be the largest building stone in the world is located further north along the tour. It is part of a row of stones in the Western Wall known as the "Master Course." It measures 41 feet in length, eleven and one half feet in height, and is 11 to 15 feet deep. It weighs approximately 370 tons! The Western Wall was built without any mortar or cement. The massive stones of the "Master Course" were used to stabilize the entire Western Wall.

One of the most emotional parts of this tour is when the group comes to a section of the wall which is directly opposite the Holy of Holies in the Temple. People stop and pray at this location and put in notes (kvitlech) into the cracks of the wall.

The tour continues past a Hashmonean water cistern, aqueduct and a Herodian "Struthion Pool." There was a fortress located at the northwest corner of the Temple Mount. It was originally called "Baris" or Tower of Chanan'el. It is mentioned in the Book of Nechemiah. The "Baris" was used as a palace by the Hashmoneans.

The tour continues to a Herodian Street, complete with paved stones and several columns. At one time, there was an open-air promenade which ran the full length of the Western Wall–485 meters. There are piles of paving stones at the quarry at the northern end of the tunnel tour. These stones, as well as stones the size and shape similar to the Herodian stones at the Kotel, are still waiting to be laid down. Apparently, the Roman armies were rapidly approaching the city and the workers all fled.

The tour concludes at the metal turnstile exit at the Via Dolorosa. These tunnels have been excavated following the Six Day War in 1967. They were not opened into the Arab sector of the Old City until the day after Yom Kippur in 1996. The result was an immediate flare-up within the Arab population in Israel. The Arabs claimed that the Israelis were excavating directly beneath the mosque known as the Dome of the Rock on the Temple Mount. Many people were killed dur-

ing the riots which followed.
Note: Reservations are required for the Tunnel Tours. Call (02) 627-1333 for further information. Visiting hours are arranged in advance. It is recommended to have a tour guide (supplied at no extra charge) for the Tunnel Tours. Entrance to the Tunnel Tours is on the left side of the Kotel area (before you enter the "prayer" area–*before* the gate).

GATES OF THE OLD CITY
There are eight gates into the Old City...
1. JAFFA GATE, located at the start of Jaffa and Hebron Roads, is the most accessible entrance from the new city. Before 1870, the massive doors were locked at sunset every night. This was to protect the city inhabitants from bandits outside the city walls.
2. ZION GATE is closest to King David's tomb on Mount Zion. There are many bullet-holes around the Zion Gate. In May 1948, there was a major battle here. Reinforcements of Israeli troops failed to arrive in time and a few days later, the Old City fell into Jordanian hands.
3. DUNG GATE is where the Old City's trash used to be thrown. It is the closest gate to the Western Wall. It was near the Siloam Pool during the Second Temple period.
4. GOLDEN GATE (Gate of Mercy) has been walled up for centuries. According to Jewish tradition, it will be opened at the "End of Days." There are two doorways at this location. One is called the "Gate of Repentance" and the other is called "The Gate of Mercy."
5. LION'S GATE (St. Stephen's Gate) was built by Sultan Suleiman, after being told in a dream to build a wall around the entire city, unless he wanted to be killed by lions. There are carved lions above this gate.
6. HEROD'S GATE (Flower Gate) is named after the king who did extensive building in

Jerusalem. Herod's palace was located near this entrance.
7. DAMASCUS GATE is named after the road that starts here. It is inscribed by the builder, Suleiman the Magnificent. It leads to the oriental market in East Jerusalem. It was once the most neglected entry point into the Old City. It was the site of a major taxi stand for many years. In the 1980s, the plaza was restored and redesigned into a terraced landscape garden.
8. NEW GATE was opened in 1889 to facilitate access to the Old City's Christian Quarter. This gate was sealed from 1948 to 1967 since the international boundary between Israel and Jordan was located along Ha'tsankhanim Street. It was called "No Man's Land." The Mandelbaum Gate was nearby.

RAMPARTS WALK
It is possible to walk along the ramparts of the Old City walls. The Jaffa Gate to the Damascus Gate section includes a visit to the ancient Roman Gate, excavated under the Damascus Gate. This walk is very popular during the fast day of Tish'a Ba'av, which commemorates the destruction of the two Holy Temples on the same day.

TOWER OF DAVID
(Museum of the City of Jerusalem)
Just inside Jaffa Gate, which serves as the main entrance to the Old City from west Jerusalem, is the Citadel or Tower of David. In reality, the structure has little to do with King David; it was built by Herod who named its three towers after his wife Mariamne, his brother Phaesal, and his friend Hippicus. It was so impressive that Titus let it stand after burning the city. The Mamelukes and later Suleiman reinforced it, adding its familiar minaret.
The museum's permanent exhibition is

Just to the left of the Kotel is an interior space which is used for prayer and study. The blue wall on the extreme left marks the beginning of the Tunnel Tour. Wilson's Arch is above this space.

housed in several guard rooms of the old Citadel, and tells the eventful 3,000-year-long story of Jerusalem. Each room is devoted to a particular period and highlights the central events of the time. The exhibit embraces a wide range of visual aids like models, replicas, holograms, dioramas, and various media techniques. Hours are Sunday-Thursday 10:00-4:00, Saturday & Holidays 10:00-2:00. For further information Tel. (02) 626-5333.

CHAMBER OF THE HOLOCAUST
The Chamber of the Holocaust is located in a cellar of a building at Zion Gate near King David's Tomb. The candle-lit room is dedicated to the six million Jews who perished during the Holocaust. There are one thousand tablets commemorating all of the European communities which are bereft of Jews due to the Nazi regime. Hours are Sunday-Thursday 8:00-5:00, friday 8:00-1:00. For further information Tel. (02) 671-6841.

BURNT HOUSE OF KATHROS
This was the home of the Bar-Kathros, *cohain* or priest who lived during the Second Temple period. The Temple was destroyed in 70 C.E. by Titus. This house was also "burnt"

at that time. The charred wood, broken pottery, and furnishings offer vivid evidence of the last moments of ancient Jewish life. A stone scale has the name of the priestly family, Kathros, which lived in this house. There is a skeletal arm of a woman in the kitchen who apparently was struggling to escape the fire. The Burnt House is located beneath a modern building in the Jewish Quartor of the Old City. The Burnt House is located at Seven Arches. Hours are Sunday-Thursday 9:00-5:00, Friday 9:00-1:00. For further information Tel. (02) 287-3211.

CARDO MAXIMUS

The Romans designed their cities with a "Cardo" (literally, a heart). The Cardo was a major boulevard with porticos and shops on either side. A sixth century mosaic map of Jerusalem, which was found in 1897 in Madaba, Jordan, depicted the Cardo running from what is known today as the Damascus Gate in the north towards the Zion Gate in the south. It was an impressive boulevard–72 feet wide, with a central roadway of 36 feet, and a colonnade of 18 feet on each side.

The restoration project is 590 feet long. It consists of a housing complex above the Cardo with 37 apartments. The construction program "from the top down" was devised to complete the residential units early. A superstructure to carry the residences was built, enabling archaeologists to continue work while construction of the units above took place.

The Cardo is accessed primarily on the eastern side, from the lower level, from Street of the Jews. It has modern shops set into the old vaults, and an array of archaeological displays. These include portions of the walls of the city from the Israelite and Hashmonean periods, a great hall and façade of a Crusader building, and an exposed section of the Cardo, serving an open courtyard.

ROMAN SQUARE MUSEUM

The Roman Square Museum is located at the Damascus Gate. The museum displays a copy of the sixth century Madaba Map (from Madaba, Jordan), which is the earliest extant blueprint of Jerusalem's layout. It shows the Cardo Maximus, the main thoroughfare lined with Roman columns. The map has aided archaeologists in concluding that the Cardo recently unearthed in the Jewish Quarter is not part of the Roman original, but a Byzantine addition. Hours are Saturday-Thursday 9:00-4:00, Friday 9:00-2:00.

WOHL MUSEUM (Herod's Mansions)

This museum contains archaeological excavations of the wealthy residential quarter of Herodian Jerusalem. On display are mosaic floors, mikvehs, bathhouses, stone furniture, and ornamental artifacts. Hours are Sunday-Thursday 9:00-5:00, Friday & Holidays 9:00-1:00. For further information Tel. (02) 628-3448.

THE ISRAELITE TOWER

There are remains from the destruction of the First Temple in 586 B.C.E. There is a tower of the wall gate from the Babylonian siege and late Hashmonean fortifications. Hours are Sunday-Thursday 9:00-5:00, Friday & Holidays 9:00-1:00. For further information Tel. (02) 628-8141.

SIEBENBERG HOUSE

When the Siebenberg family began renovating their home in the Jewish Quarter, they found the remains of ancient dwellings, aqueducts, and burial vaults dating back to the days of King Solomon as well as the Second Temple period. There is a brief slide presentation followed by a tour of the excavations in the basement which includes water cisterns, mikvehs, royal burial chambers and mosaic tiles dating back three thousand years. Tours are by reservation only. The Siebenberg House is located in the Old City Jewish Quarter at 5 Beit Hasho'eva Alley. For further information Tel. (02) 628-2341.

TEMPLE INSTITUTE

There is a copy of the Ark of the Covenant and of gold and silver vessels used in the Holy Temple. There are also audio-visual presentations. The Temple Institute is located at 19 Misgav Ladach Street. For further information call (02) 689-4119.

FOUR SEPHARDIC SYNAGOGUES

The synagogue of Rabbi Yochanan ben Zakkai, Elijah the Prophet, the Central Synagogue, and the Istanbuli Synagogue were built in 1586 by Sephardic Jews who were fleeing the Spanish Inquisition. The Muslim law warned Jews that their synagogues must not be taller than the surrounding houses. In order to achieve a "lofty" interior, the synagogues were entrenched deep underground.

It has been said that when the Messiah arrives, he will enter the synagogue of Elijah the Prophet, blow the shofar which is kept

A vaulted window in the four Sephardic synagogues with stained-glass globes.

Construction underway of the new Hurva Synagogue in the Old City of Jerusalem.

for him high on a window ledge, and announce the Redemption. He will then take a cruse of oil, which is also kept there, and light the menorah in the Holy Temple.

Rabbi Yochanan ben Zakkai prayed in the synagogue which bears his name. Rabbi Yochanan lived during the time of the Roman conquest of Jerusalem and requested from the Roman commander to permit the opening of a yeshiva in the town of Yavneh. The Elijah the Prophet and Istanbuli ('Stanbuli) Synagogues contain exquisite 16th century Arks removed from Renaissance-period synagogues in Livorno and Pesaro, Italy. During the War of Independence, the Jordanians used these synagogues as a garbage dump. They have all been restored and are used daily.

HURVA SYNAGOGUE

Plans to build the Hurva Synagogue began in 1700, when Rabbi Yehuda Ha'chassid came from Poland with hundreds of his students. He started building a synagogue next to the Ramban Synagogue but died shortly thereafter. His unfinished synagogue became known as the Hurva (ruined) Synagogue.

In 1850, a majestic domed synagogue was constructed on this site. It was totally destroyed by the Jordanians in the War of Independence. Since the 1970s, all that remained of that beautiful synagogue was a solitary white limestone arch. The noted American architect, Louis Kahn, was commissioned to design a new Hurva Synagogue following the liberation of the Old City in the Six Day War. His exciting preliminary plans and sketches have been put "on hold," since the architect's death in the early 1970s. In 2007, a "new" Hurva Synagogue is being built in the original domed design on this site.

OLD YISHUV COURT MUSEUM
This museum belongs to the Weingarten family, whose ancestors lived here in the 19th century. The living quarters, household items, a baby's cradle and kitchens are all original. Two synagogues located in this house, Ohr Ha'chayim and Ari Ha'kadosh, have been restored. In 1534, the famous Kabbalist, Rabbi Yitzchok ben Shlomo Luria, was born in one of the ground-floor rooms.
The museum is located at 6, Or Hayim Street. Hours are Sunday-Thursday 9:00-2:00. For further information Tel. (02) 628-4636.

RAMBAN SYNAGOGUE
Rabbi Moshe ben Nachman (the Ramban) arrived in Jerusalem in 1267 after being threatened with death by the Catholic Church in Spain. He renovated an ancient synagogue which dated from the Ga'onic period. This synagogue is still in use. It is located on Ha'yehudim Street.

LAST BATTLE FOR THE OLD CITY MUSEUM
On May 28, 1948, the Jewish Quarter in the Old City of Jerusalem Quarter in the Old City of Jerusalem fell into the hands of the Jordanian Legionnaires. Photographs of John Philips, who accompanied the Jordanian Army, depict the surrender of the Jews and all its aspects. There are images

of the total destruction of the ancient synagogues and Jewish institutions in the city. There are also photographs showing the restoration projects following the Six Day War. Hours are Sunday-Thursday 9:00-5:00, Friday 9:00-1:00. For further information Tel. (02) 628-8141.

LEV HAROVA
This museum contains a photographic exhibit about life in the Jewish Quarter during the War of Independence. There is an audio-visual show about the rebuilding of the Jewish Quarter following the Six Day War. Lev Harova is located on Street of the Jews, adjacent to the Cardo. Hours are Sunday-Thursday 9:00-5:00, Friday 9:00-1:00.

DAVID PALOMBO MUSEUM
The Palombo Museum displays works by the noted Israel sculptor, David Palombo. He crafted the entry gate to the Knesset and contributed works to Yad Vashem. The museum is located on Mount Zion. Hours are Sunday-Thursday 9:00-1:00, Friday 9:00-11:00. For further information Tel. (02) 671-0917.

YESHIVA PORAT YOSEF
Moshe Safdie was approached by the dean of this yeshiva overlooking to Kotel. He was asked to design a series of stained-glass windows for his new Hebrew school building. The architect informed the rabbi that the origins of stained-glass windows come from the Gothic cathedrals in Europe, and is in reality, a Christian concept. The dean insisted on stained-glass windows, so Moshe Safdie decided on an innovative solution. He would design a series of glass domes and skylights. A glass prism would be installed in the center of each dome. When the sunlight struck the prisms, the rays would be refracted into the colors of the rainbow, the spectrum–from red to violet. On overcast days, there would be no light refraction, and it would just create a natural white color.

RUINS OF TIFERETH ISRAEL
In the late 18th century the first Ashkenazic Chassidim arrived in Hebron. They moved to the Old City of Jerusalem in the 19th century. The owner of the first Hebrew printing press in the city, Rabbi Israel Bak, purchased land to build a magnificent synagogue for these people. The huge synagogue was built but without the final dome since contributions ran out. In 1869, the Austrian emperor, Franz Josef visited Jerusalem, after having participated in the opening of the Suez Canal. He desired to visit some of his Jewish Chassidic subjects. When he was shown the beautiful unfinished synagogue he inquired why it had no dome. The reply he received was, "Your majesty the Emperor, the synagogue has doffed its hat for you." The emperor took the hint and donated the necessary funds to complete the dome.

Tifereth Israel was officially inaugurated in 1872. It was named after Rabbi Israel of Ruzhin, the founder of the Ruzhin and Sadagora Chassidic dynasties. Its design was modeled after the ancient synagogue at Bar'am, in northern Israel.

The synagogue was used as a position for the defenders of the Jewish Quarter during the War of Independence. At 1:00am on May 21, 1948, the Jordanian army dynamited the Tifereth Israel Synagogue. To this day, the ruins are kept intact as a memorial to those who died defending the Old City in 1948.

THE WIDE WALL
Remnants of the wall King Hiski'yahu built in the 8th century B.C.E. to guard against attack from Sanheriv, King of Assyria are located at the intersection of Tifereth Israel

Map of the Jewish Quarter in the Old City Of Jerusalem

written and edited by Yael Mali | translated by Avi Goodman | graphic design: Ayelet Tikotzky

Bikur Cholim Hospital

The Western Wall

The Hurva Square

The Open Cardo

Yeshivat HaKotel

Yeshivat Porat Yoseph

Batei Machaseh Square

Private Parking

Batei Machaseh Road

27 The "Tekuma" Park

Museums

1. Wohl Archaeological Museum - the Herodian Quarter
2. The Burnt House
3. The Israelite Tower
4. The Cardo
5. The 1949 Jewish Quarter Defender's Exhibition
6. The 1948 Jewish Quarter Battle Memorial Site
7. Old Yishuv Court Museum
8. The Western Wall Tunnels

9. The Temple Institute
11. the Siebenberg house
16. Model of Jerusalem in the First Temple Period

Guided tours (and activities)

12. Genesis Jerusalem
13. Archaeological Seminars
14. The Hymie Moruss Community Center and Visitors Center for people with special needs
15. The Ben tzvi Institute

Historical sites

17. The "Hurva" Synagogue
18. the "Wide Wall"
19. Remains of "Tiferet Yisrael" Synagogue
20. The Four Sepharadic Synagogues
22. Memorial for the defender and inhabitants of the Jewish quarter in 1948
23. The Rothchild House-offices of the Company for Reconstruction and Develpment of The Jewish quarter
24. Batei Machaseh Square
25. Remains of German Crusader Hospice
26. Remains of the Byzantine period "Nea" Church
27. The "Tekuma" Park
28. The Synagogue of the "Holy Ari" and the "Our Hachayim" Synagogue

and Plugat Ha'kotel Streets.

RACHEL YANAIT ben TZVI CENTER
One can find a model of Jerusalem as it was during the period of the First Temple. There are exhibits of archaeological finds dating back to King David's time and a light and sound show of the City of David and Jerusalem during Biblical times. Hours are Sunday-Thursday 9.00-4.00. For further information Tel. (02) 628-6288.

YARD SETTLEMENTS MUSEUM
This museum reflects the life of the old settlements from the 8th century until the Jewish Quarter fell to the Jordanians in 1948. Hours are Sunday-Thursday 9:00-2:00. For further information Tel. (02) 628-4636.

MUSEUM OF PSALMS
Artist Moshe Tzvi Berger has spent the last several years painting his interpretation of all of the Psalms. The Museum of Psalms is located at 9, ha-Rav Kook Street in the Old City. Hours are Sunday-Thursday 10:00-4:00, Friday 10:00-1:00. For further information Tel. (02) 623-0025.

THE MURISTAN
This was the residence of the Hospitaler knights, who had moved here from the Temple Mount. This order, established during the First Crusade, is also called the Order of St. John. These knights, entrusted with caring for the health of the Crusaders and pilgrims, erected a hospital here. It was deserted in the 16th century. It is located on Muristan Street.

VIA DOLOROSA
This was the way followed by Jesus bearing his cross on his back to the place of crucifixion. This is one of the holiest sites in Christianity. From the 8th to the 12th century, the procession began from the room of the Last Supper on Mount Zion, and proceeded north of Golgotha. The present route of the Way of the Cross was set in the Crusader period, in the 13th century. It begins at St. Stephen's Gate and winds its way westward towards the Church of the Holy Sepulcher. This is the route Jesus walked from the place of his trial to the place of his crucifixion. There are 14 stations on the Via Dolorosa, nine along the route and five inside of the Church of the Holy Sepulcher.

CHURCH OF THE HOLY SEPULCHER
The Church of the Holy Sepulcher is held by Christian tradition to mark the location not only of Jesus' tomb but also of the Crucifixion on Golgotha (Cavalry). The Christian community of Jerusalem held liturgical ceremonies at the Holy Sepulcher as early as 66 C.E.

MUSEUM OF THE FRANCISCAN CONVENT
This museum contains artifacts from collections of ancient Christian sites. There is a 17th century model of the Church of the Holy Sepulcher. Hours are Monday-Saturday 8:00-11:45 & 2:00-4:00. Admission is free. This museum is located in the Muslim Quarter in the Churches of Blame and Flagellation at the Second Station on the Via Dolorosa. For further information Tel. (02) 628-2936.

ARMENIAN MUSEUM
The Armenian Museum is located in St. James Street in the Armenian Quarter of the Old City. The museum contains thousands of artifacts arranged in thirty rooms. There are ancient maps, jeweled crosses, miters, mosaics, woodcuts, household and agricultural objects, and rare manuscripts. Hours are Monday-Saturday 9:30-4:30. For further

information Tel. (02) 628-2331.

GREEK ORTHODOX MUSEUM
The Greek Orthodox Museum is located in the Christian Quarter of the Old City. It is housed in a 12th century restored building. The museum contains antiquities, archaeological artifacts, and liturgical objects of the Holy Land. There are sarcophagi found in the so-called "Herod Family Tomb." Visits are by prior arrangement only. Call (02) 628-4917 for further information.

KING DAVID'S TOMB
To reach King David's tomb, walk out the Zion Gate, proceed down a narrow alley bounded by high stone walls and turn left. Near King David's tomb is a doorway and flight of stairs leading up to the Upper Room or Coenaculum. This is the site where Jesus sat with his disciples to celebrate his "Last Supper," the Passover *seder.*

SOLOMON'S QUARRIES
(Caves of Zedekiah)
Solomon's Quarries, located near the Damascus Gate, is said to have been used as escape route by King Zedekiah fleeing from the Babylonians. It was also the quarry from which the stones for Solomon's Temple were taken. The entrance to the quarries is located between Herod's and the Damascus Gates.

ABSALOM'S & ZECHARIAH'S TOMBS
These magnificent tombs are located just below the eastern walls of the Old City. They date from the Second Temple period. Absalom was the son of King David. The tomb of Zechariah the Prophet is built like a pyramid, with three pillars on its side. These tombs are located in the Qidron Valley, at the foot of the Mount of Olives. This is the place where all of the dead will arise when the Messaiah arrives.

MOUNT OF OLIVES
Between the eastern walls of the Old City and the Mount of Olives are several important Christian sites...
• The Church of the Agony is where Jesus prayed before being arrested.
• The Garden of Gethsemane is where Judas betrayed Jesus.
• The Chapel of the Ascension marks the spot where Jesus ascended into heaven.

HEZEKIAH'S TUNNEL
The Gihon Spring has been the sole source of water since the early Bronze Age. It is unique in that it is a pulsating spring and gushes water, instead of producing steadily flowing water. Three tunnels channeling this water were dug over the centuries. King Hezekiah dug one tunnel in 700 B.C.E. to link the Gihon Spring, outside the city walls, with the Pool of Siloan within. The pool today waters the fields of Silwan, the nearby Arab village, which contains remains from Biblical and Second Temple periods.
The Siloan Channel is believed to have been built during King Solomon's reign in the 10th or 9th century B.C.E. The Siloan Channel originates in the Gihon Spring, travels down the Kidron Valley and empties into the Siloan Pool. In 1867, a British officer Charles Warren discovered an underground water tunnel system. It has become to be known as Warren's Shaft. The system consists of four parts: the stepped tunnel, the horizontal curved tunnel, the 14-meter vertical shaft, and the feeding tunnel.
Note: Do not attempt to tour these tunnels on your own. They should be toured only with a group and tour guide. For further information Tel. (02) 628-8141. Hours are Sunday-Thursday 9:00-5:00, Friday 9:00-1:00.

CABLE CAR MUSEUM
A cable extended from a room in 17, Hebron

Road to the bottom of the Valley of Hinom. This was during the War of Independence. The Jewish defenders operated a cable car along this cable and transported food, gear, and the wounded. The cable was lifted (and made tight) at night and lowered during the day so they would not be spotted "air-lifting" supplies by the Jordanian army. Hours are Sunday-Thursday 9:00-4:00, Friday 9:00-1:00.

Outer wall of the Old City of Jerusalem, near the Kotel.

Tour #2 Jerusalem
New City Tour

AGRICULTURAL MUSEUM

This museum demonstrates agricultural methods from ancient times to the present. It is located at 13 Heleni Ha'malka Street. The building was originally built to house Russian Orthodox pilgrims before the Bolshevik Revolution. Hours are Sunday-Friday 8:00-1:00. Take BUS #5, 6, 18, 21.

AMMUNITION HILL MUСEUM

This hill, known as Giv'at Ha'tach'moshet, was the site of a major battle in the Six Day War. Before the war it was Jordan's most fortified strategic position in the city, controlling much of northern Jerusalem and the approaches to Mount Scopus. It was captured by Israeli troops in a bloody battle. The museum is housed in a reconstructed Jordanian bunker. Hours are Sunday-Thursday 8:00-6:00, Friday 8:00-2:00. For further information Tel. (02) 582-8442. Take BUS #4, 9, 25, 26.

BEIT AGNON

This is the house of S.Y. Agnon, winner of the Nobel Peace Prize for literature. It contains his study and extensive library, pictures, a display of his books, and a reproduction of his Nobel Prize certificate. The Beit Agnon is located at 16, Rechov Klausner in the Talpiyot section. Hours are Sunday-Thursday 9:00-12:00. The nearest bus is #7.

BELZER BAIS HA'MEDRASH

The Belzer Bais Ha'medrash is the great synagogue belonging to the Belzer Chassidim. It was designed to be a replica of the Great Belzer Synagogue which was destroyed by the Nazis during World War II. Some people say that this is one of most beautiful synagogues in the world. There are members of the Belzer Chassidim throughout the world, including New York, Montreal, London and Antwerp. The Belzer Bais Ha'

medrash is located on Shamgar Street in the Kiryat Belz section. Inquire about tours inside the ground floor facilities.

BIBLE LANDS MUSEUM

The Bible Lands Museum is located opposite the Israel Museum on Granot Street. Ancient artifacts chronicle the civilization and lands during the Biblical period. There are multimedia interactive computer programs as well as educational and musical programs for adults and children. This museum houses the private collection of Dr. Elie Borowski, an antiques collector from Canada.

There are lecture programs on Wednesday evenings and Saturday nights feature music, wine, and cheese programs. Hours are Sunday-Tuesday & Thursday 9:30-5:30, Wednesday 9:30-9:30, Friday 9:30-2:00. The Bible Lands Museum is located at 25, Granot Street. The nearest bus lines are #9, 17, 24. For further information Tel. (02) 561-1066.

BIBLICAL ZOO

An imaginatively landscaped zoological park built on 62 acres surrounded by mountains and a glorious view. The Tisch Family Zoological Gardens have a central lake and monkey islands. Visitors can view a wide variety of animals in spacious enclosures without any bars. There are species mentioned in the Bible as well as rare and endangered species. There is a Bibleland Wildlife Preserve,
and African and South American enclosures. There are small animals from the desert to the rainforest, a large aviary, a penguin exhibit, and Lemur land. Be sure to see the computerized Visitors Center. There is a zoo train for the kids (except on Saturday). The schedule for feedings of animals on Saturday is as follows: 11:30-chimpanzees; 12:00 - penguins; 1:00-bears; 1:30-giraffes,

The Belzer Bais Hamedrash was modeled after the one destroyed during the Holocaust in Europe.

2:00-lions; 3:00-lemurs. Petting the animals is daily from 11:00-4:00.

The Biblical Zoo is located near the Jerusalem Mall (Canyon) in the Manhat section. Hours are Sunday-Thursday 9:00-5:00, Friday & Holidays 9:00-3:00, Saturday 10:00-5:00. For further information Tel. (02) 643-0111.

BLOOMFIELD SCIENCE MUSEUM

The Bloomfield Science Museum is located near Hebrew University at Giv'at Ram. This is an interactive museum with "hands-on" scientific and technological experiments. One of the exhibits deals with the celebration of motion–the physical laws that guide movement.

Hours are Monday-Thursday 10:00-6:00, Saturday 10:00-3:00. The nearest bus lines are #9, 28. For further information Tel. (02) 654-4888.

BOTANICAL GARDENS

The Botanical Gardens are located on Burla Street on the campus of Hebrew University in the Givat Ram section. The gardens were opened in 1953 as a scientific project of the university. They are located at the southern end of the campus. Hours are Sunday-Thursday 10:00-2:00. For further information Tel. (02) 679-4012. There are Botanical Gardens in the Mount Scopus campus of the Hebrew University as well.

CHAGALL WINDOWS

The Chagall Windows are located in the synagogue of the Hadassah Medical Center in the Ein Kerem section. The synagogue was built in 1962. The glorious stained-glass windows represent the twelve tribes of Israel. Tours of the Chagall Windows are given Sunday-Thursday at two separate time slots, 8:00-1:15 and 2:00-3:30. For further information Tel. (02) 677-6271.

DOLL COLLECTION

There is a large collection of dolls dressed in national costumes from all over the world. This collection is housed in the International Cultural Center for Youth (ICCY). They are located at 12-A Emek Refa'im Street. Hours are Sunday-Friday 8:00-3:00.

THE GREAT SYNAGOGUE

The Great Synagogue of Jerusalem is located just to the right of Heichal Shlomo on King George Street. The cornerstone was laid in June, 1969. The interior design incorporates elements of a Sephardic synagogue and creates a theater-in-the round effect. Yet, the service itself follows the Ashkenazic ritual and includes the world's best cantors and a 30-man professional choir.

As one enters the building on street level, one passes a collection of hundreds of *mezuzot* which were donated from Jewish communities around the world. Those communities also donated the millions of shekalim which were used in the construction of this Great Synagogue. As one proceeds up the staircases one enters the main sanctuary. There are glorious white marble finishes throughout the building. The Ark consists of three openings, each containing no less than ten Torahs adorned with the finest silver ornaments. There is a 60-foot-high stained glass window along the Eastern wall above the Ark depicting the creation of the earth.

When Cantor Naftali Herstik recites the closing verses of *uve'nucha yo'mar* (while putting the Torah back into the Ark) in a falsetto intonation (*kope shtimmel*), and the choir accompanies in a very soft-spoken dialogue, it is as if the angels are singing! It is quite breathtaking.

Sometimes after Sabbath morning services, the congregation is invited downstairs for a kiddush. Not many people are aware that

Feeding the swans in the Jerusalem Biblical Zoo.

Friendly sculptural creatures covered with mosaic chips in Jerusalem's Biblical Zoo.

the "kiddush room" is actually the synagogue's bomb shelter. There are no windows, but it is decorated quite handsomely. That space is also used as the daily *beit ha'medrash* (chapel).

Be sure to visit the Yeshurun Synagogue, just up King George Street. It was designed in the mid-1930s in the Bauhaus style and served as the "Great" Synagogue before the present one was completed. They still have visiting cantors.

HAAS PROMENADE

The Haas Promenade is located in the North Talpiot section. One can see Jerusalem in all its glory–the Old City walls, the New City, and the ancient villages. They all blend into one panoramic view of this glorious city. The Hass Promenade is just east of Derech Hevron, at the intersection of Daniel Yanovsky.

HALL OF HEROISM
(Heichal Ha'gvurah Museum)

The Hall of Heroism is located in the Russian Compound. It was once the world's largest hotel, accommodating as many as 10,000 Russian pilgrims to the Holy Land. Following the Revolution of 1917, the Russian church went bankrupt and then rented the facilities to the British. The British transformed the compound into a maximum

Elegant mansion along Ha'nevi'im Street.

security prison for the entire country. Members of the Jewish underground, from the Haganah, Etzel, and Lehi, were imprisoned here. The original prison yard, cells, and gallows are still intact. Be sure to see the escape tunnel used by Jewish underground fighters.

The Russian Compound housed Israel's Supreme Court from 1948-1992. The Supreme Court moved to its new home next to the Knesset in 1992. The Russian Compound is located near Jaffa Road (turn northeast at Chesin Street). It is near the New City Hall complex at Safra Square. Hours are Sunday-Thursday 9:00-4:00, Friday 9:00-1:00.

HA'NEVI'IM STREET

Jaffa Street has been a major commercial thoroughfare for more than 150 years. The Street of the Prophets, Ha'nevi'im Street, which runs parallel to Jaffa Street on the north, from the Damascus Gate to the Davidka Square, is quite another story. It was called the "Street of the Consuls" by the inhabitants of the city, because of the many foreign consulates located on it. It was also known as the "Street of the Hospitals," because of the hospitals flanking it.

This was a very prestigious location and many famous people had residences on this street including the researcher of Jerusalem, Conrad Schick; the English painter, Holman Hunt; the poetess, Rachel; Empress Zaudito; and Baron Edmond de Rothschild. In the late 1980s, there were several plans to widen the street or to build a major highway along this route. These plans were met with stiff opposition.

HECHT SYNAGOGUE -
HEBREW UNIVERSITY (Mount Scopus)

Mount Scopus is the site of Jerusalem's premier university, the Hebrew University. It was designed in the 1930s by the noted architect, Eric Mendelsohn. The old Hadassah Hospital was located on this mountain as well. Mount Scopus' location has made it a valuable goal in many famous battles of the city. There are outstanding views of the Old City from this location. If you look east, you will see an unbelievable view of the Judean Desert.

The Hecht Synagogue is located in the "Ruach" Building (Section 3). It is located near the main dining hall. It may be a bit hard to find. But if you go around 4:00pm, afternoon prayers (*mincha*) are held daily. You will see people with kippot going in for services. Just ask them where the shul is. Once you're in this Hecht Synagogue, you won't believe your eyes. Instead of an Ark along the western wall of the synagogue (since this synagogue is on the east side of the Old City, one is required to face towards the Kotel–in this case, one would be facing west!), there is a very large picture window. You are looking out at the Old City from the east. It's just spectacular. There are two mini-Arks on either side of the picture window which contain the Torahs. The women's section is located upstairs, behind the oversized circular cut-outs.

To the left of the Old City, there is a volcanic-shaped mountain in the distance. That is Herodion, the man-made palace and fortress designed by King Herod. It is located near Bethlehem in the Judean Desert.

The Lerner Sports Complex of Hebrew University serves the students as well as the general public. The complex includes an Olympic-size pool, fully equipped fitness center with 80 machines, and a health club offering massage treatments. The tennis courts are located adjacent to the Lerner Sports Complex. For further information Tel. (02) 588-1234.

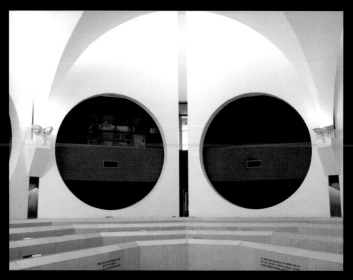

Women's balcony in center of circles in Mount Scopus' Hebrew University Hecht Synagogue.

The Holy Ark in the Hecht Synagogue at Mount Scopus Hebrew University consists of a floor-to-ceiling picture window overlooking the Old City of Jerusalem–looking west.

HEROD FAMILY TOMB
The tomb of King Herod's family is located behind the King David Hotel. The entrance was sealed by rolling a stone to prevent the tomb from being pillaged.

HERZL MUSEUM
Mount Herzl is located at the end of the Beit Hakerem section of Jerusalem. It is the burial site of Theodor Herzl (1860-1904), the Austrian journalist who founded the Zionist movement. A large black granite monolith marks Herzl's tomb. Other national leaders of Israel, including Zev Jabotinsky, Levi Eshkol, Golda Meir, and Yitzchok Rabin (1922-1995), are also buried on Mount Herzl. The Military Cemetery is located on the northern slope of the ridge.

The Herzl Museum contains a replica of Herzl's Vienna study with his own library and furniture. Admission is free. Hours are Sunday-Thursday 9:00-5:00,
Friday 9:00-1:00. Take bus #17, 17A, 18,20, 21, 23, 24, 26, 27, 39, 40, 99. For further information Tel. (02) 651-1108.

ISRAEL MUSEUM
The Israel Museum was founded in 1965. It is situated on a landscaped 20-acre campus opposite the Knesset. The Israel Museum has emerged as one of the leading comprehensive museums worldwide. While its permanent collection–comprising nearly 500,000 objects–represents cultures from around the globe and all periods of time, a significant portion has special relevance to the institution's setting in Jerusalem. Its extensive holdings of Biblical, Jewish, early Christian and Islamic archaeology, as well as Jewish ceremonial art and ethnography, rank among the finest worldwide.

The museum's extraordinary fine arts collection ranges from the Old Masters to contemporary art. Additionally, the fields of Israeli Art, Asian and Oriental Art, the Arts of Africa, Oceania, and the Americas, Prints and Drawings, Photography, and Architecture and Design are represented. The Billy Rose Art Garden was designed by the Japanese-American sculptor, Isamu Noguchi. It contains works by Picasso, Rodin, and Henry Moore. The Floersheimer Pavilion contains Impresionist art with works by Renoir, Monet, Degas, Gaugin, and Matisse.

The Israel Museum consists of five main separate components: the Bezalel Art Museum, the Samuel Bronfman Biblical and Archaeological Museum, the Billy Rose Art Garden, the Shrine of the Book, and the Ruth Youth Wing.

The Judaica Wing contains ceremonial artifacts from Jewish communities throughout the world. Be sure to see the reconstructed 18th century Italian synagogue from Vittorio Veneto and the 18th century German synagogue. There are Chanukah menorahs, silver Torah ornaments, spice boxes and an exhibit of costumes worn by Jews in the lands of the Diaspora. The detailed miniature model of Jerusalem during the time of the Second Holy Temple has been moved from the former Holyland Hotel in Bayit V'gan to the Israel Museum.

The Shrine of the Book contains the Dead Sea Scrolls. The scrolls were discovered in 1947 by a Bedouin shepherd looking for a goat which strayed into a cave above the Dead Sea at Qumran. The Shrine of the Book is designed to resemble the onion-shaped clay jar covers or lids in which the Dead Sea Scrolls were discovered. Included in this treasure trove are two copies of the Book of Isaiah, letters written by Bar Kochba, and fragments of scrolls from Masada.

The Shrine of the Book is designed to recreate the feeling of one of the caves in which the scrolls were found: a tunnel-like entrance slopes down to the main chamber on the lower level. In the event of an aerial bombing of the building, the Dead Sea Scrolls are automatically lowered into a bomb-proof concrete bunker.

The Ruth Youth Wing is designed specifically for kids who are encouraged to "please touch the exhibits." There are puppet and magic shows, children's concerts and films, and lots of kids stuff.

Hours are Monday & Wednesday 10:00-4:00, Tuesday & Thursday 10:00-9:00, Friday 10:00-2:00, Saturday 10:00-4:00 (Note: Saturday tickets must be purchased in advance–before the Sabbath.) The nearest bus lines are #9, 17, 24 . For further information Tel. (02) 670-8811.

JASON'S TOMB

This tomb, also known as the Alfasi Cave, was discovered in 1956 while foundations for a new house were being dug. The burial cave is estimated to date from the early first century B.C.E. Cooking pots, food, and gambling dice were found at the site, leading archaeologists to believe that the people of that period believed in the afterlife. Jason was one of the wealthy people of Jerusalem who seems to have been a sea merchant. These findings are based on wall paintings on the site. Note the pyramid over the porch and eight shaft graves in the burial chamber. Jason's Tomb is located on Alfasi Street in the Rechavia section.

JERUSALEM BIRD OBSERVATORY

The Israeli government has allocated a one-acre plot of prime real estate, between the Knesset and the Supreme Court. The site is one of the few traditional birdwatching areas in Jerusalem that has not been harmed by development. For further information Tel. 053-869488.

JERUSALEM ARTISTS' HOUSE

This was the original site of the Bezalel Academy of Arts and Design which was founded in 1906. There are exhibitions of art, concerts of classical music, and jazz programs. The Bezalel School is presently located at the Hebrew University. The Jerusalem Artists' House is located at 12, Shmuel Ha'nagid Street. The nearest bus lines are #4, 7, 8, 9, 19, 48. Hours are Sunday-Friday 10:00-1:00 & 4:00-7:00, Friday 10:00-1:00, Saturday 11:00-2:00. For further information Tel. (02) 625-3653.

JERUSALEM CENTER FOR PLANNING IN HISTORIC CITIES

In the short time since its establishment, the Center has become a laboratory for developing and testing new techniques for architects and planners. It houses the 1:500 three-dimensional model of the expanded central area of Jerusalem, designed to facilitate study and testing of the city's development options and which is used by teams of architects and planners.

The model was created at the initiative of Jerusalem City Engineer Amnon Niv and built by engineer Dick Harvey and students of architecture at the Technion Institute of Technology in Haifa, over a period of seven years. The Center is located at Safra Square, 1. Hours are Sunday-Thursday 11:00-2:00. For further information Tel. (02) 629-7731. Reservations are recommended.

JERUSALEM MUNICIPALITY COMPLEX - SAFRA SQUARE

Before 1993, the Municipal offices of Jerusalem were scattered throughout the city. The Jerusalem Municipal Complex brings all of the city offices within one new site at Safra Square. It is named in honor of Yaakov and Esther Safra. The 4,000 square meter main square has become a popular public plaza which is used for gatherings, demonstrations, and public fairs. Tours of the new City Hall complex are given every

"United Buddy Bears" in Safra Square is a display of 132 bear sculptures which have been painted by artists from all around the world. They represent peace and friendship to all countries. This is a worldwide traveling exhibit.

Monday at 10:00am. For further information Tel. (02) 629-5981 or 624-1379.

KENNEDY MEMORIAL
There are two memorials located near Ein Kerem. The Kennedy Memorial is shaped like a giant tree trunk cut off at its base and designed in concrete. The second memorial is dedicated to Arthur Rubinstein, the noted pianist. The memorial is shaped like a giant piano keyboard.

KING DAVID HOTEL
The King David Hotel was built by Egyptian Jews in 1930. It served as a British base of command in the Mandate period. The entire right wing of the hotel was destroyed in a bomb attack, set off by the Jewish underground in 1946. Today, the King David Hotel is a five-star luxury hotel. Its guests include kings and queens, as well as many diplomats and foreign dignitaries while they are visiting Israel.

KING DAVID MUSEUM
The King David Museum is located on Mount Zion, near the Holocaust Cellar (Havitat Yerushalaim Street). The museum

displays the life of King David through modern art. The museum is operated by volunteers at a nearby yeshiva. For further information Tel. (02) 671-6841.

KNESSET

Israel's Parliament, the Knesset, is housed in this $7 million modern building. It was financed by the Rothschild family of England and was built in 1966. The magnificent bronze menorah outside the Knesset was designed by the British artist Benno Elkan. It is decorated with themes from Jewish history. The entranceway, a grillwork of hammered metal, is the work of the Israeli sculptor David Palombo, who also designed the dramatic doors at Yad Vashem. There is a 24-foot-high Chagall mosaic and tapestry in the reception hall.

Tours are given on Sunday and Thursday from 8:30-2:30. The Knesset is in session Monday through Wednesday from 4:00-9:00. Gallery tickets are available. Be sure to bring your passport for all visits to the Knesset.

LIBERTY BELL GARDEN

A replica of the Liberty Bell, complete with its crack, was presented by the City of Philadelphia to the City of Jerusalem in honor of the American Bicentennial in 1976. Both the original bell in Philadelphia and its replica were cast in England. The main archway is dedicated to hubert Humphrey, "A warm friend of Israel."

L.A. MAYER MUSEUM OF ISLAMIC ART

The L.A. Mayer Memorial Museum of Islamic Art displays a significant collection of ceramic ware, figurines, glass and metalwork, calligraphy, miniatures, paintings, jewelry, and artifacts from the Islamic world from the 7th to the 19th century. There are samples from Sassanian and Early Islamic Art, the High Period of Islamic Art (the period between the 12th and 14th centuries), Later Iranian Art, Ottoman Art, and Moghul Art. The watch and clock collection, assembled by the late Sir David Salomons, contains sample watches, music boxes, richly decorated automata from the 18th and 19th centuries, and scientific instruments.

The museum is located at 2, Ha'palmach Street. Hours are Sunday-Monday & Wednesday-Thursday 10:00-3:00, Tuesday 10:00-6:00, Friday 10:00-2:00, Saturday & Holidays 10:00-2:00. The nearest bus is #13. For further information Tel. (02) 566-1291.

MENACHEM BEGIN HERITAGE CENTER

The visitor to this interactive museum is lead through 15 to 20 rooms and mini theaters which contain a wide variety of rare photographs, film clips, theatrical re-enactments, documents and artifacts. The tour starts in the streets of Brisk, the town where Begin was born, continues to Warsaw where he studied, and in Vilna where he was arrested and sent to a Soviet prison camp. From there visitors continue to the secret headquarters of the Irgun where actions were planned against the British. Then on to the period when Begin was the leader of the Opposition. Visitors become part of an election rally and witness the Likud victory in 1977. There are moving moments when the Egyptian leader Anwar Sadat comes to Israel and speaks in the Knesset, Begin receives the Nobel Peace Prize, and the bombing of the nuclear reactor in Iraq by the Israeli Air Force. But the saddest moment of this interactive tour is when they announce the passing of Menachem Begin, the 6th Prime Minister of Israel.

The Menachem Begin Heritage Center is located at 6 Nakhon Street, in the area of Yemin Moshe, Mishkenot Sh'ananim and the Scottish Church of St. Andrews. Hours are Sunday-Thursday 9:00-4:00, Friday

9:00-12:30. For further information Tel. (02) 565-2020.

MODEL OF ANCIENT JERUSALEM

A scale model of Jerusalem (1:50 of true size) during the Second Temple period is located on the grounds of the Israel Museum. Note the massive walls, lavish palaces, elegant citadels, arched bridges and hillside homes that surrounded the Temple. It was masterminded by Professor Avi Yona of the Hebrew University according to historical documents and contains authentic building materials.

NAHON MUSEUM OF ITALIAN ART

Over the centuries many small Jewish communities throughout Italy had lost their Jewish populations. This was due to several factors. One reason was because the younger generation moved to the large cities to attend the universities and get better jobs. The other reason was because the older generation had died and there was nobody to take over the Jewish institutions. Many ancient synagogues were closed in this process. Luckily, their furnishings had not been destroyed or dismantled. In the 1950s, Israel asked the Italian government if they

18th century Holy Ark and Bimah from the Tempio Spagnola of Padua, Italy is located in the Jerusalem's Heichal Shlomo.

would send these holy furnishings to the new Jewish state. Italy agreed to this request and sent the furnishings of more than 44 ancient synagogues to various locations in Israel. Below is a list of some of these locations:

BAT YAM - Heichal Yaakov Synagogue
• *17th century Holy Ark from Ancona.*

BNEI BRAK - Ponovez Yeshiva
• *18th century Holy Ark from the Great Italian Synagogue of Mantua, located in the main sanctuary of the yeshiva.*
• *19th century Holy Ark from Moncalvo.*

HAIFA -
Central Synagogue of Kiryat Shmuel.
• *1756 Holy Ark from Reggio Emilia.*

JERUSALEM -
Hapoel Ha'mizrachi Synagogue
• *18th century Holy Ark from Corregio.*

JERUSALEM -
Heichal Shlomo Synagogue
• *18th century Holy Ark and Bimah from the Tempio Spagnola of Padua.*
• *Other furnishings from the Casas Synagogue of Mantua are located in the Wolfson Museum upstairs.*

JERUSALEM - Israel Museum
• *18th century Holy Ark from Vittorio Veneto.*

JERUSALEM - Nahon Museum of Italian Art
• *17th century Holy Ark, Bimah, benches, and women's partition from Conegliano Veneto.*
• *17th century Holy Ark from San Daniele del Friuli.*
• *1543 Holy Ark from Mantua-Sermide.*

JERUSALEM - Synagogue of the Knesset
• *17th century Holy Ark from Soragna.*

JERUSALEM - Komemi'ut Synagogue
• *1727 Holy Ark from Busseto.*

JERUSALEM -
Maale High School (Beit Medrash)
• *18th century Holy Ark from Mantua.*

JERUSALEM - Machon Gold Seminary
• *18th century Holy Ark from Pisa.*

JERUSALEM -
President's Residence (Rechavia)
• *18th century Holy Ark from Saluzzo.*

JERUSALEM -
Four Sephardic Synagogues (Old City)
• *16th century Holy Ark from Livorno*
• *16th century Ark from the Italian Synagogue in Pesaro.*

KARMIEL - Synagogue of Karmiel
• *18th century Holy Ark from Pitigliano.*

KEREM b'YAVNEH - Yeshiva
• *16th century furnishings from the Spanish Synagogue of Florence.*
• *17th century Holy Ark from the Matir Asurim Synagogue, Florence.*

KIRYAT SANZ - Central Synagogue
• *1650 Holy Ark from the Italian Synagogue of Pesaro.*

MERCAZ SHAPIRA - Yeshiva Or Etzion
• *Holy Ark from Pesaro, 1700.*

NETANYA - Giv'at Meir Synagogue
• *18th century Holy Ark from Cento.*

NESS ZIONA - Ayanot Agricultural School
• *Synagogue furnishings from ancient synagogue of Carpi.*

RAMAT GAN - Yad Giborim Synagogue
• *19th century Holy Ark from the Tempio Italiano, Florence.*

RAMAT GAN - Synagogue
• *16th century Holy Ark and furnishings from Trino.*

RECHAVA (Lachish Zone) - Synagogue
• *Holy Ark from Bozzolo, 1802.*

TEL AVIV - Beit Yesha'yahu Synagogue
• *1795 Holy Ark from Mantua.*

TEL AVIV -
Central Synagogue (Rassco-Tzafon)
• *18th century marble Holy Ark from Trieste.*

The Nahon Museum of Italian Jewish Art is located at 27 Hillel Street. Hours are Sunday, Tuesday-Wednesday 9:00-5:00, Monday 9:00-2:00, Thursday-Friday 9:00-1:00. For further information Tel. (02) 624-1610.

MUSICAL INSTRUMENTS MUSEUM

This museum is located in the Rubin Academy of Music, There are musical instruments from ancient to modern times on display. The museum is located at Peres Smolensky Street in the Giv'at Ram section. Hours are Sunday-Thursday 9:00-1:00. For further information Tel. (02) 663-6232.

NATURAL HISTORY MUSEUM

The nature museum has various displays in different areas of natural and environmental sciences and the human body. There are dioramas dealing with the mammals, fowl, and reptiles of Israel. There are special dinosaur displays, the meaning of color in nature, garden parasites, nests and eggs, and a section about natural gems. There are push-button displays about anatomy. Learn what the various parts of the brain do, take your blood pressure, or move the bones on a skeleton. This museum is great for kids. The Nature Museum is located at 6, Mohilever Street. Hours are Sunday, Tuesday, Thursday 8:30-1:30, Monday & Wednesday 8:30-6:00, Saturday 10:00-2:00. The nearest bus lines are #4, 14, 18. For further information Tel. (02) 563-1116.

RABBI KOOK MUSEUM

This museum is devoted to the life and writings of Rabbi Kook, one of first Orthodox Zionist rabbis in the country. He lived in the early part of the 20th century. The museum is located at 9, Rav Kook Street. Hours are Sunday-Thursday 9:00-3:00, Friday 9:00-12:00. For further information Tel. (02) 623-2560.

ROCKEFELLER ARCHAEOLOGICAL MUSEUM

The Rockefeller Archaeological Museum was built in 1927 with the help of the American millionaire, John D. Rockefeller. It is recognized by its stately octagonal tower and is located near the Damascus Gate in East Jerusalem. It is now part of the Israel Museum. The original Dead Sea Scrolls were located here in 1947 and were under Jordanian control until 1967. The building still has bullet holes from the battle for Jerusalem in the Six Day War.

The Rockefeller Archaeological Museum contains one of the most extensive collections of archaeological finds in the Middle East. Much of the treasure was excavated in the areas of Acre and the Galilee by American and European archaeologists in the 1930s. Pottery, tools, and household items from the Iron Age, Persian, Hellenistic, Roman, and Byzantine eras. The south gallery contains the skull of Carmel Man, who lived many thousands of years ago.

The Rockefeller Archaeological Museum is located at Sultan Suleiman Street. The nearest bus lines are #1, 2. Hours are Sunday-Thursday 10:00-3:00, Saturday 10:00-2:00. For further information Tel. (02) 628-2251.

SACHER PARK

Gan Sacher or Sacher Park is a large strip of green parkland separating government buildings such as the Supreme Court and the Knesset from the neighborhood of Nahla'ot on the other side of Ben Zvi Boulevard. The park contains the "Bonsho," a large Japanese bell presented to the city as a symbol of everlasting peace and is engraved with the quote, "Pray for the peace of Jerusalem. They shall prosper that love thee as well."

MOSHE SAFDIE'S DAVID CITADEL HOTEL

This hotel was conceived in the spirit of the great opera houses of Europe. Like *La Scala* in Milan or the *Great Opera House* in Paris, the eight-story hotel forms a horseshoe, a dress circle of boxes focusing toward the stage–the Old City of Jerusalem. Just a stone's throw away unfolds the grand view of the massive city walls, the Citadel, David's Tower, and beyond, the golden Dome of the Rock, and the Mount of Olives. On either side of the horseshoe, two parallel wings protrude toward the Old City, accommodating rooms with oblique views. These wings terrace towards the east, forming trellised roof gardens from the suites opening onto them. Along King David Street, the entrance is defined by a grand arcade in the scale of the great Roman aqueducts, protected from the elements by a cantilevering glass canopy which fans out of the building. The building fits harmoniously into its historic setting. Its walls are constructed of traditional roughly hewn golden Jerusalem limestone, its roofs and canopies sheathed in pewter colored leaded copper. Inside the hotel, richly patterned stone floors, beechwood paneling and stenciled wood ceilings create a fresh and contemporary character, yet strongly rooted in the traditions of Jerusalem and the Mediterranean. The David Citadel Hotel is located at 7, King David Street.

SHAI AGNON HOUSE

Shai Agnon, the noted Israeli poet who won the Nobel Peace Prize for Literature, lived at 16, Klauzner Street. His house is now a museum which contains an exhibit about his life and works. Hours are Sunday-Thursday 9:00-1:00. The nearest bus line is #7. For further information Tel. (02) 671-6498.

SKIRBALL MUSEUM

Hebrew Union College newest building in its Jerusalem campus was designed by the noted Israeli-American architect, Moshe Safdie. The museum contains artifacts collected from excavations in Tel Dan, Gezer, and Aro'er. The Skirball Museum has branches in New York City and Los Angeles. It is located at 13, King David Street.

SUPREME COURT OF ISRAEL

From the establishment of the State of Israel until 1992, the Supreme Court was housed in rented quarters in Jerusalem's Russian Compound. In 1984, Yad Hanadiv (The Rothschild Foundation, which also built the Knesset building) offered to build a permanent residence for the Supreme Court in the government precinct of Jerusalem.

The architects, Ada Karmi-Melamede and Ram Karmi of Tel Aviv, were commissioned to design the project. Their design incorporated the concepts of law and truth which are translated into straight lines. Justice is represented by circles and curves, referred to a passage from Psalms (23:3).

The visitor ascends the main staircase of a Jerusalem passageway and faces a panoramic window overlooking the Nachla'ot neighborhood, Sachar Park, and downtown Jerusalem. Natural light enters through glass walls, windows, and skylights, and is one of the main architectural elements of the building's design. The pyramid is the area which defines the formal entrance to the Supreme Court. The legal library, built on three levels, surrounds the entrance under the pyramid.

In the foyer, of the Courtroom wing there is a contrast and blending of the "old" and the "new." On the right is a modern white Mediterranean wall with seating areas for the public. The natural stone wall on the left is reminiscent of Jerusalem's historical building style. The entrances to the five courtrooms are designed in the shape of gates. In Biblical times, the law courts were held at the gates of the city. There is a passage outside the main entrance of the Supreme Court which leads to the Knesset via the Wohl Rose Garden. Tours of the Supreme Court are given daily in English. The Supreme Court is located at Shaarey Mishpat Street, Kiryat David Ben-Gurion.

Tours are given in English at 12:00 (except in July-August). For further information Tel. (02) 675-9612.

TAX MUSEUM

This is the world's only museum devoted entirely to the history of taxation and collection in ancient Israel, during the Diaspora, and in Israel today. Admission is free. The Tax Museum is located at 32, Agron Street. The nearest bus lines are #18, 21. Hours are Sunday-Thursday 9:00-3:00. For further information Tel. (02) 625-8978.

THEATER ARCHIVES AND MUSEUM

The Israel Goor Theater Archives and Museum is a museum of the theater in Israel. Visitors can learn about sets, directing, acting, and costumes that are involved in the making of a dramatic performance. There are exhibits about posters, models of sets, photographs, and paintings.

The Theater Archives and Museum is located at Hebrew University, Mount Scopus campus, in the Humanities Building. Admission is free. The nearest bus lines are #4-A, 28. Hours are Sunday, Wednesday-Thursday 9:00-1:00, Monday 9:00-5:00. For further information Tel. (02) 588-3986.

YAD VASHEM

The new Holocaust History Museum at Yad Vashem opened on March 15, 2005. It took ten years to build and covers some 4,200 square meters or just over an acre. Yad Vashem will use this new museum as its main platform for imparting the Holocaust legacy to its visitors. The victims are the focus, instead of being portrayed as anonymous objects being acted upon by their persecutors, and visitors will leave with a wider perspective on the protection of humanity's basic values and Jewish identity.

World-renowned architect Moshe Safdie designed a unique building for the new museum. "The story of the Holocaust has no equal," Safdie says, "I felt that it cannot be accommodated in a conventional building. I wanted it to be like an archaeological remnant. Responding to Yad Vashem's request to preserve the pastoral character of the Mount of Remembrance, and that the Hall of Remembrance maintain its centrality. I conceived of a prism-like structure that cuts through the mountain from the south, extending 200 meters to the north."

At the end of the museum's historical narrative is the Hall of Names—a repository for the Pages of Testimony of millions of Holocaust victims, a memorial to those who perished. In a separate room, visitors can conduct searches of the digitized Central Database of Shoah Victim's Names. Also on line at www.yadvashem.org

Visitors enter the Hall in the circular space between two reciprocal cones onto an elevated ring-shaped platform between them. Surrounding the platform is the circular repository, housing the Pages of Testimony collected so far, with empty spaces for testimonies not yet submitted—room for six million Pages in total.

A basic guideline for the new museum's design was to create a visitor's route dictated by the evolving narrative. As such, Safdie devised a central walkway (prism) with underground exhibition galleries by a series of impassible gaps, created by museum designer Dorit Harel, extending along the breadth of the prism floor. Displaying items from different events, the gaps symbolize turning points in the Holocaust, and serve as chapter headings for the evolving narrative of the exhibition. Subtly illuminated by skylights, nine chapters (galleries) depict the history of the Holocaust through exclusive and new presentation techniques.

Yad Vashem is the national memorial dedicated to the six million Jews who perished during the Holocaust. The Avenue of the Righteous Among the Nations is framed by a path lined with carob trees that bear plaques inscribed with the names of non-Jews who risked their lives saving Jews during the Nazi era. This leads to the memorial. The heavy entrance gate to the Hall of Remembrance (Ohel Yizkor), designed by Dezalel Schatz and David Palombo, is an abstract tapestry of jagged, twisted steel. Inside is a huge stone room, like a crypt, where an eternal flame flickers over the names of Nazi death camps.

The Hall of Names contains an agonizingly long list of all known Holocaust victims. The Art Museum houses drawings and paintings made in the ghettos and in the concentration camps by Jewish prisoners. The most powerful exhibit at Yad Vashem is the Children's Memorial, where mirrors are used to create a spark of light for every child who perished; a recorded voice recites the name and age of each young victim. The Children's Memorial was designed by Moshe Safdie.

Below Yad Vashem is the Valley of Destroyed Communities, commemorating the 5,000 European Jewish communities that were wiped out during the Holocaust. It was literally dug out of the natural bedrock and was designed by Dan Zur and Lipa Yahalom.

There is a sculpture designed by Nathan Rapoport in front of the Warsaw Ghetto Square–Wall of Remembrance. The Pillar of Heroism commemorates Jewish resistance during the Holocaust. It was designed by Buki Schwartz.

The Cattle Car - Memorial to the Deportees serves as a monument to the millions of Jews herded onto cattle-cars and transported from all over Europe to the extermination camps. An original German cattle-car given to Yad Vashem by the Polish authorities stands at the center of the memorial

site. This exhibit was designed by Moshe Safdie.

Admission to Yad Vashem is free. Hours are Sunday-Thursday 9:00-4:30, Friday 9:00-3:00. For further information Tel. (02) 644-3400.

ANNA TICHO HOUSE

In tho oarly part of the 20th century this was the home and office of Avraham Ticho, Jerusalem's humanitarian eye doctor. It was one of the first houses built outside the Old City. His wife, Anna, was a noted artist. The gallery, now a branch of the Israel Museum, displays Anna Ticho's paintings. Be sure to see the exquisite collection of Dr. Ticho's Chanukah menorahs upstairs.

The Anna Ticho House is a museum, library and kosher coffee house. There are also musical concerts given on several occasions. It is located at 9, Harav Kook Street. Museum hours are Sunday-Friday 10:00-5:00. There is an outdoor kosher cafe on the premises. For further information Tel. (02) 624-5068.

TIME ELEVATOR

Traveling through 3,000 years of history, visitors experience an enthralling multi-sensory adventure as they discover ancient layers of Jerusalem's history and meet different historical figures. Using advanced technology, the Time Elevator features kinetic seats, three giant screens, special auditorium scenery, and an astounding variety of special effects from the best in 6-D multimedia from ITA. This same company is used at EPCOT in Florida.

The kinetic seat system lets the viewer feel completely "swallowed-up" inside the history of Jerusalem and feel a complete part of the Jerusalem experience–soaring over the city, moving through many underground tunnels, bursting into the besieged city with Titus' fearsome army, or narrowly escaping Zedekiah's Cave like the king himself. Each kinetic seat is able to move in six different directions. For pregnant women and those suffering from motion sickness, dizziness, or heart problems, the auditorium contains twelve stationary seats in addition to the ninety kinetic seats. The tour guide in the program is the noted Israeli actor, Topol (from "Fiddler on the Roof" fame).

The Time Elevator is located at Beit Agron, 37 Hillel Street. Hours are Sunday-Thursday 9:00-9:00, Friday 9:00-3:30, Saturday 9:30-4:00. Tel. (02) 625-2227.

TOMBS OF THE SANHEDRIN

The tombs of the Sanhedrin are located at Sanhedrin Street, near Shmuel Ha'navi Street (in the Sanhedria section). The pediment, dating from the first century C.E., is decorated with pomegranates and other fruits between stylized acanthus leaves. The large tomb chamber inside the entrance contains two rows of small shaft tombs, one over the other. The Sanhedrin was the supreme Jewish religious and civil council.

TOURJEMAN POST MUSEUM

This old Turkish house was turned into a fortress and used as an Israeli command post during the 1948 War of Independence up until 1967. The museum is dedicated to the history of the divided City of Jerusalem that existed during that period. It is located near the former "Mandelbaum Gate" which divided Jerusalem until 1967. The museum features an audio-visual display and a movie, "Jerusalem–A Divided City Reunited." The Tourjemon Post Museum is also known as the Museum of the Seam. It is located at Shivtei Yisrael and Shmuel Hanavi Streets. The nearest bus lines are #1, 11, 12, 27, 99. Hours are Sunday-Thursday 9:00-4:00, Friday 9:00-1:00. For further information Tel. (02) 627-7061.

UNDERGROUND PRISONERS MUSEUM

The building was constructed in 1858 as a Russian pilgrim's hotel for women. During the British Mandate period (1918-1948), the building was converted into a central prison. Apart from common criminals, there were hundreds of Jewish underground fighters from the Haganah, Irgun, and Lechi imprisoned in this facility. The museum exhibits life in the prison, tells the stories of the underground groups and their members, and perpetuates the memory of those who were executed here by the British.

The Underground Prisoners Museum is located at 1, Mishol Ha'gevurah Street, near Safra Square (City Hall). Hours are Sunday-Thursday 8:30-4:00. For further information Tel. (02) 623-3166.

WINDMILL MUSEUM

Sir Moses Montefiore, a philanthropist from England, visited Israel seven times during his 101 years of life. He wanted to assist the poor people who lived in unsanitary conditions in the Old City of Jerusalem. In 1855, he purchased a plot of land opposite the Jaffa Gate and across from the Sultan's Pool. He created the first settlement outside the walls of Jerusalem, Mishkenot Sha'ananim. He constructed a building with twenty apartments and a windmill to provide a livelihood for those who settled here. Montefiore sent all the equipment for the mill and building materials for the houses from England by ship and then overland by camel. He was assisted in building the neighborhood by a bequest from Judah Touro, a wealthy Jew from New Orleans, Louisiana (USA).

About twenty housing units were built in 1860, each consisting of two rooms–a kitchen and a storeroom. In addition, two synagogues (one for Sephardim and one for Ashkenazim), a mikveh, a public oven, and the first well with a water pump in the country.

For security, the residences were designed as two buildings, one above the other, and were enclosed by a high stone wall. The windows and doors all faced towards the Old City. The crenelated edge of the roof of the building mirrors the walls of the Old City. In the next four years, Montefiore purchased an adjoining plot of land and expanded the quarter, calling it Yemin Moshe.

There is a museum devoted to the life of Sir Moses Montefiore in the windmill. The original carriage used to transport Sir Moses and his wife, Lady Judith, was destroyed by a terrorist who set it ablaze about 20 years ago. Yemin Moshe is today one of the most exclusive neighborhoods in the city and has become an artists colony. There is another windmill in Jerusalem. It is located just to the left of the Prima Kings Hotel on Ramban Street, off King George Street.

The Windmill Museum is located between King David Street and Mount Zion. Hours are Sunday-Thursday 9:00-4:00, Friday 9:00-1:00. The nearest bus lines are #4, 4-A, 18, 24. For further information Tel. (02) 629-2222.

WOHL ROSE GARDEN

There are fifteen acres containing a rich variety of rose species from all over the world. The park is located near the Knesset and the Supreme Court. The nearest buses are #9, 24.

Street scene in Me'a Shearim.

Drying clothes on the lines above a courtyard in Me'a Shearim, just like they did in the shtetlech of Europe.

JERUSALEM BUS ROUTES (Subject to change)

Route #1
Central Bus Station
Binyanei Ha'umma
Me'a Shearim
Shivtei Yisrael
Ha'nevi'im
Sultan Suleiman
Derech Jericho
Kotel - Western Wall

Route #4
French Hill
Ramat Eshkol Yecheskel
Straus Street
King George Street
Emeq Refa'im
Yochanan ben Zakai
Jerusalem Shopping Mall

Route #4A
Mount Scopus (Hebrew University)
Same as Route 4
(excluding French Hill)
Derech Raziel
East Talpiyot
Jaffa Road
King George Street
Emek Refa'im
Pierre Koenig
Derech Chevron
Har Homa

Route #6
East Pisgat Ze'ev
Sderot Moshe Dayan
Sderot Cha'im Bar Lev
Chayl Hahandasa
Jaffa Street
Central Bus Station
Sderot Herzl
Shmuel Beyth

Ha'rav Herzog
Jerusalem Shopping Mall

Route #8
Pisgat Ze'ev
Sderot Moshe Dayan
Cdorot Lovi Eshkol
Bar Ilan
Yirmiyahu
Jaffa Road
King George Street
Keren Hayesod
Derech Chevron
Derech Raziel
East Talpiyot

Route #11
Ramat Shlomo
Sderot Yig'al Yadin
Sderot GoldaMeir
Ezekiel Street
Ha'nevi'im Street
Jaffa Road
Giv'at Sha'ul
Negiara Street
Kanfei Nesharim
Har Nof

Route #12
Hadassah Hospital
Giv'at Masu'a
Jerusalem Shopping Mall
Derech Moshe Bar'am
Derech Chevron
Derech Raziel
East Talpiyot

Route #14
Ramat Beit Hakerem
Shaarei Zedek Hospital
Sderot Herzl

Jaffa Road
King George Street
Emek Refa'im
Pierre Koenig
Derech Chevron
Har Homa

Route #18
Kiryat Ha'yovel
Sderot Herzl
Jaffa Road
King David Street
Emek Refa'im
Yochanan ben Zakai
Jerusalem Mall

Route #19
Mount Scopus
Sderot Levi Eshkol
Ezekiel
Ussishkin
Derech Aza
Ha'rav Herzog
Jerusalem Shopping Mall
Golomb
Tahon
Hadassah Medical Center

Route #20
Giv'at Masu'a
Hantke
Sderot Herzl
Jaffa Road
Jaffa Gate

Route #25
Nevai Yaakov
Ezekiel
Hanevi'im
Central Bus Station

Route #27
Central Bus Station
Sderot Herzl
Hantke
Hadassah Medical Center

Route #28
Mount Scopus -
Hebrew University
Sderot Levi Eshkol
Bar Ilan
Yirmiyahi
Hebrew University -
Giv'at Ram

Route #32
Ramot
Sderot Golda Meir
Shaarei Yerushalayim
Jaffa Road
King George Street
Derech Aza
Ha'rav Herzog
Jerusalem Shopping Mall
Dov Yosef
Gilo

Route #33
Har Nof
Kanfei Nesharim
Sderot Herzl
Bayit Ve'gan
Jerusalem Shopping Mall
Dov Yosef
Gilo

Route #35
Har Nof
Kanfei Nesharim
Jaffa Road
Ha'nevi'im
Ezekiel
Sderot Golda Meir
Ramot

Route #38
Kotel - Western Wall
Ma'aleh Ha'shalom
Ha'emek
Gershon Agron

King George Street
Nathan Straus
Ha'nevi'im
Shiftei Yisrael
Jaffa Road
Into the Old City
Kotel - Western Wall

Continues outside Old City
walls back to King George
Street.

Route #99
City Tour Bus

Jerusalem's "Monster" children's slide is located in Kiryat Hayovel. Just ask the bus driver on the No. 18 bus for the "Monster."

Jaffa Street near the Davidka Monument and Machaneh Yehuda Market. The modern Chalon (window on) Yerushalayim Building with its cut-out section is in the background.

JERUSALEM LIGHT RAIL - RAFEVET KALAH

There is a master plan in the works to design a system of light rail lines throughout Jerusalem. It will basically remove all of the buses from the streets and replace them with ultra-modern trolleys. At the entrance to Jerusalem, as one enters the city from Route 1, there is a new white suspension bridge which was designed by Santiago Calatrava (the designer of the new Transportation Center at New York's World Trade Center site). He designed another suspension bridge in Petach Tikvah. The Jerusalem Light Rail is scheduled to open around 2012.

The first route will start at Har Herzl. The Light Rail will cross over the New Harp Suspension Bridge and curve onto Jaffa Road. It will proceed past the Jerusalam Municipality at Safra Square, turn left at the Old City and travel along Rechov Hatznachanim (what used to be the wall separating Jewish and Arab Jerusalem or the old Mandelbaum Gate). It will continue north along Sderot Haim Bar Lev and terminate in Pisgat Ze'ev.

A new high-speed rail line from Tel Aviv to Jerusalem via Modi'in is presently under construction. It will take only 28 minutes between both major cities. The plans call for the route to go "under" Canada Park, and hug Route 1. It will not ascend the mountain as you approach Jerusalem but will terminate underground at the Central Bus Station. These plans have been put on "hold" until further notice.

They restored the old railroad route from Tel Aviv to Jerusalem in April 2005. It was originally built in 1892 by the Ottoman government. For a truly exciting railroad trip, catch the train in Tel Aviv. East of Beit Shemesh, the train winds through the steep Judean Hills as it approaches Jerusalem. The ride may be a bit long, nearly two hours since you have to change trains in Beit Shemesh and wait for a connecting train, but the views are just spectacular. It's like riding through the Grand Canyon.

NEW CABLE CAR TO THE KOTEL

The City of Jerusalem is going to construct a new cable car line, similar to the ones at Masada, Rosh Hanikra, Haifa, and Kibbutz Menara (near the Lebanese border above Kiryat Shemona) – to the Kotel. The starting point will be at the old railroad terminal in Emek Refa'im. It will run outside the Old City walls to the Dung Gate. These plans are "on hold."

הגשר

גשר הרכבת הקלה בכניסה לירושלים. התערוכה.
י"ד בשבט - י"א באדר, תשס"ד. 5.2-4.3.2004 בניין העירייה, ירושלים

he new Harp Bridge designed by Santiago Calatrava for Jerusalem's Light Rail–Rakevet Kal

Artist rendering of the new Jerusalem Light Rail crossing over Santiago Calatrava's Harp Suspension Bridge as it proceeds north from Har Herzl to Jaffa Road.

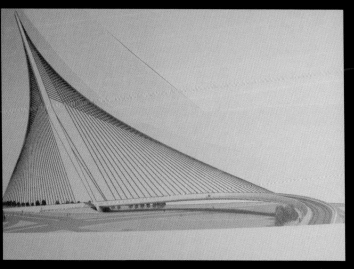

Rendering showing the elegant curve of the Harp Suspension Bridge.

Construction of the Harp Suspension Bridge near the central bus station in 2007. Note the blue sign below the bridge, which notes the disruption of regular traffic due to the building of the new Rafqvet Kallah- Jerusalem's Light Rail system.

SIR ISAAC & LADY EDITH WOLFSON MUSEUM

The Wolfson Museum is located on the fourth floor of Heichal Shlomo, the former seat of Israel's Chief Rabbinate. The Chief Rabbinate moved to a new building behind the new Central Bus Terminal. The museum contains over 5,000 Jewish ceremonial objects including Torah scrolls, maps, coins, and ceremonial objects. There are dioramas of scenes in Jewish history, a collection of Purim "groggers," and a kernel of wheat, inscribed with the morning prayers.

The synagogue, located on the first floor, contains a lovely Ark and Bimah brought from the 17th century Spanish Synagogue in Padua, Italy. Heichal Shlomo is located at 58 King George Street, just to the left of the Great Synagogue of Jerusalem. Admission is free. The nearest bus lines are #4, 7, 8, 9, 14, 19, 31, 32, 48. Museum hours are Sunday-Thursday 9:00-1:00, Friday 9:00-12:00. For further information Tel. (02) 624-7112.

THE JERUSALEM DIG

The Mufti of Jerusalem has excavated vast amounts of debris from under the Temple Mount in order to construct a vast underground mosque. This debris contains remnants of Jewish history dating from the Holy Temple periods. It was all dumped in a nearby garbage pile. The public has been invited to help sift through this holy debris and find bits and pieces of Jewish life from thousands of years ago.

Digging and sifting fees are 15 shekels for up to five hours, free for those who stay more than five hours. For further information Tel. (02) 627-4365.

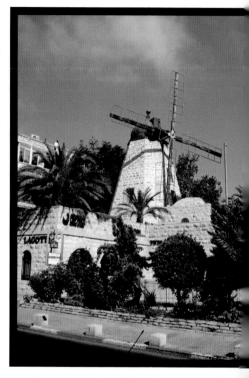

One of two windmills in Jerusalem. This is located behind the Prima Kings Hotel

Kosher Dining

Kosher food establishments in Israel must display a valid Certificate of Kashrut. This certificate or *Te'udat Kashrut*, must be renewed every three months. Be sure to look for this certificate and check the date. No responsibility, therefore can be taken for the absolute accuracy of the information in this guide, and travelers are advised to obtain confirmation of kashrut claims. Although every effort has been made to ensure accuracy, changes will occur after this guide has gone to press. Particular attention must be drawn to the fact that kosher food establishments change hands often and suddenly, in some cases going over to a non-kosher owner. All of the restaurants listed below are closed on the Sabbath. Rabbinical supervisions are in brackets.

Ahavat Ha'iam (Fish) Paz Gas Station on Ben-Zvi Avenue [Mehadrin] Tel. (02) 623-6767
Al Dente (Italian/Dairy) 50, Ussishkin Street [Rabbinat Yerushalayim] Tel. (02) 625-1479
Almora (Southern Indian/Meat)
Yishuv Even Sapir [Rabbinat Mateh Yehuda] Tel. (02) 643-1186
Angelo (Italian/Dairy/Fish)
9, Horkanos Street [Rabbinat Yerushalayim] Tel. (02) 623-6095
Atcha (Meat) 9 Joel Solomon Street [Rabbinat Yerushalayim] Tel. (02) 623-6603
Bagel Bite (Dairy) 84, Derech Beit Lechem [Rabbinat Yerushalayim] Tel. (02) 671-6890
Beit Ha'ma'ayan (Fish/Dairy)
14 Ha'ma'ayan Street [Rabbinat Yerushalayim & Mehadrin] Tel. (02) 644-8840
Belinda Coffee Shop (Dairy)
9, Diskin Street (Wolfson Center) [Mehadrin] Tel. (02) 624-5717
Benny's Dagim (Dairy) 1, Mesilat Yesharim Street [Mehadrin] Tel. (02) 625-2403
Bonkers Bagels (Dairy)
2, Tifereth Israel Street (Old City) [Rabbinat Yerushalayim & Mehadrin] Tel. (02) 627-2590
Brunch Bagel (Dairy) 2, Ezer Yoldot Street (Ge'ula) [Badatz] Tel. (02) 500-4001
Buffalo Steakhouse (Meat)
54 Emek Refa'im Street [Rabbinat Yerushalayim] Tel. (02) 561-1325
Burger Deli (Meat) 16 Shamgar Street (Rav Shefa Mall) [Badatz] Tel. (02) 500-3070
Cafe Bagina (Garden Cafe) (Dairy)
74, Beit Lechem Road [Rabbinat Yerushalayim] Tel. (02) 672-0825
Cafe Inbal (Meat) 25-D Ein Kerem [Rabbinat Yerushalayim] Tel. (02) 644-6533
Cafe Neeman (Dairy)
Malcha Mall [Rabbinat Yerushalayim & Mehadrin] Tel. (02) 679-1515
Caffit (Dairy) 35, Emek Refa'im Street [Rabbinat Yerushalayim] Tel. (02) 563-5284
Canela (Meat) 8 Shlomzion Hamalka Street [Rabbinat Yerushalayim] Tel. (02) 622-2293
Coolinary (Meat) 31 Emek Refa'im Street [Rabbinat Yerushalayim] Tel. (02) 566-2671
Corus Al Ha'esh (Meat/Fish Grill) 43, Yirmiyahu Street Tel. (02) 538-6061
Corus Dairy (Dairy) Center One [Mehadrin] Tel. (02) 538-3507
Corusin (Chinese/Meat) Jerusalem Mall, Malkha [Mehadrin] Tel. (02) 679-1088
4 Luntz Street [Mehadrin] Tel. (02) 624-2042
Cup 'O Joe (Dairy) 38 Keren Ha'yesod [Rabbinat Yerushalayim] Tel. (02) 561-0555

Darna (Moroccan/Meat) 3, Horkanus Street [Mehadrin] Tel. (02) 624-5406
1868 (Dairy) 10, King David Street [Rabbinat Yerushalayim] Tel. (02) 622-2313
Eldad Vezehoo (French/Meat)
31, Jaffa Road [Rabbinat Yerushalayim] Tel. (02) 625-4007
El Gaucho Steakhouse 22, Rivlin Street [Rabbinat Yerushalayim] Tel. (02) 624-2227
(Argentinian/Meat) Note: Not all branches are closed on Shabbat.
Eshel Avrohom (Meat)
9, Yirmiyahu Street [Rabbinat Yerushalayim & Mehadrin] Tel. (02) 537-3584
Ethio-Israel (Ethiopian/Meat)
5, Elyashar Street [Rabbinat Yerushalayim] Tel. (077) 622-3994
Eucalyptus (Meat) 7, Horkanus Street [Rabbinat Yerushalayim] Tel. (02) 623-2864
Gabriel (French-Fusion/Meat)
7, Shimon Ben Shetach [Rabbinat Yerushalayim & Mehadrin] Tel. 902) 624-6444
Ginger Noodle Bar (Meat) 103, Herzl Boulevard [Mehadrin] Tel. (077) 211-4440
Goldie (Meat) 5, Yoel Solomon [Rabbinat Yerushalayim & Mehadrin] Tel. (02) 623-3255
Gong (Japanese/Sushi Bar/Meat)
33, Jaffa Road [Badatz & Rabbinat Yerushalayim] Tel. (02) 625-0818
Grill Bar (Meat) 1, Ha'soreg [Rabbinat Yerushalayim & Mehadrin] Tel. (02) 622-3761
Grill on the Terrace (Meat) Inbal Hotel [Rabbinat Yerushalayim] Tel. (02) 675-6688
Ha'Finjan (Meat)
149, Agrippas Street [Rabbinat Yerushalayim & Mehadrin] Tel. (02) 622-2241
Ha'mishpacha (Meat) 12, Yoel Solomon [Rabbinat Yerushalayim] Tel. (02) 623-6886
Hapetilia (Meat)
17, Hauman Street (Lev Talpiot) [Rabbinat Yerushalayim] Tel. (02) 679-8994
Ha'tajeen (Moroccan/Meat)
15, Yad Ha'rutzim Street [Rabbinat Yerushalayim] Tel. (02) 625-4036
Heimisha Essen (Meat)
19, Keren Kayemet Street [Rabbinat Yerushalayim] Tel. (02) 563-9845
Hess (Meat) 9, Heleni Ha'malka [Badatz & Mehadrin] Tel. (02) 625-5115
Holy Bagel (Fish/Dairy) 39, Jaffa Road [Badatz] Tel. (02) 672-0844
Holyland Park Cafe (Dairy) Holyland Hotel [Rabbinat Yerushalayim] Tel. (02) 642-0905
Joy Grill & Beer (Meat)
24, Emek Refa'im Street [Rabbinat Yerushalayim] Tel. (02) 563-0033
Keyara (Meat) 8, Ramban Street [Rabbinat Yerushalayim & Mehadrin] Tel. (02) 566-3271
Kohinoor (Indian/Meat)
Holiday Inn Crowne Plaza [Rabbinat Yerushalayim] Tel. (02) 653-6667
Korea House
23, Joel Solomon Street [Rabbinat Yerushalayim & Mehadrin] Tel. (02) 625-4756
La Boca (Meat)
46, Emek Refa'im Street [Rabbinat Yerushalayim & Mehadrin] Tel. (077) 214-7755
La Carossa
7, Shatz Street (Montefiore Hotel) [Rabbinat Yerushalayim & Mehadrin] Tel. (02) 623-0056
La Guta (French/Oriental/Meat/Fish)
18, Rivlin Street [Rabbinat Yerushalayim] Tel. (02) 623-2322

Little Italy (Italian/Dairy)
38, Keren Ha'yesod Street [Rabbinat Yerushalayim] Tel. (02) 561-7638
Little Jerusalem-Anna Ticho (Dairy/Fish)
9, Ha'rav Kook Street [Rabbinat Yerushalayim] Tel. (02) 624-4186
Lugar (Meat) 6, Rabbi Akiva Street [Rabbinat Yerushalayim] Tel. (02) 622-1616
Luigi (Italian/Fish/Dairy)
12, Yoel Solomon Street [Rabbinat Yerushalayim] Tel. (02) 623-2524
Macaroni (Dairy) 28, King George Street [Rabbinat Yerushalayim] Tel. (02) 623-5533
Marvad Ha'ksmamim (Magic Carpet) (Yemenite/Meat)
16, King George Street [Rabbinat Yerushalayim & Mehadrin] Tel. (02) 625-4470
42, Emek Refa'im Street Tel. (02) 567-0007
Malcha Tech Park
Masryk (Fish) 31, Emek Refa'im Street [Rabbinat Yerushalayim] Tel. (02) 563-6418
Menorah Coffee Bar (Dairy)
87, Ha'yehudim Street (Old City) [Rabbinat Yerushalayim] Tel. (02) 628-9944
Montefiore (Italian/Dairy)
The Windmill (Yemin Moshe) [Rabbinat Yerushalayim] Tel. (02) 623-2928
Muscat (Italian/Dairy) 24, Kanfei Nesharim [Mehadrin] Tel. (02) 652-4414
New Deli (Meat) 33, Hillel Street [Nachlat Yitzchok] Tel. 1 700 700 788
Nina's Bagel Cafe (Dairy) 7, Paran Street [Badatz & Mehadrin] Tel. (02) 581-5434
Norman's Steak 'N Burger (Meat)
27, Emek Refa'im Street [Mehadrin] Tel. (02) 566-6603
Olive Bar & Restaurant (Meat) 36, Emek Refa'im Street [Rabbinat Yerushalayim] Tel. (02) 561-1102
Olive & Fish (Meat) 2, Jabotinsky Street [Rabbinat Yerushalayim] Tel. (02) 566-5020
Osaka (Japanese/Fish/Sushi)
7/23, Sapir Center [Rabbinat Yerushalayim & Mehadrin & Badatz]
Pera e Mela (Italian/Dairy) 6 Safra Square [Rabbinat Yerushalayim] Tel. (02) 623-0280
Pninat Hayam (Dairy/Fish)
7, Hatenufa Street [Rabbinat Yerushalayim] Tel. (02) 673-6746
Primavera (Italian/Dairy/Fish) Sheraton Plaza Hotel [Mehadrin] Tel. (02) 629-8666
Quiche Cafe (Dairy/Vegetarian) 2, Ha'palmach Street Tel. (02) 563-7969
Rachmo Cafeteria (Meat) 16, Yoel Solomon Street Tel. (02) 624-0468
Ragu (Italian/Meat) 41, Derech Beit Lechem Tel. (02) 673-0760
Rimon Cafe (Dairy) 4, Lunz Street [Rabbinat Yerushalayim] Tel. 1 599 501 030
Rimon Meat Restaurant (same as above)
Sbarro Pizza (Dairy) 35, Jaffa Street (new location) Tel. (02) 623-2678
Selina (Dairy/Fish) 24 Emek Refaim [Rabbinat Yerushalayim] Tel. (02) 567-2049
Shakespeare (Dairy/Fish)
2, Betar Street (Arnona) [Rabbinat Yerushalayim] Tel. (02) 673-2715
Sheyan
8, Ramban Street (Windmill) [Rabbinat Yerushalayim & Mehadrin] Tel. (02) 561-2007
Sophia (Italian/Dairy) Inbal Hotel [Rabbinate Yerushalaim] Tel. (02) 675-6689

T'mol Shilshom (Dairy & Bookstore)
5, Yoel Solomon Street [Rabbinate Yerushalayim] Tel. (02) 623-2758
Vaqueiro (South American/Meat)
54, Ha,nevi'im Street [Rabbinate Yerushalayim] Tel. (02) 624-7432
Village Green (Vegetarian) 33, Jaffa Road [Rabbinate Yerushalayim] Tel. (02) 625-3065
Yo Ja (Japanese/Meat)
25, Emek Refa'im Street [Rabbinate Yerushalayim] Tel. (02) 561-1344

Happenings in Jcrusalem

ISRAELI FOLK DANCING
• **Matnas Armon Ha'netziv** (Sunday) 8:00pm Mimi Kogan Tel. (052) 370-6395
• 11, Rechov Bezalel (Sunday) 8:00pm Yael Shim'oni Tel. (02) 678-1529
• 137, Sde Herzl Matnas Ziv (Monday) 7:15pm David Zilka Tel. (02) 642-2695
• 243, Jaffa Road (Tuesday) 7:30pm Malka Bachar Tel. (03) 966-8133
• **Beit Ha'kerem** (Tuesday) 8:45pm David Zilka Tel. (02) 642-2695
• **Beit Ha'noar**
105, Rechov Herzog (Tuesday) 6:00pm Boaz Cohen Tel. (02) 624-4368
　　　　　　　　(Wednesday) 8:00pm Avner Naeim Tel. (02) 678-2261
　　　　　　　　(Thursday) 8:00pm Haim Zemach Tel. (02) 536-1197
　　　　　　　　(Saturday) 9:00pm Avner Naeim
• Nostalgia Session at **Beit Ha'noar** (First Monday each month) Avner Naeim

Women-only Sessions
• 9, Rechov Aharoni (Sunday) 7:30pm Mali Cohen Tel. (02) 993-2307
• 4, Elazar Ha'gadol Street (Monday) 8:00pm Roni Broza Tel. (02) 642-3419
• **Beit Sefer Maimon** (Tuesday) 7:00pm Sarit Doron Tel. (02) 641-3342
　　　　　　　　　　(Wednesday) 7:30pm Zvia Waill Tel. (02) 999-5556

THEATERS & CONCERT HALLS
Beit Shmuel 6, Shama Tel. (02) 620-3455
Center Stage Theater
Mercaz Ha'magshimim Hadassah 7-A, Dor v'Dorsgav Tel. (02) 561-9165
Gerard Behar Center 11, Bezalel Tel. 902) 560-5755
Hama'abada (The Lab) 28, Hebron Tel. (02) 673-4116
Hazira Performance Art Theater Talpiot Tel. (02) 673-3814
Hirsch Theater Beit Shmuel, King David Tel. (02) 620-3427
Jerusalem Music Center Mishkenot She'ananim Tel. (02) 623-4347
The Jerusalem Theater 20, Marcus Tel. (02) 560-5755
Khan Theater 2, David Remez Tel. (02) 671-8281
Pargod Theater 94, Bezalel Tel. (02) 625-8819
Targ Music Center Ein Kerem Tel. (02) 641-4250
Train Theater Liberty Bell Gardens Tel. (02) 561-8514

NIGHTCLUBS
Note: These establishments may not serve kosher foods.
Barood Bar Restaurant 31, Jaffa Tel. (02) 625-9081
Fink's King George & Histadrut Tel. (02) 623-4523
Mike's Place 37, Jaffa Tel. (0522) 670-965

COMEDY CLUB
Off the Wall Comedy
(Little Coffee House in Baka) Yehuda & Hevron Tel. (0508) 755-688

Former yeshiva along Rechov Straus,
near the Bikor Cholim Hospital.

Will the real chassid please stand up.
Street scene in Me'a Shearim.

Tour #3 - Judean Hills

NOTE: Some of the stops on this tour are now under the control of the Palestinian Authority. It is strongly advised to check in advance with the Israeli military authorities whether it is safe to visit these sites.

Rachel's Tomb

Rachel was the Matriarch not buried with her husband, Jacob, in the Cave of Machpéla in Hebron. According to the Bible, Rachel died in Efrat, which is on the way to Bethlehem. Rachel's Tomb is located just to the north of Bethlehem, and just to the south of the Gilo section of Jerusalem. There are daily buses (except Saturday) to Rachel's Tomb from the central bus station in Jerusalem. The modest dome over the site as well as the prayer hall were rebuilt by Sir Moses Montefiore in 1841. Montefiore was a renowned philanthropist who lived in Ramsgate, England. When his wife, Lady Judith, died he designed her mausoleum (located next to the Ramsgate Synagogue) as an exact replica of Rachel's Tomb in Israel. Ramsgate is located in the once-lavish seaside resort along the English Channel, just north of Dover. The former Montefiore Estate has been sold to developers. New condominiums are being built along its "White Cliffs." The synagogue and its adjoining mausoleum are in danger of being demolished. There were plans on removing both structures and bringing them to Israel where they would be rebuilt. Those plans have not been carried out as of this date.

Bethlehem

Bethlehem is best known, especially to Christians, as the birthplace of Jesus. Manger Square was once a crowded place with thousands of pilgrims coming during the Christmas season. In recent years, those pilgrims have numbered only a few dozen. This is due to the violent situation of the most recent intifada. The Church of the Nativity contains the Grotto of the Nativity, a

Rachel's Tomb in 1900. Today, it is surrounded by an Israeli military compound.

low, irregularly shaped marble chamber which, according to tradition, is the actual birthplace of Jesus.

Herodion

Herodion (Har Hordus) is a cone-shaped mountain located five miles east of Bethlehem on the edge of the Judean Desert. In 40 B.C.E., Herod was forced to flee from Jerusalem. A decisive battle proved victorious for Herod at this location. In honor of this victory, Herod had his engineers "build" this mountain. The 100-meter-high "man-made" mountain became a memorial to the battle. It housed Herod's summer palace, but also served as a fortress, and ultimately was the site where Herod was buried.

Today, to reach the summit, there is a gently sloped road winding upwards around the mountain. Originally, the only way up was from the north, where two hundred steps of the whitest marble were constructed. Opposite this grand staircase was the rest of the palace grounds called Lower Herodion. Herod's engineers succeeded in overcoming the aridity of the desert by building an aqueduct from the spring near Solomon's Pools, south of Bethlehem, all the way to Herodion.

There are 37 additional acres in Lower Herodion which contain the remains of an enormous pool. It measured 70 by 45 meters and was four meters deep. The pool served as a reservoir for water brought in by the aqueduct and as a swimming pool for hot summer days.

Herodion was used by the Zealots in the first revolt against Rome. They, too, committed suicide before the Romans captured the fortress, similar to the events at Masada and Gamla. The followers of Bar Kochba used Herodion during their rebellion. This group constructed a series of tunnels or bunkers built into the mountain.

The mountain fortress today contains the remains of Herod's summer palace, a Roman bathhouse, synagogue, mikveh, and four round observation towers. Note: This area has been closed as a restricted military zone. For further information about Herodion National Park Tel. (03) 776-2251.

Gush Etzion

GUSH ETZION MUSEUM

Four kibbutzim along the road from Jerusalem to Hebron were in the center of battles in the War of Independence. Two hundred and fifty Israeli soldiers were killed in those battles. The Israelis were forced to retreat. In 1967, the region was liberated by the Israeli Defense Forces. Jews returned to their former settlements in the area known as Gush Etzion or the Etzion Block. The Gush Etzion Museum displays the heroic stories of these people. Hours are Sunday-Thursday 8:30-1:00, Friday 8:30-11:00. For further information Tel. (02) 693-5233.

Hebron

TOMB OF THE PATRIARCHS

Hebron is the highest of the four Jewish Holy Cities (Hebron, Jerusalem, Safed, and Tiberias) at an altitude of 1,030 meters above sea level. The Cave of Machpéla (Tomb of the Patriarchs) is located in Hebron. Abraham purchased this cave as a family burial site after his wife, Sarah, died. In Biblical times, Hebron was known as Kiryat Arba, *District of the Four*. This refers to the four married couples who are buried in the cave: Abraham and Sarah, Isaac and Rebecca, Jacob and Leah, and Adam and Eve. Tradition has it that Adam and Eve lived in Hebron after their banishment from the Garden of Eden. Rachel, Jacob's second wife, is not buried here but is rather buried on the way to Bethlehem.

Inside the Tomb of the Patriarchs are stone cenotaphs which are empty. The Patriarchs' gravesites are actually 18 meters below the synagogue and mosque level and are sealed off. The shaft leading down to the gravesites is marked by a brass plate in the Hall of Isaac.

The magnificent structure housing the Tomb of the Patriarch was built by King Herod about 2,000 years ago, in the Second Temple period. It is the largest building in Israel to be preserved from that period with every stone intact. When the Byzantines and later Crusaders captured Hebron, the building was converted into a church. During the Moslem period, it was turned into a mosque. The crenelated parapet was added to the façade during the Mameluke conquest.

During this period, until after the Six Day war in 1967, Jews were not permitted to enter the Tomb of the Patriarchs. They were restricted to the top seven steps east of the building. Today, the Tomb of the Patriarchs serves as a synagogue and a mosque. Following the attack on the mosque by a Jewish soldier, Baruch Goldstein, on Purim day about several years ago, security has been tightened. A new concrete partition separates the synagogue from the mosque. Jews are now permitted to pray at the synagogue on all days except Friday, the Moslem Sabbath.

The historical Jewish Quarter (ghetto) of Hebron was established in 1540. It was built around a courtyard, with the grand Avraham Avinu Synagogue at its center. There were nine synagogues in Hebron, two religious schools for children, three yeshivot, religious courts, the Beit Hadassah Hospital (established in 1893), a mikveh, two guest houses, two bakeries, inns, and other public institutions.

In 1912, the lavish home of a wealthy Turkish Jew, Beit Romano, was purchased by Rabbi Shalom Schneerson of Chabad. It became the noted Torat Emet Lubavitch Yeshiva. Nearly 600 Jews lived in relative harmony with their Arab neighbors in Hebron until Saturday, August 24, 1929. At about 9:00 in the morning the Arabs of Hebron and the neighboring villages ganged up in the streets and called for a massacre of the Jews. Sheikh Taleb Morke and other notables took the lead, proclaiming in the name of the Mufti "that the day had come to kill and annihilate all the Jews, from young to old, and that the religious leaders had said that they could take the Jews' women and property."

The rioters went from house to house unhindered, indiscriminantly killing and slaughtering young and old, men and women. They set fire to the synagogues, Beit Hadassah Hospital, and other buildings. A total of 69 Jews were murdered in this pogrom. If it were not for a few kind-hearted Arab neighbors who hid many Jews in their homes, the entire community of nearly 600 Jews would have been wiped out. There was another anti-Jewish riot in the city in 1936. Hebron remained *Judenrein* (with Jews) until the Six Day War in 1967.

There are about 400 Jewish settlers living in the Old Jewish Quarter of Hebron. There is a small museum located in the former Beit Hadassah Hospital. The exhibit presents a history of the former Jewish community of Hebron. The nearest Jewish settlement is located just outside Hebron in Kiryat Arba. There are about 5,000 Jews living in that town.

Tour #4 - Dead Sea

Dead Sea

Israel is located at the junction of three continents; Africa, Asia, and Europe. It is on one of the earth's major geological fault lines, the Syrian/African Rift. The fault line begins in southern Turkey and northern Syria, extends southward through Syria's Bak'aa Valley and continues through Israel's Hula Valley, Sea of Galilee, Jordan River Canyon, Dead Sea, and past Eilat, into the Red Sea. It continues all the way to Lake Victoria in Malawi, Africa.

At one time, in geologic time, the cliffs on the Israeli side of the Dead Sea were level with the cliffs on the opposite side, in Jordan. The middle section then "dropped down," via major geologic fault activity in the Pleistocene era, creating a "Rift Valley" which today contains the Dead Sea. There was once an ancient lake, whose waters reached 700 feet above the present level of the Dead Sea, called Lashon (Tongue) Lake. Over the centuries, the level of this lake dropped to its present level. There is evidence of the water receding along the cliff-faces on the banks of the present Dead Sea.

It is this rift that has given shape to the mountains and valleys, and it is the reason why you can stand at the Sea of Galilee, 700 feet below sea level, and look up toward the north and see Mount Hermon towering 9,000 feet above sea level. It is also the reason for the earthquakes and volcanic eruptions over the centuries, as well as for the mineral hot springs around the shores of the Sea of Galilee and the Dead Sea.

The Dead Sea is the lowest spot on the surface of the earth. It lies 394 meters or 1,292 feet below sea level. The lowest point in the United States is in Death Valley, California, which lies only 282 feet below sea level. In recent years, sink-holes have appeared along the shores of the Dead Sea. This is due to the diversion up north of the Jordan River by Israel.

Jericho

NOTE: Some of the stops in this area are now under the control of the Palestinian Authority. It is strongly advised to check in advance with the Israeli military authorities whether it is safe to visit these sites.

HEROD'S WINTER PALACE
Jericho, 820 feet below sea level, is reputed for its mild and warm climate in the winter with a very scanty rainfall. Even in ancient times the wealthy of Jerusalem and other parts of Israel wintered here, leading a life of great luxury and ease. King Herod constructed his winter palace, Kipros, in Jericho. The palace was built just west of Jericho, on the south side of Wadi Kelt (Nahal Perath). There are remains of a magnificent hall, a circular frigidarium of a bathhouse, an Olympic-size swimming pool, and several mikvehs. Mark Anthony, the Roman ruler, removed the Jericho Valley from Herod's hands and gave it to his beloved Cleopatra of Egypt. Nearby, Wadi Kelt is today a very popular hiking area. Be sure to see the St. George Monastery built into the rock formations of Wadi Kelt. In the spring, there are beautiful waterfalls in the area.

HISHAM'S PALACE
Caliph Hisham built his palace in 724. It was destroyed during an earthquake just before Hisham moved in. The site contains exquisite floor mosaics, bathhouses, heating systems, pools, and saunas. The Rockefeller Museum in Jerusalem has a model of what the entire palace looked like before the earthquake.

"SHALOM AL YISRAEL" SYNAGOGUE
The sixth century synagogue near Jericho contains a beautiful floor mosaic with details of a menorah, lulav, and shofar and a unique Hebrew inscription, *Shalom Al Yisrael*,

"Peace upon Israel." Several years ago, the synagogue was "manned" by yeshiva students but they were surrounded by Palestinian Authority police units. The students have since vacated the premises.

Salt crystals exposed as the Dead Sea evaporates.
Courtesy Ministry of Tourism. Photo by Itamar Greenberg.

Kibbutz Almog

HOUSE OF THE SCRIBE

This museum has replicas of some of the more famous and interesting scrolls found at Qumrom, the Essenes vast library and home. Part of the permanent exhibit is a multi-media presentation and an explanation of the mysteries surrounding the Essenes and Qumron. Kibbutz Almog also offers guided tours to the Qumron Caves, several monasteries and the Judean Desert. Hours to the museum are by appointment only. For further information Tel. (02) 994-5211.

*Driving east from Jerusalem on Route 1, go to the **Almog Junction.***

Qumron Caves

In 1947, a Bedouin shepherd was looking for a goat which had wandered from the flock. He threw a stone into a cave in the side of a cliff and heard it smash some pottery. He had discovered a collection of earthernware jars containing two thousand year old parchment manuscripts. The largest was a seven meter long ancient Hebrew text of the Book of Isaiah. Many of these Dead Sea Scrolls are now on display in the Israel Museum. In 1949, archaeologists uncov-ered the village of the sect which wrote the Dead Sea Scrolls. The site was settled by the Essenes, a Jewish sect whose members were disillusioned by the corruption and Hellenization of their fellow Jerusalemites and therefore sought refuge in the cliffs of the Judean Desert. The archaeological site contains a small fort, a large room where writing tables and small inkpots were found, mikvehs, and water reservoirs. The Qumron National Park is open Sunday-Thursday 8:00-6:00. For further information Tel. (02) 994-2235.

*Turn right and go south along Route 90 to the **Qumron Caves.***

Ein Feshkha

The oasis of Ein Feshkha (Ein Zukim) is where the Essenes grew their food. It is located three kilometers south of the Qumron caves. Ein Feshkha today is a popular bathing site, where you can swim (float) in the Dead Sea and later wash off the salt and minerals in the fresh water of the Ein Feshkha springs. For further information Tel. (02) 994-2355.

*Continue driving south along Route 90 to **Ein Feshkha.***

Kibbutz Mitzpeh Shalem

MURABBAT CANYON

The Murabbat Canyon is located near Kibbutz Mitzpe Shalem

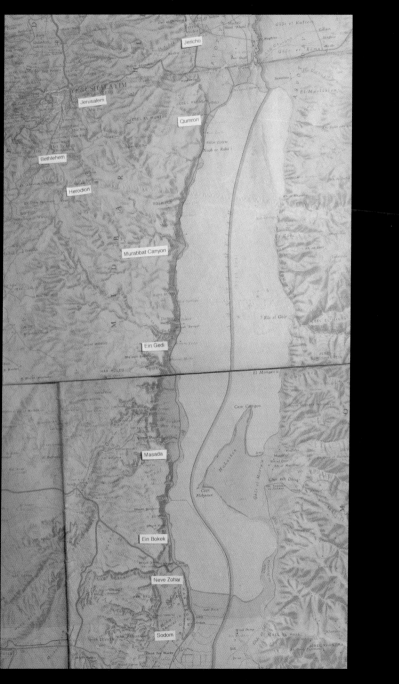

Jericho

PRUSHALAYIM
Jerusalem

Qumron

Bethlehem

Herodion

Murabbat Canyon

Ein Gedi

Masada

Ein Bokek

Neve Zohar

Sodom

Courtesy Survey of Israel.

and its field school. There are caves where additional first and second century scrolls have been discovered. These caves were used by followers of Bar Kochba during the revolt in 135 C.E. Do not attempt to go hiking on your own in these sheer cliff rock formations. Adults can learn cliff rappelling off the Mitzukay Dragot cliffs. The two-day rappelling course is about $120. Jeep tours in the Judean Desert are also available at the kibbutz.

Ein Gedi

Ein Gedi is an oasis in the wilderness formed by a stream of pure water that emerges from underground springs in the mountainside and comes down a deep wadi, forming glorious clear pools at the foot of waterfalls. Ein Gedi was the site where David hid in a cave from the wrath of King Saul in Biblical times. There are remains of an ancient synagogue near Kibbutz Ein Gedi. On the floor of the synagogue are mosaic tiles in the design of a peacock. Upon further digging, archaeologists discovered an even earlier synagogue underneath. Its floor mosaic shocked many on the team. Its design was that of a swastika! That design was simply a geometric pattern commonly used in designs of antiquity. Kibbutz Ein Gedi was established as a border settlement in 1948.

*Continue driving south along Route 90 to **Ein Gedi**.*

KIBBUTZ EIN GEDI BOTANICAL GARDEN
Even people who have no real affinity to desert scapes admit that the Ein Gedi oasis is a sight not to be missed. Imagine an oasis with over 800 unique and rare species of trees, shrubs and flowers from all over the world. The result is a one-of-a-kind, exotic and well-tended botanical garden containing Biblical plants such as myrrh and frankincense, rare trees such as baobab, tropical plants from the rainforests, date palms and other palm trees, fruit trees, local plants such as the Sodom apple, and many more. Nearby is the Cactus Park, with a rare collection of 1,000 species of cactus and desert plants from around the world. The houses are set among this exotic flora, providing a rare and picturesque way of life for members of Kibbutz Ein Gedi. For further information call (08) 659-4222.

EIN GEDI HOT SPRINGS & SPA
On the shores of the Dead Sea, at the foot of the Judean Hills to the west, and facing the Mountains of Moab to the east, at the lowest spot on earth, nature has created thermo-mineral

springs with healing properties found nowhere else.The water temperature in the Ein Gedi Spa is a constant 38 degrees C. The high concentration of salts in the water, ten times higher than anywhere else, creates the Dead Sea's famous floating effect, providing a sense of weightlessness and soothing warmth. You can relax and get mud baths or dip in a sulfer pool. For further information call (800) 844-4007.

DODIM CAVE

More adventurous hikers can attempt the 50-minute hike to the Dodim (Lovers) Cave. From the Nahal David waterfall, take the trail up the hill. At the top, follow the path to the Ein Gedi spring, and then continue to the Dodim Cave.

A metal ladder attached to the cliff provides access down to the cave. The water of Nahal David runs through the cave, making it well worth the trip, but please be extremely careful. The cave is at the top of the Ein Gedi waterfall. Do not approach the edge! For further information Tel. (08) 658-4585.

*There are many hiking trails throughout the **Ein Gedi Nature Reserve**..*

NAHAL ARUGOT

For the real nature-lover, the less known Nahal Arugot is recommended. From the parking lot, follow the path to the Hidden Waterfall, which drops into a deep pool in a secluded canyon. The hike to the waterfall takes one hour.

EIN GEDI HIKING TRAILS

Many hiking trails begin in Ein Gedi. Best known are the trails to the Hever Caves and Ma'ale Iss'im (Essenes Ascent), the trail to the Dry Canyon and Mount Yishai, and the trail to Ma'ale Ein Gedi and Ma'ale B'nei Ha'moshavim. For information about these hikes, inquire at the Ein Gedi Field School. Hikers on these trails should be accommodated by an experienced guide.

NAHAL DAVID NATURE RESERVE

The main path of the reserve follows the riverbed as it climbs to the Nahal David waterfall. The hike to the waterfall and back takes about 40 minutes. Hidden pools in the rich foliage along the way make the trip extra refreshing.

Date palms are harvested along the Dead Sea near Ein Gedi.

Masada

Proceed south along Route 90 until you reach **Masada**.

Masada is located in the Judean Desert. The region represents a mountain wilderness with an apparently chaotic landscape of innumerable valleys of all kinds. Many of them are canyons cut in harder rock exposed along the geologic fault lines. The higher-lying portions form a maze of mostly flat-topped hills. These hills appear as badlands. It was mainly this type of relief and the absence of productive soils–that throughout historical times rendered it a region of desolation and a refuge for fugitives from the law and prevented any permanent settlement.

Masada is located 12 miles south of Ein Gedi and about 20 miles north of Sodom, opposite the Ha'lashon (the tongue-shaped peninsula on the Jordanian side) of the Dead Sea. The great flat-topped mount or mesa projects from the rest of the mountain range and rises a sheer 320 meters (1,300 feet); its plateau measures about 650 meters by 220 meters.

There are four main periods which have left their mark on Masada. The Hashmoneans built a fortress, palace, water storage systems, and roads between 100 and 60 B.C.E. King Herod undertook major construction projects throughout Israel between 37 and 4 B.C.E. Most of what is present today on Masada was built by Herod. The Zealots moved onto Masada during the Great Revolt, from 66 to 74 C.E., in order to escape from the Roman legions. They redesigned some of the buildings and also built new housing. The last group to inhabit Masada were Christian monks during the Byzantine period.

Herod erected a defense wall with 37 watch towers 75 feet high around the rim of the Masada plateau. At the northeastern corner, looking out across the Dead Sea, he built a most extraordinary three-tiered, hanging palace-villa. Access to the middle and bottom terraces was by a staircase invisible from the outside, enclosed in a shaft scooped out of the rock. He kept the top of the mesa clear for cultivation and stored water from the winter flash floods in large rock cisterns which were filled by way of aqueducts from the escarpment behind the mesa. The smooth plaster lining of these cisterns is still intact. Storage chambers for grain, dates, wine, and oil were also built into the fortress. Since this region is in an exceptionally dry climate, it was possible to store food for many years.

When Jerusalem fell to Titus in 70 C.E., a band of Jewish patriots, called Zealots, numbering nearly one thousand with their women and children and led by Eliezer ben Ya'ir, fled to Masada. They were pursued by a huge Roman force under General Flavius Silva, who encircled the mountain and, for

*While hiking along the cliffs near the Dead Sea
one can often see a Nubian Ibex.*
Courtesy Ministry of Tourism

three years, tried in vain to storm the fortress. The besieging Tenth Legion numbered some 10,000 legionaires and about 15,000 auxiliaries and slaves. They built eight encampments around Masada, so well constructed that they stand to this day.

The Romans then laid siege to the fortress and built a siege-wall measuring close to five kilometers around the mountain to prevent anyone escaping or receiving any food and supplies from the outside. They then proceeded to construct a huge earthen ramp from the western side of the mesa at an angle to a height of 100 meters. The ramp, a wooden form onto which soil was poured and pressed in place, has survived in the arid desert climate to this day.

On the ramp, 50 meters from the table-top of Masada, the Romans built their war engines; a battering ram built on top of a solid square platform. When the Romans finally breached the stone walls of Masada, they discovered that the Jews in the meantime had built another wall opposite the same spot–a wall of earth, invincible to battering rams which can break rigid stone walls only. To prevent the earth from being scattered, the Zealots poured it over a wooden frame. The Romans set this wall on fire. The Romans waited until the next morning to capture their stubborn enemy on Masada.

That evening, the Zealot's leader, Eliezer ben Ya'ir, assembled all the people on Masada–nine hundred and sixty men, women, and children–and ordered each man to slaughter his family in order not to be taken into slavery by the Romans. When the Romans came to capture the fortress the next morning, instead of being greeted by a battle-cry, they were greeted by an unnerving silence. At first they suspected a trap. But upon finding the hundreds of dead bodies, they felt no glory of victory.

Two women and five children, who had hidden in a cave, came out and des-cribed the mass suicide pact of the previous evening. Josephus explains, "When the Romans came upon the rows of dead bodies, they did not exult over them as enemies but admired the nobility of their resolve, and the way in which so many had shown in carrying it out without a tremor, an utter contempt of death." In recognition of the symbolic importance of the site, young soldiers being inducted into the armored corps of the Israel Defense Force today swear their oath of allegiance atop the fortress and vow, "Masada shall not fall again!"

Access to the top of Masada is by convenient cable cars. For those more adventuresome, there is the Snake Path, where hikers ascend at 4:00am and reach the summit to view the sunrise over the Dead Sea. Both of these ascents are from the eastern or Dead Sea side of the mountain. On top of Masada be sure to see the Zealot's living quarters in the casement wall, the ancient synagogue, mikveh, three-tiered palace, Roman bathhouse, storehouses, western palace with its beautiful mosaics, and huge water cisterns. **During the summer season, be sure to drink plenty of water and definitely wear a hat or head covering for protection against the scorching sun.**

There is a road to the backside of Masada–site of the ancient Roman earthen ramp built up to the top of the mountain. On that western slope of Masada there is a sound and light show presented at 9:00pm (April-August) and at 7:00pm (September-October) on Tuesdays and Thursdays. These programs are given in Hebrew but headsets in English are available. Access to the western slope of Masada is only via Arad. This road (Route 3199) does not link up with the main Dead Sea road, Route 90. For further information Tel. (08) 658-4207.

Ein Bokek

This part of the southern Dead Sea is renowned for its minerals and thermal baths. Several luxury hotels have been constructed to accommodate the many visitors. The mineral springs have been in use since the first century C.E. The healing waters are believed to cure a spectrum of ailments, from skin disease to lumbago, arthritis, and rheumatism. The clinics offer sulfur baths, mineral baths, salt baths, and mud baths. It is said that Cleopatra used Dead Sea mud for her "facials." There are additional health spas in nearby Neve Zohar.

*Proceed south along Route 90 until you reach **Ein Bokek**.*

MAZAD BOQEQ
On the western side of Route 90, opposite Ein Bokek, is an archaeological site which contains ruins of Israelite and Roman fortresses.

Neve Zohar

BEIT HAYOZER MUSEUM
The Beit Hayozer Museum in Neve Zohar contains an exhibition depicting the history of the Dead Sea area and the various processes involved in the extraction of its minerals. The museum is only open to groups, by prior arrangement. For further information Tel. (057) 957-545. Nearby are ruins of a Byzantine fortress called Mazad Zohar.

*Proceed south along Route 90 to **Neve Zohar**.*

Sodom

PILLAR OF SALT
Mount Sodom was formed as a displacement block or a salt plug that took its shape via geologic faulting and erosion. It is 11 kilometers long, 2 to 3 kilometers wide and over 230 meters above sea level. In short, Mount Sodom is one big piece of salt. This is the site of the destruction of Sodom and Amorah. Abraham pleaded to spare the cities and was allowed to take his nephew, Lot, and his family on the condition that nobody "looks back" to see the destruction-
in-progress. Lot's wife took a quick look back and was turned into a Pillar of Salt.
According to local guides, Lot's Wife is located about 1.5 kilometers north of the "Ladder" trail. Look for signs on the road. Be sure to go into the Flour Cave (Me'arat Ha'kemach), which is actually powder-white limestone dust, and looks just like flour.

Continue past Neve Zohar along Route 90 to Sodom and the Dead Sea Works.

Tour #5 - Central Israel

Beit Zayit

*This tour starts in the western part of Jerusalem, just west of Har Nof and the Hadassah Medical Center. There is a small town called **Beit Zayit**.*

DINOSAUR FOOTPRINT

The remains of a dinosaur footprint are located behind the water tower in Beit Zayit.

Betar

Betar was the site where the Jewish rebels led by Bar Kochba made their last and desperate stand against the Roman legions in 135 C.E. There are archaeological remains of the Roman army camp. Betar is also known as Battir, an Arab village on the site. It is located just south of the old Jerusalem-Tel Aviv Railroad line.

The next stop may be off limits to tourists since it is near Bethlehem and requires military approval for entry. It is located due west of the Gilo section of Jerusalem.

American Independence Park

The American Independence Park is a project of the Jewish National Fund. It is located near Moshav Nes Harim, about 10 miles west of Jerusalem. The park contains the ruins of a Crusader fortress and a memorial to the United States "Space Shuttle Challenger" which exploded in mid-air about one minute after "lift-off" from Cape Canaveral, Florida. The park also contains the Nahal Sorek Nature Reserve and the magnificent Sorek Stalgtite Cave.

*From Jerusalem's Ein Kerem section, take Route 386 towards Bar Giyora. At the Bar Giyora Junction turn right onto Route 3866 past Nes Harim until you reach the **American Independence Park**.*

Moshav Kesalon

SOREK (AVSHALOM) CAVE

This cave was discovered by chance during a routine quarrying operation. The cave is over 90 meters long and about 80 meters wide. There are magnificent stalagtite and stalagmite formations. A stalagtite forms over many centuries when rains seep from the ceiling of a cave. A drop of water with dissolved limestone drips from the ceiling. It evaporates before it reaches the floor. It remains as a spot on the ceiling until, after millions of drops, the dissolved limestone creates magnificent limestone columns. There is a "floating" path in the cavern and extraordinary lighting. Photographs are strictly forbidden since exposure to flashes damages the mineral   formations. There is a slide presentation about the geology of the cavern and a guided tour. It is possible to hike to the Sorek Cave from Nes Harim (about 7 kilometers) or take an Egged tour bus from Jerusalem which takes you directly to the caverns. To find Sorek Cave on the

*Continue on Route 3866 to 3855 and then to Route 38, just north of Beit Shemesh. Turn right at Eshta'ol Junction onto Route 395. Continue east to **Moshav Kesalon**. Look for signs to the "Scroll of Fire."*

map, follow the old railroad tracks west of Jerusalem. As the tracks wind through the Judean Hills, the caverns are about two-thirds of the way towards Beit Shemesh. Sorek Caves are open Sunday-Thursday 8:30-3:00, Friday 8:30-12:30. For further information Tel. (02) 992-5756.

DAVID & GOLIATH
The valley just south of the Sorek Caves is called the Valley of Elah. This was the site where David used a sling-shot to kill the giant, Goliath. Today, the spot is marked by a giant satellite dish on a kibbutz.

Beit Guvrin

*Doubleback to Route 38, turn left and go south past Beit Shemesh, all the way to the end–to the Nekhusha Junction, turn right onto Route 35. In Beit Guvrin, look for signs for the **Beit Guvrin Caves**.*

BEIT GUVRIN CAVES
These bell-shaped caves are actually man-made, created by ancient Roman quarrying operations. There are also ruins of many historic periods, notably the Crusader ruins on either side of the road. These caves are located near Kibbutz Beit Guvrin, about 20 kilometers south of Beit Shemesh. For further information Tel. (07) 681-1020.

Moshav Amatziah

*Take Route 35 west to the Lachish Junction. Turn left onto Route 3415. Go past Lachish for about 8 kilometers to **Moshav Amatziah**.*

BAR KOCHBA CAVES
The Bar Kochba (Hazan) Caves were discovered in 1980 near Moshav Amatziah. More than 35 rooms are connected by a network of tunnels spanning approximately 750 feet. The Bar Kochba rebels transformed these underground caverns into a military camp from 132-135 C.E. There are more than 100 similar caverns throughout Israel in which Bar Kochba and his men hid during the war. They are all connected by a network of tunnels which contained food storehouses, water cisterns, oil press es, and workrooms. Some of the sites are located around the Herodion fortress, in the Judean Desert, near Gush Etzion, and in the Galilee.

Latrun Junction

*Doubleback to Route 38. Go north all the way to Route 1. Turn left and go west to the **Latrun Junction**.*

LATRUN MEMORIAL
Latrun is located midway between Jerusalem and Tel Aviv, along Route 1. It was a key position on the route to Jerusalem and Joshua, Judah Maccabee, the Muslims, and the Crusaders all fought here. There is a monastery and remains of

a Crusader fortress. During the War of Independence it was the site of bloody battles. From Latrun, Arab forces in 1948 closed the only road by which food supplies could have been brought to the besieged inhabitants of Jerusalem. The Arab Legion held this strategic junction against numerous Haganah attacks. Eventually, the Israelis secretly constructed a new passage, called the Burma Road, outside the range of the Arab guns in order to bring food to the starving residents of Jerusalem. Parts of the old Burma Road are still there. Go back east towards Jerusalem on Route 1 to Sha'ar Ha'gai Junction. Turn right on Route 38. The very first road on the right (located about one half kilometer) was the old Burma Road.

The rusting red vehicles on the side of Route 1 today testify to those who never made it up the hill to Jerusalem. Latrun remained in Arab hands until the 1967 Six Day War.

ARMORED CORPS MUSEUM
The Latrun Museum serves as a memorial for the fallen soldiers of the Armored Corps. There is an exhibit of military vehicles and weapons from the different periods of Israeli Defense Force battles. Hours are Sunday-Thursday 8:30-4:30, Friday 8:30-12:30, Saturday & Holidays 9:00-4:00. For further information Tel. (08) 925-5268.

Mini Israel

Visitors to Israel may not have the time see all of the sites in the country. Mini Israel was designed to highlight 350 sites throughout the country in miniature scale models built at 1:25 scale. This is similar to Madurodam in Amsterdam, Holland. There are enough models to stimulate kids as well as adults. Several models have moving parts and have sound effects. A model of the Temple Mount has about 200 squatting Arabs (each about three inches in height). When the sound of the muezzin calls them to prayer, they all bend over in unison. There are people skiing down Mount Hermon, a windmill farm to generate electricity on the Golan Heights, an animated soccer game near Tel Aviv. There are detailed architectural models of modern skyscrapers in Tel Aviv, the Tomb of the Patriarchs in Hebron, and the Western Wall in Jerusalem. There is a replica of Masada and the Roman legion building an earthen ramp before it breaks the upper walls with its battering ram. But if you take a closer look at this model, it's actually a replica of the making of a television movie about Masada. There are miniature camera crews shooting from different angles at this scene. There are model rail

At the junction of Route 1 and Route 3, turn west and follow the signs to Mini Israel.

roads in Tel Aviv, jets at Ben Gurion Airport, and live fish in the Underwater Observatory model in Eilat. There's something for everyone. Mini Israel is designed in plan in the shape of a Star of David. There are little hills and valleys. It is handicapped accessible. There are motorized golf carts available. Mini Israel is located in the Ayalon Valley across from the Latrun Armored Corps Memorial. Hours are Sunday-Monday & Wednesday-Thursday 9:00-6:00, Tuesday & Saturday 9.00am-11;00pm, Friday 9.00-6:00. It is recommended to come to Mini Israel an hour or two before sunset. Many of the models light up after dark. It's like going to two separate parks—one in daylight, the second with special lighting effects. For further information Tel. (08) 922-2444.

Canada Park

Take Route 3 east to Canada Park.

Canada or Ayalon Park is devoted to the history of agricultural life. It is covered with trees and vegetation characteristic of farming in Israel in the time of the Mishnah and Talmud. The park, well-tended by the Jewish National Fund with monies contributed by Canadian Jews, stretches over the entire eastern edge of the Ayalon Valley and Judean Hills range. There are plans on building the extension of the Tel Aviv-Ben Gurion Airport-Jerusalem railroad underneath Canada Park. But it is being met with fierce protests from environmentalists.

Modi'in

Continue northeast on Route 3 to Route 443, turn left and go west to Modi'in.

Modi'in was the birthplace of the Hashmonean family, who led the revolt against the Syrian-Greek Empire, which controlled Judea in the second century B.C.E. The revolt started when an official of the empire came to Modi'in to order the people to sacrifice pigs on a pagan altar. The revolt, led by Judah Maccabeus, started when the officials of the empire were killed. It quickly spread over all of Judea, resulting in the recapture of the Holy Temple and the restoration of Jewish worship in Jerusalem.

Today, there is a beautiful park in Modi'in with a model of a village of the period of the revolt. There are replicas of ancient agricultural implements. Some claim that the tombs of the Hashmoneans is located in Modi'in. Others claim that the graves are more characteristics of the Roman rather than the Hellenistic period. At Chanukah, the festival commemorating the revolt, a torch is lit at Modi'in and carried in relays to Jerusalem to light candles at the Kotel (Western Wall).

Neot Kedumim

BIBLICAL LANDSCAPE RESERVE

Neot Kedumim is located halfway between Jerusalem and Tel Aviv. It is a unique endeavor to re-create the physical setting in the Bible in all its depth and detail. Far more than a "garden" showing various Biblical plants, Neot Kedumim embodies the panorama and power of the landscapes that helped shape the values of the Bible and provided a rich vocabulary for expressing them. The Bible conveys its ideas not in abstract terms, but through a clear and vivid record of long human interaction with the land of Israel. Neot Kedumim draws on a variety of disciplines—such as Bible scholarship, botany, zoology, geography, history, and archaeology—to bring the Bible and its commentaries to life.

Drive west of Modi'in along Route 443 for about 15 kilometers to Neot Kedumim.

Literally with the Bible in one hand and a spade in the other, Neot Kedumim has constructed a network of natural and agricultural landscapes bearing names that indicate their textual source: Forest of Milk and Honey, Dale of the Song of Songs, Isaiah's Vineyard, Fields of the Seven Varieties, and many more.

Thousands of tons of soil were trucked in and spread on the eroded hillsides, reservoirs were dug to catch runoff rainwater, and ancient terraces were restored. Habitats were created for such varied species as cedars from the snow-covered mountains of Lebanon and date palms from Sinai desert oases. Hundreds of varieties of Biblical and Talmudic plants; wild and domesticated animals; ancient and reconstructed olive and wine presses, threshing floors, cisterns, and ritual baths bring to life the literal roots of the Biblical tradition in the soil of the land of Israel.

By reuniting text and context, Neot Kedumim opens up before the visitor Israel's nature as the idiom of the Bible. The symbols, prayers, and holidays of the Jewish and Christian heritage, observed and preserved for thousands of years, blossom in a new and colorful dimension in Neot Kedumim, the world's only Biblical landscape reserve. Hours: Sun-Thur 8:30-4:00, Fri and Holiday eves 8:30-1:00. For further information Tel. (08) 977-0777.

Tour #6
Tel Aviv - Jaffa

Jaffa - Tel Aviv

Jaffa is one of the world's oldest cities. According to tradition, its name originates from *Yefet*, the son of Noah. Jonah fled from Jaffa port only to be swallowed by a whale. Cedars of Lebanon were brought into the Port of Jaffa on their way to Jerusalem. Those cedars of Lebanon were used in the construction of the Holy Temple.

The development of Israel's largest city began with Jewish settlement in Yaffo (anglicized as Jaffa) in 1820, when a Jewish traveler from Constantinople settled here. Jaffa at that time served as Palestine's major port and the arrival destination for immigrants, mainly North African merchants and craftsmen, who merged with the local Arab community. Shortly thereafter, enough Jews had settled in Jaffa to create the first two exclusively Jewish neighborhoods just to the north, Neveh Tzedek in 1887 and Neveh Shalom in 1891. As the Jewish population in Jaffa continued to increase, settlers founded a suburb in this area to the north.

On April 11, 1909, they parceled out their newly acquired land north of Jaffa with the assistance from the Jewish National Fund, naming the area Ahuzat Bayit. They purchased 32 acres, and, under the leadership of Meir Dizengoff, 60 families staked their claims. One year later, the suburb's name was changed to Tel Aviv. Its first main streets included Herzl Street, Ahad Ha'am Street, and Rothschild Street; are still busy thoroughfares.

By 1921, Tel Aviv had blossomed into a separate town from Jaffa and had become home to 15,000 residents. By the outbreak of World War II, Tel Aviv was a small metropolis of 100,000 people and played host to two million Allied soldiers who passed through during the war. Although most of Israel escaped the ravages of that war, Tel Aviv was bombed by Italian and Vichy French planes.

In 1948, as the British were pulling out of Israel, the Israelis launched an attack against Jaffa, from which Arab guerrillas and snipers had been firing indiscriminately at Tel Aviv. During the battle, much of Jaffa's Arab population fled. Jaffa returned to Israeli hands during the War of Independence.

In 1949, Jaffa and Tel Aviv were merged into one city. Old Jaffa was reconstructed and renovated in 1963, with cobbled paths and alleys twisting through the massive stone fortifications surrounding the city. Tel Aviv has grown to be the center of culture, business, haute couture, and nightlife in Israel. While the city itself holds only some 350,000 residents. Tel Aviv's sizeable metropolitan district contains over two million people.

Jaffa

CLOCK TOWER

This Ottoman Clock Tower on Yefet Street was built in 1906 by a Turkish sultan and marks the entrance to the city. The tower's stained-glass windows each portray a different chapter in the port city's history. On Wednesday mornings at 9:30 there are free guided tours of the ancient port which start at the Clock Tower.

COLLECTION HOUSES

The museum documents information about the history of Jewish defense activities in the homeland beginning as early as the Hibat-Zion movement in 1881, and continuously updated to the present. The museum's collection comprises a variety of exhibits, some of them are the only remaining samples worldwide. Many articles of the extensive

Ancient port of Jaffa.
Courtesy Ministry of Tourism.

rifle and pistol collection were donated by Jews from the four corners of the world who sent their personal weapons to help defend the young country during the critical stages of the War of Independence. Unique, one-of-a-kind, innovations produced by the armament experts during the War of Independence are also on display.

A large section is devoted to enemy weapons captured during the wars, including the two coastal guns positioned by the Egyptians in 1956 near the Strait of Tiran, which resulted in the Sinai War of 1956 (Suez Operation). There are also many Russian-made weapons used by the Arab armies and Palestinian terror groups. The tank shed contains a collection of tanks from the first "Sherman" tank used by the Israel Defense Forces (IDF), to the modern Israeli-made "Merkava." There are also several captured tanks which have been introduced into active service with the IDF. The Collection Houses are located at 35 Eilat Street (corner Elif'elet). For further information Tel. (03) 517-2913.

JAFFA MUSEUM
Erected in the 18th century, the Jaffa Museum was once the Turkish governor's headquarters and the local prison. The museum contains archaeological exhibits from more than thirty years of excavations. The Jaffa Museum is located at 10, Mifratz Shlomo Street. Hours are Sunday-Monday & Wednesday-Friday 9:00-1:00, Tuesday 4:00-7:00, Saturday 10:00-1:00.

ILANA GOOR MUSEUM
This museum is located on the third floor of the artist's residence. The building was constructed in 1740. There are exhibitions of paintings, sculptures, and furniture of Israeli and foreign artists. The Ilana Goor Museum is located at 4, Mazal Dagim Street. Hours are Sunday-Saturday 10:00-4:00. The nearest bus lines are #10, 25, 46, 88. For further information Tel. 903) 683-7676.

ISRAEL DEFENSE FORCES HISTORY MUSEUM
35 Eilat Street   Tel. (03) 517-2913
The IDF History Museum is located in the old railway station in Jaffa. There are films, maps, photographs, documents. There is a "Davidka" mortar (which made alot of noise but nothing more), a "Napoleonchik " cannon, and armored cars which were used in breaking the blockade around Jerusalem during the War of Independence. Hours are Sunday-Thursday 8:30-3:30.

Tel Aviv

The City of Tel Aviv was founded in 1909, with Jaffa joining the municipality in 1949. It was constructed based on an urban plan by Sir Patrick Geddes. Tel Aviv-Jaffa is home to 400,000 residents, spread over an area of 50 square kilometers. With over 50% of jobs in banking and finance, Tel Aviv is the country's business center. A world-class cultural center, Tel Aviv-Jaffa provides a rich and varied offering of art, music, dance, theater, fashion, and cuisine.

In the 1920s, many children of European-born immigrants sent their children to a new school of architecture in Weimar (and later in Dessau), Germany–the Bauhaus. It was founded in 1919 by Walter Gropius. The school's aim was to fuse all the arts under the concept of design. Gropius engaged some of the best architects and artists of the day including Paul Klee, Mies van der Rohe, and Le Corbusier. The school was closed on April 11, 1933 by the Nazis. The Bauhaus

When these Bauhaus-trained students returned to Tel Aviv, they created nearly 4,000 buildings (constructed between 1931-1956). Bauhaus architecture was concerned with the social aspects of design and with the creation of a new form of social housing for workers. Bauhaus gained a foothold in Tel Aviv since there was no real entrenched architectural style.

Tel Aviv has the largest number of cooperative workers' apartments in the country (an urban kibbutz). The aim was to provide residents with as much equality in living quarters. These blocks of apartments, operated almost as self-contained units. Residents had a variety of services right on the premises including a post office, canteen, and kindergarten. There was also a common yard where residents could grow their own vegetables. The cooperative building on the corner of Frishman, Dov Hoz, and Frug Streets were built for the trade union movement. It was once the headquarters of the Haganah.

Many of the Bauhaus-style buildings were simple three-story structures, often built on concrete stilts known as pilotis. This allowed the wind to blow the dust and sand from the street under the building rather than through the windows. The first building in Tel Aviv which was built on stilts was designed by Ze'ev Rechter in 1933 and is located at 84 Rothschild Boulevard.

Bauhaus architecture became common in Tel Aviv for a variety of reasons. Architects who worked locally, had strong ties to the European architectural developments of the day. There was also a need to build cheaply and quickly because of the growing metropolis. The local building technology of the time was not sophisticated. Reinforced concrete was easy to work with and did not require skilled workers. Some of the Bauhaus-trained architects included Dov Carmi, Richard Kauffmann, Pinchas Hueth, Arieh Sharon, Josef Neufeld, Genia Averbuch, and Eric Mendelsohn. In 1934, Genia Averbuch designed Dizengoff Circle as a social gathering place on street level with palm trees and a beautiful fountain. The present design of Dizengoff Square is raised above the traffic congestion. It was redesigned in the 1980s. In 1936, Eric Mendlesohn designed the private residence of Israel's first president, Chaim Weizmann. It is located in Rehovot.

Some of the characteristics of Bauhaus-style architecture are:
• Lack of ornaments from earlier architectural styles e.g. Moorish, Romanesque, or Classical.
• Use of assymetry and regularity versus symmetry.
• Use of long and narrow horizontal windows.
• Some buildings look "streamlined," with gentle curves.
• Use of circular or porthole windows.
• Use of flat roofs, which were used as social gathering points in the building.
• Most Bauhaus buildings are colored white.

There are now about three thousand Bauhaus-style buildings in Tel Aviv. Fifteen hundred buildings are scheduled to be restored to their original state. On June 6, 2004, UNESCO declared Tel Aviv a "World Heritage Site" for its treasure of Bauhaus architecture. Tel Aviv's "White City" is home to more buildings designed in the Bauhaus style than anywhere in the world.

BAUHAUS CENTER

The Bauhaus Center in Tel Aviv is located at 99, Dizengoff Street. Architectural tours of the most elegant Bauhaus-inspired buildings are given. For tour information Tel. (03) 522-0249.

The colorful Yaakov Agam fountain in Dizengoff Square. In the background is the Hotel Cinema. It was originally designed as the Esther Theater in 1939 by Magidovitch. It was named after "Esther" Nathanel, a Jewish immigrant from Aden. There are plans for removing the tunnel below.

Pelzman House, located at 18, Bialik Street,

BAUHAUS ARCHITECTURE TOUR
This is one of several simplified Bauhaus Architecture tours near the junction of Rothschild Boulevard and Mazeh Street...

• #84, Rothschild Boulevard (corner Mazeh Street) was designed as the Engel House in 1933 by Ze'ev Rechter.

• #82, Rothschild Boulevard was built in 1932 and designed by Yossef and Ze'ev Berlin–a father and son architectural firm.

• #81, Rothschild Boulevard was designed by Moshe Cherner in 1931.

• #83, Rothschild Boulevard was designed in 1928 by architect Yossef Berlin and his sculptress wife, Miriam.

• #87, Rothschild Boulevard was designed by Karl Rubin in 1936.

• #89 & #91, Rothschild Boulevard was built in 1935 and was designed by Pinchas Hütt.

• #93, Rothschild Boulevard is known as the Magnet House. It was designed by Yehudau Megidowitz in 1934.

• #5, Engel Street. Known as the Aghinsky House, was designed by architect Shmuel Barkas in 1934.

• #8, Engel Street is known as the Handel House. It was built in 1936 and designed by Schwartz & Hirsch.

• #9, Engel Street was designed in 1933 by Shevah Shaprinsky.

• #6, Bilu Street was built in 1935 and designed by Arieh Streimer.

• #1, Ha'gilboa Street is located at the corner of Sheinkin Street. It was designed by Lucian Korngold in 1936.

• #68 Sheinkin Street is located at the corner of Rothschild Boulevard. It was designed in 1933 by architect Yehuda Stempler.

YAAKOV AGAM SCULPTURE
The noted artist Yaakov Agam is known for his kinetic art. He designed a very unique sculptural fountain in the center of Dizengoff Square. It is called "Fire and Water." It is a round form with Agam's standard kaleidoscope of colors but it emits fire *and* water at the same time. It's quite fascinating. The problem with Dizengoff Square these days is that there are very scary people "hanging around," namely the homeless and drug addicts. There are plans on moving this fountain to a new high-rise housing complex in Tel Aviv which was also "painted" with Yaakov Agam's trademark color schemes. It is called Ne'eman Towers and is located in the Ezory Chen section of Tel Aviv. The overpass is slated to be removed, creating the original design of a large traffic circle around the park–at grade level.

TEL AVIV MODERN SKYSCRAPER TOUR
The modern skyscraper has its origins in a small medieval village in Italy called San Gimignano. The village once contained 72 fortresslike towers, each built by rival families. Today, there are 14 towers still standing. In the world of modern architecture, large corporations are "competing" for the best corporate image for their headquarters in a country. Within the last fifteen to twenty years, Tel Aviv has seen a proliferation of skyscraper construction. Each high-rise building seems to be "competing" with its rival, similar to the "Towers of San Gimignano" in medieval times. Below are some of the more significant high-rise commercial and residential towers in Tel Aviv.

• Azrieli Towers are known as Israel's "Twin Towers." One tower is circular and the other is triangular. The tallest tower is 49 floors high. There is an Observation Deck and restaurant atop the circular tower. The architects of the Azrieli Towers were A. Yaski and Y. Sivan. The towers are located at the corner of Begin and Ha'shalom Ways. There is a pedestrian bridge which crosses the Ayalon Highway and connects with the Israel Railway station. The top of the 49-story building serves as a heliport. There is a large shopping mall on the lower floors. The upper floors are commercial.

• Tzameret Towers are 34-story residential structures. They were designed by A. Yaski and Y. Sivan. They are located at 72 Pinkas Street.

• Metcal Building is located on Begin Way, directly in front of the Azrieli Towers. The 17-story building combines two structures into one. The central elevator shaft is capped with a heliport.

• Dizengoff Tower is located at 50 Dizengoff Street. It was designed by Mordechai ben Horin. Its circular 24 floors contain a large shopping mall, parking facilities, and swimming pool on the lower floors. Above is the residential section.

• Rubinstein Tower is a sleek curved 28-story blue glass high rise. It is a commercial tower designed by A. Frieberger.

• Platinum Tower is Israel's version of a post-modern "Leaning Tower of Pisa." Part of its 28 floors slant outward. This office tower was built by Reved, Honit & Dana, Engineers. It's a really cool design—partially designed in glass and partially in stone. It is located on Ha'arbaha Street.

• Millenium Tower is located adjacent to the Platinum Tower on Ha'arbaha Street. It's a 25-story commercial structure designed by Moshe Tzur.

• The Opera Tower is located at Allenby, Herbert Samuel, and Hayarkon Streets. It was designed by A. Yaski and Y. Sivan. The 25-story structure is both commercial and residential.

• Ne'eman Towers is located in the Ezorey Chen section of Tel Aviv. It was designed by architect Kna'an Shenhav with consulting artist Yaakov Agam. Agam added the lively "coloration" to its façade. There are plans on moving Agam's famous water fountain, "Fire and Water," presently located in Dizengoff Square, to this location.

• IBM Tower is located next to the Asia House. The contrast between the two buildings is quite stark. The Asia House is a white five-story free-flowing sculptural form. The IBM Tower is a massive 24-story office tower. It is located on King Sha'ul Boulevard and Weitzman Street. It was designed by Avraham Yaski.

• Africa-Israel Tower is quite unique. Half the building was designed as a rectilinear masonry structure. The other half was designed as a curved glass edifice. It was designed by Yaski & Sivan. It is located on Herzl and Ehad Ha'am Street.

• Trade Tower is located on Ha'mered Street. It was designed by A. Yaski and Y. Sivan. The building is designed as two separate components—a half-round glass tower and its counterpart, a solid masonry rectilinear structure.

• Hashmona'im Tower, located on Begin Way and Hashmona'im Street, was designed by Rapoport Architects. Its 18 floors are composed of a interesting mix of glass and masonry elements.

• Bank Le'umi Tower is best viewed at night. It is located at Lilenbaum Street and was designed by Buki Zucker. It is a circular brick and glass structure.

• El Al House was one of the earliest skyscrapers in Tel Aviv. It has 13 floors designed in massive curved concrete elements. It is located on Ben Yehuda Street and was designed by Carmi Architects. The most unique aspect of this building is the exterior concrete spiral staircase ascending 13 stories.

BEN-GURION HOUSE
17, Ben-Gurion Boulevard
Tel. (03) 522-1010   BUS #4, 5
This was the home of Paula and David Ben-Gurion. Ben-Gurion was Israel's first Prime Minister. The library comprises some 20,000 books.There is a blocked-up window in the bedroom. It was used as a bomb shelter dur-

Leon Recanati House at 35, Menachem Begin Road was designed in 1935 by Orenstein & Liaskowsy. There are commercial shops on the ground level and residential apartments above.

BETH HATEFUTSOTH - MUSEUM OF THE JEWISH DIASPORA

Tel Aviv University - Ramat Aviv
BUS #25, 45, 49, 74, 86, 274
The Beth Hatefutsoth was founded in 1979 by Dr. Nahum Goldman, founder and first president of the World Jewish Congress. This museum contains no objects from the past, but instead is a multimedia history lesson. Here is what happened to the Jewish people, and what they accomplished in their 2,500-year history of the Diaspora, between the time they were driven from Israel and when they returned. There are photographs, replicas of artifacts, films, music, maps, and scale models vividly bring to life the communities, synagogues, households, and workshops of Jews living in dozens of countries. The Memorial Column, an abstract sculpture suspended from the roof of the building, in its central space, serves as a commemoration to Jewish martrydom and the fight for survival. The book, "Scrolls of Fire," a unique work of art, devoted to the 52 episodes of persecution in the annuls of the Jewish people, is presented below the Memorial Column.

The museum has a display of 18 scale models of synagogues throughout the world including the 1153 synagogue of Kaifeng, China, the Atl-Neu Shul of Prague, the Great Portuguese Synagogue of Amsterdam, a Venice Ghetto synagogue, the Paradesi Synagogue of Cochin, India, and the Great Synagogue of Florence, Italy. The models were designed by Displaycraft, the firm which first designed several of these architectural models for the Yeshiva University Museum in New York.

The visitor can sit at a computer panel and search for information about 3,000 Jewish communities throughout the world. A computer print-out is available afterwards. On can search for family names in the 200,000 name data bank.

Guided tours are available. Hours are Sunday-Thursday 10:00-4:00 and in July-August Friday 10:00-1:00. For further information Tel. (03) 640-8000.

BIALIK HOUSE

22, Bialik Street
BUS #4   Tel. (03) 525-4530
This was the home of Israel's national poet, Chaim Nachman Dialik, during the years 1925-1934. It remains just as it was when he died. His 94 books, with translations in 28 languages, articles, letters, paintings, photographs, and an archive of hundreds of his manuscripts are also on display. Hours are Sunday-Thursday 9:00-5:00, Saturday 11:00-2:00. Admission is free.

BIBLE MUSEUM

16, Rothschild Boulevard
Tel. (03) 517-7760
The Bible Museum is located in the Dizengoff House. One wing of the museum, "The Bible in Print" contains commentaries on the Bible, books on Biblical criticism, history, geography and archaeology. Another wing , "The Bible in Art" includes paintings, sculptures, and ceramics. There are maps and photographs of the Dead Sea Scrolls. There is also an exhibit dealing with the Bible in games, on stamps, and on coins. Hours are Sunday-Friday 9:30-12:30, Wednesday also from 4:00-9:00.

ERETZ ISRAEL (Ha'aretz) MUSEUM

2, Chaim Levanon Street
BUS #24, 25, 27, 45   Tel. (03) 641-5244
The Erezt Israel or Ha'aretz Museum is located in Ramat Aviv, a suburb north of Tel Aviv. It comprises the most comprehensive storehouse of archaeological, anthropological, and historical findings in the region. It is located near Tel Aviv University and consists of eleven pavilions spread out over 30 acres. The museum lies within a large enclo-

sure that encompasses Tel Qasile, an ancient mound in which 12 strata of ancient civilizations have been discovered. Selected artifacts from this ancient mound are displayed in several pavilions...

• Alphabet Museum – The history of writing, its spread and development; pre-alphabetic, alphabetic, Hebrew alphabet; copies of important inscriptions including a Hebrew inscription from 800 B.C.E.

• Glass Pavilion – History of glass production, methods of styles, with samples of glass vessels spanning 3,000 years of civilization.

• Kadman Numismatic Pavilion – Exhibits chronicling the history of coinage and monetary systems.

• Man and His Works Pavilion – Tools and implements for hunting, agricultural industries, energy, light, writing, measuring in various materials; steam-power in agriculture, oriental market and craftsmen's stoves of the 19th century.

• Nebusthan Pavilion – Archaeological finds from temples of ancient copper production during Biblical times in the Timna Valley in the Arava, and in the Sinai.

• Lasky Planetarium – Display of "Moon Rocks" and a mezzuzah carried by an American Jewish astronaut, Jeffrey Hoffman.

Hours are Sunday-Thursday 9:00-3:00, Friday-Saturday 10:00-2:00. For further information Tel. (03) 641-5244.

ETZEL MUSEUM
38, King George Street
BUS #13, 24, 25, 26, 61   Tel. (03) 517-2044
The Etzel Museum is dedicated to the Jewish underground organization active in Palestine from 1931-1948, which retaliated against the anti-Jewish terrorist Arab attacks and rebelled against the British regime's "White Paper" policy that imposed restrictions on immigration to Palestine and its set-tlements, condemning the Jewish population to remain a perpetual minority in its own homeland.

The Etzel Museum is also known as the Museum of the Irgun Tzvai Le'umi (I.Z.L.). It has a large collection of documents that were kept in various archives throughout Israel, England, and other countries. On display are weapons used by the Irgun fighters in the underground and in the open, during their operations in Israel and in the Diaspora to liberate the homeland from the foreign yoke and to establish the State of Israel; photographs and models of sites where sabotage operations and battles took place are computerized and accompanied by audiovisual explanations.

Adjoining the Etzel Museum is the Jabotinsky Institute. This is a research institute devoted to the study of the activist trend in the Jewish Resistance Movement. Vladmir (Zev) Jabotinsky was a poet, writer, journalist, soldier, and founder dur-ing World War I, of the Jewish Legion, which helped Allenby's forces liberate Israel from Turkish rule.

Hours are Sunday-Thursday 8:30-4:00. For further information Tel. (03) 528-4001. The Etzel Museum is located in Charles Karrol Park.

GEOLOGICAL MUSEUM
12, Ha'palmach Street (Ramat Ha'sharon section) Tel. (03) 549-7185
The Geological Museum tells the geologic history of Israel including the Jordan Rift Valley, Mount Hermon, the Dead Sea, the Sea of Galilee, etc. Hours are Sunday-Thursday 9:00-4:00.

HAGANAH MUSEUM
23, Rothschild Boulevard
BUS #4, 5   Tel. (03) 560-8624
The Haganah Museum records the history of the Israeli military from the time of the

*Rooftops of Tel Aviv, looking west from Ha'yarkon Street.
In the distance (in center) are the Azrieli Towers.*

field watchmen at the turn of the century down through the War of Independence. There are photographs, documents, uniforms, scale models, and weapons. See how the Israelis hid arms inside farm machinery to escape British detection, and how the Haganah stealthily manufactured hand grenades in clandestine kibbutz workshops. Some grenades were marked with the letters "USA" stamped on them. When the British captured members of the Haganah with these grenades they wouldn't suspect that they were made locally. But, in reality, the initials stood for the Yiddish words, *unsere selbst arbeit*, "Our own piece of work!"

Beit Eliyahu is one of the houses built in Little Tel Aviv during the early days. Eliyahu Golomb, the founder and leader of the Haganah, lived here and operated from this house until his death in 1945. He devoted his life to fostering, before the establishment of the State of Israel, a Hebrew defense force. His house served as Central Headquarters of the Haganah.

After the establishment of the State of Israel, the house was purchased from its owners by a public committee of Haganah members and given to the Ministry of Defense. A new building adjacent to the house serves as the museum of the history of the Haganah. Hours are Sunday-Thursday 9:00-3:00, Friday 9:00-12:30.

HELENA RUBINSTEIN PAVILION
6, Tarsat Boulevard BUS #5, 18, 25, 63 Tel. (03) 528-7196
The Helena Rubinstein Pavilion is a branch of the Tel Aviv Museum of Art. It specializes in modern art exhibitions. It is located next to the Habima theater and the Mann Auditorium, home of the Israel Philharmonic. Hours are Monday, Wednesday & Saturday 10:00-4:00, Tuesday & Thursday 10:00-10:00, Friday 10:00-2:00.

INDEPENDENCE HALL
16, Rothschild Boulevard
Tel. (03) 517-3942
This was the home of Meir Dizengoff, the first mayor of Tel Aviv. Israel's Declaration of Independence was signed in this building on May 15, 1948. The second and third floors of the building house the Bible Museum. Hours are Sunday-Thursday 9:00-2:00.

ISRAEL THEATER MUSEUM
The Israel Theater Museum is located at 3, Melchet Street. It houses historic memorabilia and documents of the Jewish and Israeli theater. The nearest bus lines are #4, 5. Hours are Monday-Thursday 9:00-2:00.

JABOTINSKY MUSEUM
38, King George Street
BUS #13, 24, 25, 26, 61 Tel. (03) 528-7320
Zev Jabotinsky was the famous leader of Zionist movement. The history of the Revisionist Movement, the Etzel, and the Lehi underground movements are presented. There are multimedia exhibitions throughout the museum. The museum is located next to the Etzel Museum. Hours are Sunday-Thursday 8:00-4:00, Friday 9:00-1:00.

LECHI MUSEUM
8, Avram Stern Street Tel. (03) 682-0288
The Lechi Museum or Beit Ya'ir is devoted to the Lehi organization, the Fighters for Israel's Freedom. It was founded by Abraham Stern. There are exhibits which contain photographs and documents relating to the British Mandate period leading up to the War of Independence. Hours are Sunday-Thursday 9:00-3:00, Friday 9:00-12:00.

LUNA AMUSEMENT PARK (Yarkon Park)
Luna Amusement Park and Yarkon Park

have many wonderful activities for all members of the family. There are tropical gardens, boat rentals, puppet theaters, and amusement rides. Yarkon Park is located in the northern section of Tel Aviv. The nearest bus lines are #21, 28, 48. It is open daily from 10:00am-11:00pm. For further information Tel. (03) 643-3070 or 647-6133.

NAHUM GUTMAN'S MUSEUM
21, Rokach Street Tel. (03) 516-1970
The Nahum Gutman Museum is located in the old Writers' House. The museum collection emcompasses works in oil, gouache, and watercolor. There are several thousand drawings and illustrations. Hours are Sunday-Wednesday 10:00-4:00, Thursday 10:00-7:00, Friday 10:00-2:00, Saturday 10:00-5:00.

PALMACH MUSEUM
10, Haim Levanon Street (Ramat Aviv)
Tel. (03) 643-6393
The Palmach was the strike force of the Haganah, the pre-state underground defense organization which was eventually incorporated into the Israel Defense Forces after 1948. The main exhibition of the Palmach History Museum takes place underground, in a series of rooms. Groups of about 20 people are conducted through the rooms by a guide. It starts at a memorial to the fallen. It continues to a replica of Herzl Street in Tel Aviv in 1941. The multimedia experience starts here. Images of events in Europe during the World War II are projected onto the street scene.
The Palmach was created to stop the advance of the Nazis into Egypt and to protects Jews in Israel against attacks by Arabs. The next scene is in a eucalyptus grove where a group of seven new Palmach recruits are about to start their training regimen. Some trainees are assigned to blow up bridges, others to lead supply convoys to Jerusalem, or to bring in immigrant ships. There are realistic sets, sounds, lighting, special effects, and even moving rooms. The museum was designed by Zvi Hecker and Rafi Segal in 1998. The building is built to the plan of a Star of David, broken up by three crossed swords–the symbol of the Palmach. The building appears to be a bizarre agglomerate of stone masonry which could easily be mistaken for an old bunker built into the terraced hillside. This is a "must-see" museum. A museum designed in a similar format is the new Menachem Begin Heritage Museum in Jerusalem.

POSTAL AND PHILATELIC MUSEUM
2, Haim Levanon Street Tel. (03) 641-5244
The museum focuses on the history of postal services in Israel from the mid-19th century through the establishment of the State of Israel. There are multimedia displays and interactive systems. Be sure to see the red Israel postal truck from the 1940s. Hours are Sunday-Thursday 9:00-3:00, Friday-Saturday 10:00-2:00.

RABIN SQUARE
Rabin Square is located just south of the Tel Aviv City Hall, near the junctions of Gordon Street and Chen Boulevard. It is the site where Israel's Prime Minister, Yitzchok Rabin, was assassinated by an angry Israeli Jew on November 4, 1995.

RUBIN MUSEUM
14, Bialik Street
BUS #4, 16,24,25 Tel. (03) 525-5961
The Rubin Museum is located in the former home of the Israeli artist Reuven Rubin. See the artist's former studio and works of art which represent the different periods of Rubin's artistic development. There is also an audio-visual slide show about the artist's life and work. Hours are Monday, Wednesday-Friday 10:00-3:00, Tuesday 10:00-8:00, Saturday 11:00-2:00.

Tel Aviv street scene.

SCHREIBER UNIVERSITY ART GALLERY
This gallery is located on the campus of Tel Aviv University–in Entin Square, Gate #7. It is located near the main entrance of the university. There are changing exhibits relating to Modern and Israeli Art, architecture, archaeology, literature, theater, and photography. Admission is free. Hours are Sunday-Thursday 11:00-7:00. For further information Tel. (03) 640-9022.

SHALOM ALEICHEM MUSEUM
The Shalom Aleichem Museum is located at 4, Berkovich Street. He was born Shalom Rabinovich and was a brilliant Jewish writer. The house is devoted to Yiddish culture, since Shalom Aleichem wrote his works in Yiddish. There is a permanent exhibit about Shalom Aleichem's life. There are also classes for those who are interested in learning Yiddish. Hours are Sunday-Thursday 10:00-2:00, Friday 10:00-1:00. For further information Tel. (03) 695-6513.

SHALOM TOWER
The Shalom (Meyer) Tower is one of the earliest skyscrapers in Israel. It is one of the tallest buildings in the Middle East. From the 35th floor observation deck on a clear day, one can see Mount Carmel in the north, the Negev to the south, and Jerusalem in the east. When the 50-story Azrieli Tower was completed, the observation deck in the Shalom Tower was closed. The Shalom Tower was built on the site of the Herzliya Gymnasium, one of the first buildings in Tel Aviv, built in 1909. A fresco of that structure was created on the wall of the Shalom Tower. The Great Synagogue of Tel Aviv is located just a few blocks to the east of the Shalom Tower. Cantor Yossele Rosenblatt was supposed to inaugurate the new synagogue in the early 1930s but he suddenly suffered a fatal heart attack. Cantor Kwartin took his place. The nearest bus lines are #4 and #5.

SUZANNE DELLALE CENTER
Just west of the Shalom Tower, in the Neveh Tzedek section, are recently renovated buildings that comprise the Suzanne Dellale Center. Several dance and theater groups, including the Bat Sheva Dance Company and the Inbal Folklore Theater, perform in the Center. For performance schedules call (03) 510-5656. Walk through this restored section of Tel Aviv and get a sense of what the city was like in the early 1900s. There are many outdoor cafes and art galleries.

TEL AVIV ARTISTS' HOUSE
The Tel Aviv Artists' House is located at 9, Alharizi Street. It was founded in 1948 to serve as an exhibition pavilion for new Israeli artists. There are changing exhibits, painting workshops, art lectures, and a professional equipment store for artists. Hours are Monday-Thursday 10:00-1:00 & 5:00-7:00, Friday 10:00-1:00. For further information Tel. (03) 524-6685.

TEL AVIV MUSEUM OF ART
27, King Saul Boulevard Tel. (03) 696-1297 The Tel Aviv Museum of Art has four central galleries. The museum has exhibitions of 17th century Dutch masters, 18th century Italian paintings, Impressionists, post-Impressionists, and 20th century art from Europe, Israel, and the United States. There are works by Cezanne, Chagall, Dali, Monet Rodin, Picasso, and Kadinsky. The auditorium features film retrospectives, concerts and lectures. Hours are Monday Wednesday & Saturday 10:00-4:00 Tuesday & Thursday 10:00-10:00, Friday 10:00-2:00.

THE CRAZY HOUSE
The house on Ha'yarkon Street (north of Gordon) was designed in the 1980s by

architect Leon Gaignebet. It is a five-story apartment building which looks amorphic. There are all kinds of weird shapes extruding from the walls. It looks like it may have been influenced by the designs of Antoni Gaudi's *Casa Batllo* in Barcelona. But to the local Israelis, it's just the "Crazy House." Nearby, at 220 Ha'yarkon Street, is another oddity in Tel Aviv. The Melody Hotel is an elegant boutique hotel. But notice the "man" clinging onto the outside walls!

TIME FOR ART - AN ISRAELI ART CENTER

This is an art museum and a culture center for Israeli artists. There are changing exhibits of sculpture, painting and photography. The center also houses a coffee house. Time for Art is located at 36, Montefiore Street. Hours are Monday-Thursday 10:00-7:00, Friday 10:00-2:00, Saturday 10:00-5:00. For further information Tel. (03) 566-4450.

WORLD OF SCIENCE AQUARIUM

1, Kaufman Street   Tel. (03) 510-6670
View hundreds of fish from the Mediterranean Sea, the Red Sea, and around the world. Another room houses a frightening array of snakes, scorpions, reptiles, and tarantulas. The World of Science Aquarium is open daily from 10:00-7:30

Kosher Dining

Kosher food establishments in Israel must display a valid Certificate of Kashrut. This certificate or *Te'udat Kashrut*, must be renewed every three months. Be sure to look for this certificate and check the date. No responsibility, therefore can be taken for the absolute accuracy of the information in this guide, and travelers are advised to obtain confirmation of kashrut claims. Although every effort has been made to ensure accuracy, changes will occur after this guide has gone to press. Particular attention must be drawn to the fact that kosher food establishments change hands often and suddenly, in some cases going over to a non-kosher owner. All of the restaurants listed below are closed on the Sabbath. Rabbinical supervisions are in brackets.

Agvania (Dairy) 19, Shenkin Street Tel. (03) 525-6666
Alternative (Fish/Dairy)
32, Weitzman Street [Rabbanut Tel-Aviv & Mehadrin] Tel. (03) 695-0567
Apropo Alexander (Thai/Fish/Dairy) 3, Chabakuk Street Tel. (03) 544-4442
Ashrav (Persian/Meat) 20, Rothschild Street [Rabbanut Tel-Aviv] Tel. (03) 510-4777
Asia Cafe (Dairy) 4, Weitzman Street Tel. (03) 697-9989
Bari Bar (Health Bar/Dairy) 32, Ha'barzel Street Tel. (03) 644-5049
Berkana (Italian/Dairy) 32, Ha'barzel Street Tel. (03) 644-4411
Bruno (Urban Mediterranean Cuisine/Meat) Azrieli Tower, 3rd Floor Tel. (03) 609-3030
Busi (Meat Grill) 41, Etzel Street (Ha'tikvah section) Tel. (03) 688-1034
Carlton Rooftop BBQ (summer only)
Top of the World - Ha'tikvah Street Tel. (03) 520-1818
Cup O' Joe (Dairy)
2, Weitzman Street (Europe Tower) [Rabbanut Tel-Aviv] Tel. (03) 693-2005

Dalida (Dairy) 30, Sheinkin Street Tel. (03) 620-1979
Derby Fish & Grill (Meat) 14, Wallenberg Street Tel. (03) 648-0733
Dodo (Meat/Fish) 4, Heichal Ha'talmud Tel. (03) 510-7001
El Gaucho 49, Bograshov Street [Rabbanut Tel-Aviv] Tel. (03) 525-6455
    (Argentinian Steakhouse) Note: Not all branches are closed on Shabbat.
Ha'homa Ha'sinit (Chinese/Meat) 26, Mikveh Yisrael Street Tel. (03) 560-3974
Ha'pina Ha'yeruka (Dairy/Fish) 80, Rokach Boulevard Tel. (03) 642-2741
Hashagrir-Ambassador (Meat)
82 Hayarkon Street [Rabbanut Tel-Aviv & Mehadrin] Tel. (03) 516-5986
Hungarian Blintzes (Dairy) 35, Yirmiyahu Street [Rabbanut Tel-Aviv] Tel. (03) 605-0674
Kerem Hateimanim (Yemenite/Meat) 6, Frishman Street Tel. (02) 523-4586
Lilith (Fish/Dairy/Vegetarian) 42, Mazeh Street Tel. (03) 629-8772
Muldan (Meat) 98, Ha'yarkon Street [Rabbanut Tel-Aviv & Mehadrin] Tel. (03) 527-8418
Olive Leaf (Meat) Sheraton Hotel Tel. (03) 521-9300
Pacific Bistro & Sushi (Meat)
Crowne Plaza Hotel 145, Ha'yarkon Street Tel. (03) 520-1169
Papagaio Azrieli (South American/Meat)
Azrieli Center [Rabbanut Tel-Aviv] Tel. (03) 609-2000
Parperaot (Dairy/Fish) Yordei Hasira Tel. (03) 544-2774
Petrozelia (Meat Grill) 47, Rothschild Boulevard Tel. (03) 516-2468
Pizza Domino (Dairy) 4, Laskov Street Tel. (03) 695-9103
Providence (Italian/Dairy/Fish) 66, Ha'yarkon Street Tel. (03) 510-5969
Rebecca Dairy Cafe 2, Laskov Street Tel. (03) 696-2099
Shangrila (Thai/Meat) Astor Hotel Ha'yarkon Street Tel. (03) 523-8913
Shaul's Inn (Yemenite/Meat) Upstairs is less expensive. Downstairs is upscale.
    11, Eliashiv Street Tel. (03) 517-3303
Shipudei Ramat Ha'hayal (Meat Grill) 24, Ha'barzel Street Tel. (03) 649-3625
Smoky Deli (Meat) Azrieli Mall Tel. (03) 608-1116
Sushi Bar (Vegetarian) Sheraton Hotel 115, Ha'yarkon St. Tel. (03) 521-1111
Toscana (Thai/Dairy/Fish)
3, Habakuk Street [Rabbanut Tel-Aviv & Mehadrin] Tel. (03) 544-4442
Zion Exclusive (Meat) 28, Pedui'im Street Tel. (03) 517-8714

Where to Stay

Abratel Suites Hotel 3, Ge'ula Street Tel. (03) 516-9966
Adiv Hotel 5, Mendele Street Tel. (03) 522-9141
Alexander Suite Hotel 3, Ha'vakook Street Tel. (03) 545-2222
Ambassador Hotel 56, Promenade Tel. (03) 510-3993
Ami Hotel 152, Ha'yarkon Street Tel. (03) 524-9141
Armon Ha'yarkon Hotel 268, Hayarkon Street Tel. (03) 605-5271
Aviv Hotel 88, Ha'yarkon Street Tel. (03) 510-2784
Basel Hotel 156, Ha'yarkon Street Tel. (03) 520-7711
Bell Hotel 12, Allenby Street Tel. (03) 517-7011

Ben Nevet Gitta Bed & Breakfast Tel. (03) 574-2644
Best Western Regency Suites 80, Ha'yarkon Street Tel. (03) 517-3939
Carlton Hotel 10, Eliezer Peri Street Tel. (03) 520-1818
Center Hotel 2, Zamenhof Street Tel. (03) 629-6181
City Hotel 9, Mapu Street Tel. (03) 524-6253
Country Club 300, Namir Road (Glilot) Tel. (03) 699-0666
Crown Plaza Hotel 145, Ha'yarkon Street Tel. (03) 520-1111
Dan Panorama Hotel Charles Clore Park Tel. (03) 519-0190
Dan Hotel 99, Ha'yarkon street Tel. (03) 520-2525
David Intercontinental Hotel 12, Kaufman Street Tel. (03) 795-1111
Deborah Hotel 87, Ben Yehuda Street Tel. (03) 527-8282
Grand Beach Hotel 250, Ha'yarkon Street Tel. (03) 543-3333
Havakook Apartment Hotel 7, Ha'vakook Street Tel. (03) 604-2222
Howard Johnson Hotel 216, Ha'yarkon Street Tel. (03) 524-3277
Shalom Imperial Hotel 66, Ha'yatkon Street Tel. (03) 517-7002
Isrotel Tower 78, Ha'yarkon Street Tel. (03) 511-3636
Lusky Suites Hotel 84, Ha'yarkon Street Tel. (03) 516-3030
Maxim Hotel 86, Ha'yarkon Street Tel. (03) 517-3721
Melody Hotel 220, Ha'yarkon Street Tel. (03) 527-7711
Mercure Marina Hotel 167, Ha'yarkon Street Tel. (03) 521-1777
Metropolitan Hotel 11-15 Trumpeldor Street Tel. (03) 519-2727
Miami Hotel 8, Allenby Street Tel. (03) 510-3868
Nes Ziona Hotel 10, Nes Ziona Tel. (03) 510-6084
Olympia Hotel 164, Ha'yarkon Street Tel (03) 524-2184
Ophir Hotel 43, Dizengoff Street Tel. (03) 525-7350
Prima Astor Hotel 105, Ha'yarkon Street Tel. (03) 520-6666
Renaissance Hotel 121, Ha'yarkon Street Tel. (03) 521-5555
Sea.Net Hotel 6, Ness Ziona street Tel. (03) 517-1655
Sheraton Moriah Hotel 155, Ha'yarkon Street Tel. (03) 521-6666
Sheraton Hotel 115, Ha'yarkon Street Tel. (03) 521-1111
Tal Hotel 287, Ha'yarkon Street Tel. (03) 542-5500
Tel Aviv Hilton Independence Park Tel. (03) 520-2222
Top Hotel 35, Ben Yehuda Street Tel. (03) 51700941
Yamit Park Plaza Hotel 79, Ha'yarkon Street Tel. (03) 519-7111

Happennings in Tel Aviv

ISRAELI FOLK DANCING
- 3, Rechov Kehilat Kiev (Sunday) 7:30pm Miri Akuni Tel. (03) 651-2395
- **Beit Dani** (Sunday) 8:00pm Mishael Barzilai Tel. (03) 631-5191
- **Country Club Azori** Chen (Sunday) 7:00pm Sara Gutman Tel. (09) 742-8571
- **Country Gimmel** (Ramat Aviv) (Sunday) 8:00pm Batya Kronenberg
- **Country Dekel** (Sunday) 8:00pm Carmela Shlomo Tel. (03) 969-3376
- **Countrylee** (Monday) 8:00pm Pnina Aran Tel. (03) 551-0301

- **Mo'adon Bank L'eumi** (Monday) 7:00pm Malka Bachar Tel. (03) 966-8133
- **Country Club** - 35, Nachalat Yitzchok Street (Monday) 7:30pm Batya Kronenberg
- **Country Gimmel** (Ramat Aviv) 7:00pm M. Varon
- **Heichal Ha'sport Hadar Yosef** (Monday) 9:30pm Yankele Ziv Tel. (08) 970-5519
- **Bikurei Ha'itim** (Monday) 8:00pm Eran Biton Tel. (08) 855-1354
- **Country Dekel** (Monday) 8:15pm Ofer Alfasi Tel. (052) 888-6900
- 35, Nachalat Yitzchok Street (Tuesday) 7:30 Mishael Barzilai
- **Bikurei Ha'itim** (Tuesday) 8:00pm Eran Biton
- **Beit Dani** (Tuesday) 8:00pm Qadi Biton
- **Country Club Azori Chen** (Tuesday) 7:00pm Sara Gutman
- **Lidor** - 8, Kehilat Venezia (Tuesday) 8:00pm Te'am Lidor Tel. (03) 649-7065
- **Mo'adon Focus** (Wednesday) 8:30pm Ronen Gabai Tel. (052) 272-8309
- 3, Rechov Kehilat Kiev (Wednesday) 7:30pm Miri Akuni
- **Lidor** - 8, Kehilat Venezia (Wednesday) 9:00pm Te'am Lidor
- **Lidor** - 8, Kehilat Venezia (Thursday) 9:00pm Te'am Lidor
- **Country Dekel** (Wednesday) 8:00pm Oren Bachar
- **Tel Aviv University** (Thursday) 8:30pm Varda & Gal Tel. (052) 255-8331
- 35, Nachalat Yitzchok Street (Thursday) 7:30 Miri Akuni
- **Tel Aviv University** - Ulam Ha'sport (Thursday) 8:00pm Gadi Biton
- **Country Dekel** (Thursday) 7:45pm Yankele Sha'arabani Tel. (03) 648-6089
- **Lidor** - 8, Kehilat Venezia (Friday) 10:30pm Te'am Lidor
- **Lidor** - 8, Kehilat Venezia (Saturday) 10:00pm Te'am Lidor
- **Mercaz Bikurei Ha'itim** (Saturday) 8:30pm Varda & Gal

Note: There is free Israeli Folk Dancing along the Promenade on Saturdays.

THEATERS & CONCERT HALLS

Beit Lessin 101, Dizengoff Tel. (03) 725-5300
Duhl Auditorium 76, Hatikva Tel. (03) 692-7777
Einav Cultural Center 71, Ibn Gvirol (03) 521-7736
Gesher Theater 7-9, Jerusalem (Jaffa) Tel. (03) 681-3131
Habama Center Theater & Gallery 20, Carmel (Ganei Tikvah) Tel. (03) 737-5778
Habima Theater 2,Tarsat Tel. (03) 629-5555
Hasimta Theater 8, Mazal Dagim (Jaffa) Tel. (03) 681-2126
Inbal Auditorium (Suzanne Dallal Center) 5, Yehieli (Neveh Tzedek) Tel. (03) 517-3711
Israel Music Conservatory 19, Stricker Tel. (03) 517-3711
The Janice and Philip J. Karov Theater Levinsky, 11
New Central Bus Station, 4th floor Tel. (03) 688-5004
Levin Municipal Music Center 10, Shirit Israel (Jaffa) Tel. (03) 682-8393
Mann Auditorium 1 Huberman Tel. 1 700 703030
Mo'adon Hate'atron 10, Jerusalem Tel. (03) 518-4715
New Cameri Theater Shaul Hamelech Tel (03) 606-0906
Notzar Theater 39, Jerusalem Tel. (03) 518-9914
Ohel Shem Theater 30, Balfour Tel. (03) 525-2266
Room Theater 8, Harav Kook Tel. (03) 517-1818

Suzanne Dallal Center 5, Yehieli (Neveh Tzedek) Tel. (03) 510-5656
Teatron Al Hayarkon Old Exhibition Grounds Northern end of Dizengoff Street
Tel Aviv Performing Arts Center 19, Shaul Hamelech Tel. (03) 692-7777
Tmuna Theater 8, Soncino Tel. (03) 562-9462
Tzava 30, Ibn Gvirol Tel. (03) 695-0156
Yuval Carmi School Theater 37, Harav Kook Tel. 0523 366 580
ZOA House 1, Daniel Frisch Tel. (03) 695-9341

NIGHTCLUBS
Note: These establishments may not serve kosher foods.
Allenby 40 40, Allenby Tel. 0528 929 218
Artel Jazz Club 56, Allenby Tel. (03) 516-8278
Artspace 19, Menachem Begin Tel. 0523 389 053
Barby Club Tel Aviv 52, Barby Galuyot (03) 518-8123
Bella Shlomskins 13, Noah Moses Tel. (03) 609-6996
Cafe Barzilay 5, Barzilay Tel. (03) 560-3477
Camelot Club Tel Aviv 16, Sholom Aleichem Tel. (03) 528-5222
Dixie 120, Yigal Alon Tel. (03) 696-6123
Fetish@Maxim 48, King George
Fusion Mamasger & Yad Harutzim
Golden Bar 8, Rothschild Tel. (03) 516-9191
Goldstar Zappa 24, Raoul Wallenberg Ziv Towers (Ramat Hahayal) Tel. (03) 649-9550
Ha'oman 17 Tel. 0525 606 661
Hava Nagila Club Tel. (03) 544-0907
Hazira Club 45, Yitzchok Sade Tel. (03) 683-9896
Heinekin Habima Club (Habimah Theater) 2, Tarsat Tel. (03) 528-2174
Jazz Alley (Roof of Simta Theater) 8, Mazal Dagim (Jaffa) Tel. (03) 681-2126
Lanski 6, Montefiore (Shalom Towers) Tel. (03) 517-0043
(Largest nightclub in the Middle East)
Leivik House
(Klezmer & Jewish music concerts on Sat. nights) Daniel Gabai Tel. (03) 523-1830
Koltura 154, Herzl Tel. (03) 518-7289
Mike's Place 86, Herbert Samuel Tel. 0522 670 965
Mishmish 17, Lilienblum Tel. (03) 516-8178
Molly Bloom's 2, Mendele Tel. (03) 523-7419
Move 3, Hata'arukha Tel. 0526 655 001
Scores (American-style Pool Bar) Yehuda Halevy & Allenby Tel. (03) 566-2010
Shesek 17, Lilienblum Tel. (03) 516-9520
Velvet 66, Hamasger Tel. (03) 624-1204

Note: The hotest night spots in Tel Aviv are in the marina area, at the northern end of Ha'yarkon Street. There are lots of cafes and artists selling their crafts.

Tour #7 - South of Tel Aviv

TEL AVIV-YAFO

Bat Yam

Or Yehuda

Holon

Kfar Chabad

Rishon Le'zion

Lod

Palmachim

Ramla

Rehovot

Yavneh

Mazkeret Batya

Ashdod

Gedera

Revadim

Kfar Menachem

Nitsanim

Ashkelon

Kibbutz Negba

Yad Mordechai

M E D

Courtesy Survey of Israel.

Bat Yam

BAT YAM CITY HALL
Be sure to visit the unique Bat Yam City Hall. It was designed by Alfred Neumann, Zvi Hecker, and Eldor Sharon in 1964. The design is based on a figure like an inverted ziggurat, built up from "cuboctahedral" space-packing units.

BEN-ARI MUSEUM
The Ben-Ari Museum is located at 6, Struma Street in Bat Yam. Hours are Sunday-Thursday 9:00-1:00, Monday 8:00-5:00, Friday 8:00-1:00. The nearest bus line is #18.

Holon

CARICATURE MUSEUM
The new Caricature Museum in Holon is one of only eleven such museums in the world. It just opened in December, 2007. The museum features changing exhibits as well as a permanent exhibit, including the work of leading Israeli artists as Dosh, Ze'ev, fridel and Navon. The Caricature Museum is located at 4, Weizmann Street. For further information Tel. 903) 652-1849.

DESIGN MUSEUM
The new Design Museum contains dramatic sweeping steel bands which envelop the structure. It is presently under construction and is scheduled to open by the end of 2008. It was designed by Ron Arad, Israel's most outstanding architect. The distinctive concept of the new Design Museum, conceived as a landmark center of architecture, design and art, incorporates designs from industry, fashion and textile designs, visual communications, jewelry and accessory designs.

EGGED MUSEUM OF PASSENGER TRAFFIC
The Egged Museum has original buses from the 1920s to the present. It's quite a remarkable museum. The museum is located on Moshe Dayan Street. Admission is free. Hours are Sunday-Thursday 8:00-1:00, Friday 8:00-12:30. For further information Tel. (03) 555-3439.

ISRAEL CENTER FOR DIGITAL ART
The Israel Center for Digital Art has changing exhibits dealing with net.art, video art, photography, animation, and interactive sound. The Digital Art Lab is located at 16, Yirmiyahu Street. Hours are Tuesday-Wednesday 4:00-8:00, Thursday 10:00-2:00, Friday-Saturday 10:00-3:00. For further information Tel. (03) 556-8792.

ISRAEL CHILDREN'S MUSEUM
The Israel Children's Museum has exhibits which encourage children to touch the objects, feel their texture, and invites children and parents to enjoy a unique creative experience. There is a "Silence Exhibition," which allows visitors to penetrate into the world of the deaf. Visitors are equipped with a personal device that cuts them off from all sounds. A team of 30 deaf and hearing-impaired guides shows visitors around, inviting them to "hear with their eyes" and "talk with their hands." The museum is located at Mifraz Shlomo Street in Peres Park. Hours are Sunday-Tuesday & Thursday 9:00-11:30, Wednesday 5:00pm, Saturday 3:00 & 5:30, Holidays 9:30, 12:00, 3:00 & 5:30. For further information Tel. (03) 650-3000.

ISRAEL PUPPET CENTER
The Israel Puppet Center, located in a new complex of its own, incorporates a museum devoted to puppet theater, a puppetry school and a 150-seat auditorium. It is locat

ed at 13, Remez Street. For further information Tel. (03) 651-6848.

Or Yehuda

BABYLONIAN JEWRY HERITAGE CENTER
The Babylonian Jewry Museum contains 2500 years of history of the Jews of Iraq. There are items relating to the customs, liturgy, music, and dress. A rare 13th century manuscript of the Babylonian Talmud is on display. The museum is located at 83, Ben-Porat Road. Hours are Sunday-Monday & Wednesday-Thursday 8:30-3:30, Tuesday 8:30-7:00, Friday 8:30-1:00. For further information Tel. (03) 533-9278.

Kfar Chabad

This village is the headquarters of the Lubavitch Chassidim in Israel. It is located just west of Ben-Gurion Airport. The movement's leader, Rabbi Menachem Mendel Schneerson (z'l), died in 1994 in New York. An exact replica of the Rebbe's home in Brooklyn (770 Eastern Parkway—which is the world headquarters of the movement) was built in Kfar Chabad, with the expectation that when the Rebbe would come, he would feel "at home." The Rebbe never made it to Israel.

There are additional replicas of 770 Eastern Parkway. One is located in Westwood (Los Angeles), California. That building, also designed in the English Tudor style, serves as the West Coast headquarters of the Lubavitch Movement in America. Another building is located on the campus of Rutgers University in New Brunswick, New Jersey. There are additional replicas located in Milan (Italy), Brazil, Argentina, Melbourne (Australia), near Montreal (Quebec) and in the Ramot section of Jerusalem.

Rishon Le'zion

RISHON LE'ZION MUSEUM
This museum contains exhibits relating to the history of Rishon Le'zion from its inception in 1882. There are guided tours of the historic sites along "Pioneers Way" and the suburbs. There is also a light and sound show during the visit. The Rishon Le'zion Museum is located at Ha'meyasdim Square. Hours are Sunday, Tuesday-Thursday 9:00-2:00, Monday 9:00-1:00 & 4:00-7:00. For further information Tel. (03) 968-2435.

RISHON LE'ZION WINE CELLARS
A visit to the Rishon Le'zion Wine Cellars includes a guided tour of the wine cellars, an audio-visual program, visit to the metal workshop, wine-tasting and free bottle of wine or grape juice. For further information Tel. (03) 964-2021.

Kibbutz Palmachim

Take Route 4311 from Rishon Le'zion and head southwest toward Kibbutz Palmachim.

BEIT MIRIAM ARCHAEOLOGICAL MUSEUM

The Beit Miriam Archaeological Museum is located on a cliff overlooking the Mediterranean Sea in Kibbutz Palmachim. There are many artifacts which were found in the area including giant clay vessels, a mosaic floor from the Byzantine period, ancient anchors, and coins from various periods. Guided tours to nearby archaeological sites are available by appointment. The museum is open by reservation only. For further information Tel. (03) 953-8281.

Lod

Doubleback to Rishon Le'zion and continue east to Lod.

MUSEUM OF JEWISH HERITAGE

The museum contains old cooking utensils, Torah scrolls with silver casings, marriage contracts (ketuvoths), amulets, models of synagogues, and carpets woven with Jewish themes. The Museum of Jewish Heritage is located at 20, David Ha'melech Boulevard. Hours are Sunday-Thursday 9:00-4:00. For further information Tel. (08) 924-4569.

BEN-GURION AIRPORT - THE NEW TERMINAL 3

The most memorable feature of the new Terminal 3 at Ben-Gurion International Airport is the "connector" passageway. It is a very long bridge connecting the arrivals with the departure sections of the airport. It was designed by architect Moshe Safdie in 2005. It consists of two elongated parallel ramps descending and passing each other in a criss-cross design. So, when you arrive at the airport and go through the passport control, you will descend down the gently-sloping ramp. At the opposite end of the passageway, you can see departing passengers descending down the other side of the hallway. There are horizontal escalators for those who cannot walk such long distances.

The main departure waiting room is housed in a rotunda structure. It is covered by an inverted dome which drains the (winter) rainwater and cascades it from the ceiling into a pool at the center of the piazza below it. But what is most interesting about this new Terminal 3 is that when you're waiting for a 1:00am flight back to New York, and sitting in this most secure high-tech structure, all of a sudden you see a bird flying around inside the building!

Ben-Gurion Airport's circular Departure Hall with its skylight waterfall.

There is a new train station at the entrance to the Arrivals and Departure area in the new Terminal 3. There are connections to Tel Aviv, Netanya, Haifa, Be'er Sheva, Ashkelon and Jerusalem (via Tel Aviv). A new direct link has been constructed to Modiin. An extenson of that line is planned under Canada Park and then will "hug" Route 1 eastward and terminate in Jerusalem, under the Central Bus station.

Kibbutz Be'eirot Itzhak

This kibbutz is located northwest of Ben-Gurion Airport. The visitor will experience animal activities as well as lectures on historical agriculture. There are coach rides, watch cheese processing, see an ancient winery, bake a pita, donkey rides, water games and lots more. For further information Tel. (03) 907-2710

Ramla

RAMLA MUSEUM
The museum contains six exhibition rooms that trace the history of the city–from the Middle Ages to the present. The Ramla Museum is located at 112, Herzl Street. Hours are Sunday-Thursday 10:00-5:00, Friday 10:00-2:00. For further information Tel. (08) 929-2650.

Rehovot

CHAIM WEIZMANN RESIDENCE
Visit the fascinating home of Israel's first president, Dr. Chaim Weizmann. It was designed in the Bauhaus (Art Moderne) Style in 1936 by Eric Mendelsohn. Despite its square form, the house also resembles from certain angles, a ship–with its prominent cylindrical staircase and the circular windows in the solid walls. Chaim Weizmann established his home in Rehovot and inspired the development of the great scientific institute which bears his name, the Weizmann Institute of Science. He was also a famous scientist in the field of chemistry and biochemistry. The Chaim Weizmann Residence and Museum is located on the campus of the Weizmann Institute. Reservations should be made in advance. Hours are Sunday 10:00-4:00, Monday-Thursday 9:00-4:00. For further information Tel. (08) 934-4500.

CLORE GARDEN OF SCIENCE
The Clore Garden of Science is located on the campus of the Weizmann Institute. The garden enables the visitor to experience science through interactive exhibits that demonstrate the principles and natural phenomena that influence our lives. Hours are Monday-Thursday 10:00-5:00, Friday 10:00-2:00. For further information Tel. (08) 934-4401.

DONDIKOV HOUSE
This house was built by one of the founders of Rehovot, Abraham Dondikov. The restored house operates as a gallery for temporary exhibitions. There are plans on turning this building into a museum featuring the history of Rehovot. The Dondikov House is located at 32, Ya'akov Street. Hours are Sunday-Thursday 10:00-1:00 & 5:00-8:00, Friday 10:00-1:00. For further information Tel. (08) 939-0310.

REHOVOT MUNICIPAL ART GALLERY
This art gallery is named after one of the founders of Rehovot, Moshe Smilanski. The center offers various courses in the arts, workshops, and lectures. There are also changing exhibits of contemporary artists. The Rehovot Municipal Art Gallery is located

at 2, Goldin Street. Hours are Sunday-Thursday 9:00-1:00 &
3:00-8:00, Friday 9:00-1:00. For further information Tel. (08)
939-0390.

MINKOV MUSEUM
Minkov's orchard, with its "bayara" (farmyard and water well
surrounded by a wall) was one of the first orchards to be plant-
ed in Israel in 1904. Located in Rehovot, it played an important
role in the development of that town as Israel's "citrus city." The
site aims to offer a light-hearted and humorous authentic illus-
tration of the early days of citrus growing in Israel. The original
packing house and sorting shed, that dynamically present the
construction of crates, rinsing of fruit, drying, sorting, and packing, will be reconstructed so that visitors will be able to sort,
pack and buy fruit boxes they fill themselves.

Yavneh

When Jerusalem was besieged by the Romans in 70 C.E., *Take Route 410 south to*
Rabbi Yochanan ben Zakkai had himself smuggled out of the *Yavneh.*
city in a coffin. He persuaded the Roman general, Vespasian,
to spare the town of Yavneh and its sages. After the destruction
of Jerusalem, he established the Sanhedrin here, as well
destruction of Jeru-salem, he established the Sanhedrin here,
as well as a large yeshiva, Kerem b'Yavneh. At the center of the
town is the tomb of a Talmudic scholar, Rabban Gamliel.
Kibbutz Yavneh was established in 1941 on the site of ancient
Yavneh.

ATOMIC REACTOR
Israel's first nuclear research facilities were started in Rehovot.
The first atomic reactor is located near the Coastal Highway
near Yavneh. The polyganol building was designed by the late
American architect, Philip Johnson in 1960.

Gedera

HISTORY MUSEUM OF GEDERA
Gedera is the first and only settlement that was created by the
BILU Movement in 1884. Visitors can see the first school and
synagogue. The museum is located on Biluyim Street. Hours
are Sunday, Tuesday & Thursday 8:30-1:00, Monday &
Wednesday 8:30-1:00 & 4:00-6:00, Friday 8:30-12:30. For further information Tel. (08) 859-4675.

Mazkeret Batya

Take Route 40 north to Route 411. Turn right and go to Mazkeret Batya.

MAZKERET BATYA FOLKLORE MUSEUM

The Folklore Museum has an audio-visual program depicting the history of this well-preserved moshava. It was founded in 1883 by representatives of the first aliya. It was named after Baron de Rothschild's mother, Batya. The museum is located at 40, Rothschild Street. Hours are Sunday-Thursday 8:00-1:00, Friday 9:30-1:30. For further information Tel (08) 031 0525.

Doubleback to Route 40, turn left. Take Route 40 south to Route 41 and turn left. Take Route 41 to the Re'im Junction. Turn left onto Route 3 and then right onto Route 383. Go to Kibbutz Kfar Menachem.

Kibbutz Kfar Menachem

SHFELA MUSEUM

The visitor can see a reproduction of a defensive construction of a remote Jewish settlement. There are also artifacts from nearby archaeological finds. Hours are Sunday-Thursday 8:30-12:30. For further information Tel. (08) 850-1827.

Kibbutz Revadim

Doubleback to Route 3 and turn right. Continue to Kibbutz Revadim.

EKRON MUSEUM

This part of the country is associated with the Philistines, an ancient tribe also known as the "People of the Sea." Archaeological finds in the region tell their story. The Ekron Museum is located in Kibbutz Revadim. Hours are Sunday-Thursday 8:00-4:00, Friday 8:00-12:00. For further information Tel. (08) 858-8913.

Ashdod

Doubleback on Route 3 and continue to Route 41. Turn right on Route 41 and take it all the way to Ashdod.

ASHDOD MUSEUM

This museum contains audio-visual presentations. There are exhibitions about archaeology, history, and works of art by Israeli painters. The Ashdod Museum is located at 16, Hasha'yatim Street. Hours are Sunday-Thursday 9:00-4:00, Saturday & Holidays 10:30-1:00. For further information Tel. (08) 854-3092.

Take Route 4 south to the Eshkolot Junction. Turn left onto Route 232. Continue to the Hodiya Junction and turn left onto Route 3. Take Route 3 about 2 kilometers. Turn right and travel south to Kibbutz Negba.

Kibbutz Negba

THE OPEN MUSEUM–KIBBUTZ NEGBA

The visitor can see the IDF memorial, an abandoned Egyptian

tank from the War of Independence, the shell-scared water tower, and the first tractor of the kibbutz from the 1930s. There is a reconstruction of the kibbutz watch tower and stockade. Admission is free. Hours are Sunday-Saturday 8:00-8:00. For further information Tel. (08) 677-4312.

Nitsanim

MEMORIAL TO JEWISH FEMALE HEROISM

Kibbutz Nitsanim was founded in 1943 just north of Ashkelon. It was surrounded by Arab villages. In 1948, the Egyptian army attacked this kibbutz. All of the women and children were evacuated. A handful of men and several young women stayed behind to defend the kibbutz. After a 14 hour battle, the kibbutz fell. Thirty three fighters, kibbutz members and soldiers, perished in this battle. The three brave women who fell were Mira ben-Ari, Shulamit Dorczin and Deborah Epstein.

Continue going south along Route 4 to **Kibbutz Nitsanim.**

Ashkelon

THE CARLSBERG–ISRAEL VISITOR CENTER

The visit to the Carlsberg Brewery in Ashkelon entails a wonderful audio-visual presentation and a tour of the brewery. There is a visit to the museum which describes the story of beer production in ancient times. There is an unlimited beer-tasting pub on the facilities! The Carlsberg-Israel Visitor Center is located at 5, Bar Lev Avenue, in the southern industrial area of the Ashkelon. Hours are Sunday-Thursday 9:00-4:00. Reservations are required. For further information Tel. (08) 674-0727.

Continue south on Route 4 to **Ashkelon.**

Kibbutz Yad Mordechai

Kibbutz Yad Mordechai is located along the Coastal Plain, just north of the Gaza Strip. It was named in honor of Mordechai Anilewitz, a Jewish leader who died in the Warsaw Ghetto Uprising of 1943. The kibbutz was founded the same year by Polish immigrants.

The museum at Yad Mordechai was designed to commemorate the heroic defense of a small group of kibbutz members against the invading Egyptian division in the War of Independence in May, 1948. They succeeded in defending their settlement and in pushing back an army division for five days and nights. Only after running out of food and ammunition, did they leave their

Continue driving south on Route 4 to **Kibbutz Yad Mordechai.**

kibbutz settlement.

Today, there is an imposing statue of Anilewitz holding a hand-grenade, standing in defiance in front of the fallen watertower which is bullet- and shell-ridden. The statue was designed by Nathan Rapoport. In memory of this defense, a museum was built on a hilly site inside the kibbutz with a panoramic view of surrounding fields and gardens, where the defense lines and trenches were once placed.

The museum was designed by the architectural firm of Arieh Sharon and Eldor Sharon. One section of the museum is dedicated to the tragic effort of the partisans, fighting against the Nazis in the Warsaw Ghetto.

Hours are Sunday-Thursday & Saturday 10:00-4:00, Friday & Holidays 10:00-2:00. For further information Tel. (00) 072-0528.

The Sabra fruit is said to be similar to an Israeli—tough on the outside but soft and tender on the inside.

Tour #8 - The Negev

The Negev

The best time to tour the Negev is the period from October to May. In January and February, the weather in the southern parts of the Negev and in the Arava Valley is pleasant and mostly dry. In the Negev highlands, temperatures at night can be as low as 32 degrees (F). In the summer months (June through September), travel through the Negev can be enjoyable if the right precautions are taken. Temperatures can reach as high as 115 degrees (F).

To fully enjoy the desert and traverse it safely, the visitor must accept the desert code of behavior. Bring along a generous supply of water and remember to drink frequently throughout the day. Also be sure to bring enough water to cool off the car engine. If you are planning to go off the beaten track, inquire at a visitor's center about the conditions on your proposed route. And, most important, notify your hotel or friends of your plans—where you are going and when you should be expected back.

If you want to see the desert in all its splendor, you should get as far away as you can from the roads, towns, and villages. In the past, this was possible only with a great deal of hiking and in vehicles with 4-wheel drive.

For the hiker and nature-lover, the Negev offers a system of trails unparalleled throughout Israel and one of the most extensive in the world. Over 2,500 kilometers of hiking trails and paths have been marked in the Negev. Ladders and steps have been installed in secluded canyons and down exciting cliff faces, allowing the visitor to get to hidden waterfalls, swimming holes, and beauty spots that were previously unreachable.

The Negev is also a wonderland for those who prefer less strenuous activities. Luxury hotels, spas, holiday resorts, and camping villages can be found throughout the Negev. Beaches on the shores of the Mediterranean, the Red Sea, and the Dead Sea offer a wide selection of relaxing vacation possibilities.

Recently, many new alternatives have emerged. Numerous desert paths have been improved to allow passage of normal vehicles without destroying the environment. Touring facilities have been enhanced, nature trails have been marked, and historical sites have been made accessible to visitors.

Be'er Sheva

ABRAHAM'S WELL
According to legend, this is the site of Abraham's Well which is mentioned in the Bible. The site is located at 1, Derech Hebron (corner Ha'atzma'ut Street). Hours are Sunday-Thursday 8:00-4:00, Friday 8:00-12:00. For further information Tel. (08) 623-4613.

BEDOUIN MARKET
Be'er Sheva's main attraction is the Bedouin

Market which takes place on Thursdays, from 6:00am to 12:00 noon. The market is located just south of the municipal market and central bus station.

BEN-GURION
UNIVERSITY OF THE NEGEV
The Central Library of the Ben-Gurion University of the Negev is designed to contain half a million volumes and provides space for a thousand readers. The building,

*Man-made stream flows through the campus of
Ben-Gurion University of the Negev in Be'er Sheva.*

Air intakes and Siamese connections outside the Alon Building for Hi-Tech in Ben-Gurion University of the Negev.

One hundred skylights illuminate the interior of the Library of the Ben-Gurion University of the Negev.

designed to obtain light from the natural resource–the always bright Negev sky. In order to achieve this, one hundred white cupola, covered with white glass mosaics, were installed as skylights. They face north on the building's sloped roof in order to light the reading halls with pleasant diffused light.

The enclosed volumes of concrete in contrast to the white cupola, express the content of the building–being a huge storage repository of information turning toward the light. The readers are placed on three levels facing a common space which joins all the reading halls of different subjects into a whole integrating the sciences and scholars. A central vertical service core serves the librarians and connects them to their sources.

Critics of the design of the Central Library building refer the overall shape of the building as the "camel seated in a squatting position."

NEGEV BRIGADE MONUMENT

This monument, located on the northeast outskirts of Be'er Sheva, is dedicated to the members of the Palmach Negev Brigade who fell in the 1948 War of Independence. The Negev Brigade defended the Jewish settlements in the Negev from the invading Egyptian army.

The abstract concrete sculptural monument was designed by Danny Karavan. The monument, located atop a hill overlooking Be'er Sheva, consists of several structures, each inscribed with poetry, dedications, and excerpts from the battle log of the brigade.

MUSEUM OF THE NEGEV

The Museum of the Negev is located in a former Turkish mosque built in 1915. It was later known as the "Governors House." The museum chronicles five thousand years of history of Be'er Sheva. There is an elegant floor mosaic taken from a sixth century church depicting animals woven into an intricate geometric pattern. The museum holds changing exhibits from its collection of early and contemporary Israeli art. The Museum of the Negev is located at 60, Ha'atzma'ut Street. Hours are Monday & Wednesday-Thursday 8:30-3:30, Tuesday 8:30-2:00 & 4:00-6:00, Friday-Saturday 10:00-1:00. For further information Tel. (08) 628-2057.

Take Route 60 east of Be'er Sheva for about three kilometers, turn right and go to the Tel Sheva National Park.

Tel Sheva

MAN IN THE DESERT MUSEUM

There are ruins of a Roman fortress dating from 200 C.E.,

houses from the 8th century B.C.E., and a well from the 12th century B.C.E. The Man in the Desert Museum, located next to the archaeological ruins, is devoted to the life of the Bedouins. Hours are Sunday-Thursday 10:00-5:00, Friday-Saturday 10:00-1:00. For further information Tel. (08) 646-7286.

Omer

OMER INDUSTRIAL PARK

There is a unique art gallery in the Omer Industrial Park. The Open Museum consists of two halls for changing exhibits of Israeli fine art. There is also a magnificent sculpture garden displaying some of the finest works in the art world. Some of these works include Ilan Averbuch's "Berlin Dome," Shlomo Selinger's "36 Righteous Men," and Ofra Zimbalista's "Satellite Dish." Hours are Sunday-Thursday 9:00-4:00, Saturday 10:00-5:00. For further information Tel. (08) 649-2692.

Doubleback to Route 60 and proceed to the Industrial Park in Omer.

Suseya

SUSEYA (Soussia)

After emerging from the Yattir Forest you will be at the top of the Hebron Mountains (Harei Hevron). Continue on this road to Suseya–a Jewish town from the Late Roman period. The early inhabitants, like many of the local Arab villagers today, lived in caves that were dug underneath their houses. In the center of the town, a synagogue with a beautiful mosaic floor has been discovered. Suseya is one of the oldest preserved ancient Israelite cities. It existed between the 2nd and 9th centuries C.E. and housed 10,000 inhabitants. Today, the town is exhibited through an audio-visual program, pottery shop, weaving house, and oil-press. Fifteen caves have been refurbished as "Cave Dwellings."

Continue going northeast on Route 60 to the Shoquet Junction. Turn right onto Route 31 and proceed toward Arad. Go about five kilometers and turn left onto Route 316. Continue toward Yattir and Suseya. Note: This road may be a closed military road. The new southern "Security Fence" is being built here.

Tel Arad

There has been human habitation in Arad for over 5,000 years. The ancient mound of Tel Arad, located 8 kilometers west of Arad, has been excavated revealing the remains of a Canaanite town. There are also remains of an Israelite fortress dating from King Solomon's era, with a sanctuary resembling the Holy Temple in Jerusalem. For further information about the Tel Arad National Park Tel. (03) 995-7690.

Doubleback on Route 316. When you reach Route 31, turn left. Take Route 31 to the Tel Arad Junction. Turn left onto Route 2808 and go about 1.5 kilometers to Tel Arad.

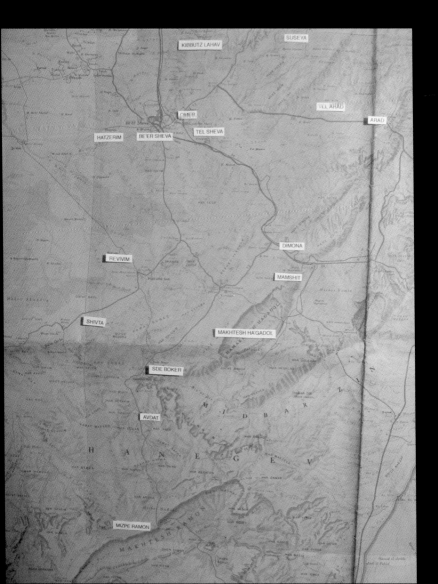

Arad

Modern Arad was developed in 1961 as a planned community with buildings designed close together around plazas. Architecturally, the plan did not work. However, Arad is ideal for asthma sufferers since it is located in the dry desert air. Arad used to sponsor an annual rock festival in mid-July. The locals referred to it as the Israeli "Woodstock" Festival. The 1995 (and all subsequent) Festival had to be cancelled after several hundred teenagers "rushed" the fence in order to get in free–just as they did in the original Woodstock Festival. However, the Israeli "rush" turned out to be disastrous. Four teenagers were crushed to death in the stampede!

ARAD MUSEUM
The Arad Museum has extensive displays and exhibitions, and creative workshops. The museum guides offer a tour of the exhibition, a talk on the Gallery, slides and creative activities, and a variety of art-related subjects. The museum is located at 28, Ben Ya'ir Street. Hours are Sunday-Thursday 9:00-5:00, Saturda y 9:00-2:30. For further information Tel. (08) 995-4409.

GLASS MUSEUM OF ARAD
This museum serves as a permanent home for the artist Gideon Fridman and other glass artists from all over the country. The museum is located at 11, Sadan Street.
Hours: Thur 10:00-5:00, Fri 10:00-3:00, Sat 10:00-7:00 or by special appointment. For further information Tel. (08) 995-3388.

SOUND & LIGHT SHOW
You can take the road northeast of Arad to the "backside" of Masada–to the site of the Roman earthen ramp, built up to the top of the mountain. On that western slope of Masada there is a Sound and Light show presented at 9:00pm (March 27–August) and at 7:00pm (September–October) on Tuesday and Thursday evenings. These special programs are presented in Hebrew but headsets in English are provided.

*Return to Route 31, turn left and continue east to **Arad**.*

Mamshit

MAMSHIT NATIONAL PARK
Mamshit is the site of a first century Nabatean city. There is an extensive network of ancient dams. Contemporary Israeli scien-

tists have tried to study these ancient waterworks and use them in new Negev projects. For further information Tel. (08) 655-6478.

Dimona

*Continue going west along Route 25 to **Dimona**.*

Dimona is a development town settled in the 1950s by North African and Indian Jews and more recently by Ethiopian and Russian Jewich immigrants.

MUSEUM OF FIGHTING GLORY
This museum is devoted to the memory of David Mudrik, a member of the partisans in the Ukraine during World War II. There are artifacts relating to the Holocaust and the Jewish partisans who fought against the Nazis. The museum is located at 14, Hadas Street. Hours are Sunday & Thursday 5:00pm-7:00pm, Tuesday 10:00-12:00. For further information Tel. (08) 655-6236.

Take Route 204 just west of Dimona and go south to Yerucham. Turn left onto Route 225.

Continue driving along Route 225, go down into Makhtesh Ha'gadol (the large crater) until the intersection of Route 206. Turn left and continue north to Route 25. Turn left on Route 25 in the direction of Dimona. There is a side road called Drerech Akravim or the Road of Scorpions. There are signs along the side of the road in several languages. The main idea behind the signs is that it is forbidden to take photographs in the area. It is also forbidden to leave the car for ANY reason. The purpose for these signs is that this is a restricted military zone. The large silver dome in the distance is Israel's Atomic Research Station!
You are now under surveillance. There are balloons overhead photographing any unauthorized vehicle. All of the fields surrounding the Atomic Research Center are mined (hence the name "Road of Scorpions"). If an airplane should happen to venture too close to this restricted air zone, it will be shot down. No questions asked!
If you want to drive through a series of hair-pin curves with stark exposed rock layers, when you get to the intersection of Route 206, turn right onto Route 227 in the direction of Route 90. Take it real slow as you descend to the lowest point on earth, the Dead Sea region.

Kibbutz Lahav

JOE ALON MUSEUM OF BEDOUIN CULTURE
This museum, located on Kibbutz Lahav, teaches about these nomadic Arabs who live in small groups, in goat-hair tents, throughout the Negev and Sinai deserts. Many bedouin are now settling down in permanent stone-built settlements. The museum contains exhibits such as an herbal garden with medicina

View from the base of the Makhtesh Ha'gadol.

These horizontal layers in the Makhtesh Ha'gadol have been lifted and folded over thousands of years. There are thousands of fish fossils in these rocks. Beware of poisonous snakes and scorpions. It is extremely hot in this crater in the summer. Temperatures can easily exceed 115 degrees!
Warning! The sharp-curved road does not have guard rails.

plants, pita baking and weaving, and Bedouin hospitality of coffee and tea. The Daroma Museum features information about ancient cultures living in caves. The museum was originally founded in the Sinai, but after Israel withdrew from the Sinai in 1979, the museum was rebuilt in Kibbutz Lahav.

Joe Alon was one of the founders of the Israel Air Force, along with Ezer Weizmann, and Motty Hod. He was born in Ein Harod in 1929. His parents were forced to return to Czechoslovakia in 1931, and in 1939 they sent Joe to England to escape the Nazis. He returned to Israel in 1948 and joined the Israel Air Force's first pilot training course.

Joe Alon became one of Israel's first jet pilots in 1953, and was appointed squadron commander of the latest jet fighters, the Ouragan in 1955. He was also the first squadron commander of the famous Mirage fighters. The peak of his career was to serve as the first commanding officer of the first airbase built from scratch by the Israel Air Force at Hatzerim.

In 1970, he was appointed Air Attaché to the Israeli Embassy in Washington, D.C. On July 1, 1973, a month before the end of his tour of duty, Joe Alon was murdered in front of his home in Washington, D.C. The case has not been solved to this day.

Kibbutz Hatzerim

THE AIR FORCE MUSEUM

The Air Force Museum is located on the Hatzerim Air Force Base, four kilometers west of Kibbutz Hatzerim. The museum exhibits planes in use by the Israeli Air Force from its inception to the present day, and other material portraying its history. The collection, which took over ten years to complete, includes over a hundred planes, twelve of which are in flying condition. A brief descriptive plaque in English stands next to each plane. An exhibition of photographs, depicting the history of the Israeli Air Force, is housed in the Heritage Building. A Boeing 707 has been converted into a hall, used to show films on the Israeli Air Force and the history of Israeli aviation. Hours are Sunday-Thursday 8:00-5:00, Friday 8:00-1:00. For further information Tel. (08) 990-6853.

*Take Route 2357 west of Be'er Sheva past **Kibbutz Hatzerim**.*

Moshav Nevatim

JEWS OF COCHIN

The Center for the Heritage of Cochin (India) Jewry is located on Moshav Nevatim. These Indian Jews came after the State of

*Take Route 25 east of Be'er Sheva for about 5 kilometers. **Moshav Nevatim** is on the left.*

Israel was created. the Jewish community of Cochin, India dates back many hundreds of years. They were merchants who originally arrived from Iraq and had commercial ties with other Jewish communities throughout the Mediterranean Sea and the Persian Gulf. The Jews of Cochin were treated with respect throughout their long history. There was never any anti-Semitism. If you go to Cochin today, there are still several exquisite synagogues, which now serve mainly as museums. There are only a handful of Jews left in Cochin. A tour of the moshav includoo the I leiilaye Cenler, synagogue, and greenhouses.

Kibbutz Sa'ad

Take Route 25 west of Be'er Sheva. Kibbutz Sa'ad is located about five kilometers east of Gaza.

STRONGHOLD OPPOSITE GAZA
This museum in Kibbutz Sa'ad is located in the only building which remained as a "safe-house" while battling the Egyptian army during the War of Independence. Ironically, the Jewish settlements in the Gaza Strip have been evacuated and this kibbutz is once again on the "front lines." History does repeat itself. Hours are Sunday-Thursday 8:00-4:00, Friday 8:00-1:00. For further information Tel. (08) 680-0267.

Kibbutz Magen

At the Sa'ad Junction, take Route 232 south to the Magen Junction. Go to Kibbutz Magen.

MUZOOLOGI
Kibbutz Magen has a beautiful Zoological Park. The Muzoologi contains exhibits of fauna, birds, mammals and reptiles. There are 11,000 specimens of Mollusks from 30 countries on display. Tours of the exhibits are available by advanced reservations. Hours are Sunday-Thursday & Saturday 10:00-4:00, Friday 10:00-2:00. For further information Tel. (08) 998-3039.

Kibbutz Revivim

Take Route 40 south from Be'er Sheva to the Mash'abim Junction. Turn right onto Route 222 and proceed to Kibbutz Revivim.

MIZPE REVIVIM MUSEUM
The Mizpe Revivim Museum is located in a restored fort that served the founders of the kibbutz as their living quarters. The kibbutz was founded in 1943 and was one of the pioneer settlements formed for the purpose of conducting agricultural experiments, for the further settling of the Negev, and the conquest of the desert. Hours are Sunday-Thursday 9:00-3:00, Friday 9:00-1:00, Saturday 9:00-4:00. For further information Tel. (08) 656-2570.

There are over one hundred vintage aircraft in the Israel Air Foce Museum at Hatzerim

Kibbutz Sde Boker

*Doubleback to Route 40, Turn right and continue south to **Kibbutz Sde Boker.***

HOME OF DAVID BEN-GURION

Kibbutz Sde Boker is located about 50 kilometers due south of Be'er Sheva. It was established in 1952 and produces olives, apricots, kiwis, and other fruit for domestic and international markets. It also produces wheat, corn, and livestock.David Ben-Gurion, Israel's first prime minister, was a passionate believer in the development of the Negev. He joined the kibbutz in 1953. He lived and worked here until his death in 1973, at the age of 87. He and his wife Paula, are buried here. Many of his books and papers may be seen in the Paula and David Ben-Gurion Hut.

Hours are Sunday-Thursday 8:30-4:00, Friday 8:30-2:00, Saturday & Holidays 9:00-3:00. For further information Tel. (08) 656-0469.

A branch of the Ben-Gurion University of the Negev has been established at Sde Boker. A modern library containing 750,000 documents associated with Ben-Gurion is located here. The institute also serves as a center for the study of desert areas such as applied geobotanics to low-water desert architecture and hydroponics.

Ein Avdat

*Take the dirt road which leads from Midreshet Ben-Gurion to the **Ein Avdat** Canyon.*

EIN AVDAT CANYON HIKE

From the parking lot, follow the path up the canyon to the spring of Ein Avdat (there is a fee). The waters of the spring collect in a deep pool at the bottom of a small waterfall. Continue up the canyon (via the secluded steps on the right side of the canyon wall), to the Ein Ma'arif waterfall. From the top of the canyon, a series of ladders leads up the cliff wall. To save time, one member of the hiking party should return to the car while everyone is climbing and bring it around to the upper parking lot.

AQEV SPRING HIKE

For those with 4-wheel drive vehicles, a trip to the Aqev Spring is highly recommended. At the small bridge where the road to the Ein Avdat Canyon crosses Nahal Zin, a jeep track branches off to the east along Nahal Zin. Follow the track to the intersection with the track that leads into Nahal Aqev. Drive into Nahal Aqev, to the end of the track. Then walk along the 300-meter path to the spring.

Ein Aqev can also be reached via the hiking trail, marked in green, that climbs via Ma'ale Divshon to the Avdat Plateau. It is

Hiking in the Ein Avdat Canyon.
Courtesy Ministry of Tourism. Photo by Itamar Greenberg.

*Take Route 40 north of Sde Boker to Route 211. Turn left and go about 17 kilometers to a fork in the road. Turn left and go to **Shivta** National Park.*

Shivta

SHIVTA NATIONAL PARK

Shivta was one of the six Nabatean-Byzantine cities which existed in the Negev between the first and seventh centuries C.E. It was not an enclosed city (fortified by a city wall).

Avdat

*Doubleback to Sde Boker and continue driving 5 kilometers south along Route 40 to **Avdat**.*

AVDAT ARCHAEOLOGICAL SITE

This is the site of a 3rd century B.C.E. Nabatean city which was located at the intersection of the caravan routes from Petra (Jordan) to Eilat. It once thrived as a rest stop for travelers, and as a strategic base for their raids. From Avdat, they could see caravans as far away as Mizpe Ramon or Sde Boker. The site was later captured by Romans and then by Byzantines.

Petra was the capital of the Nabatean kingdom. They were involved with international trade—at that time, between lower Arabia and the Fertile Crescent. Their capital of 30,000 people was ravaged by several major earthquakes over the centuries. All that remains of ancient Petra are the magnificent rock-hewn burial tombs, carved into the rosy Nubian sandstone cliffs.

The ancient city of Petra is located in Jordan, about 60 miles north of Aqaba. It is located about 20 miles due east of Har Eshet, in Israel's Negev. Over the years, Israeli hikers would "sneak" into Jordan to see the spectacular ruins at Petra. Several years ago, a few Israeli teenagers attempted to see the ruins for themselves. They hiked across the Arava, crossed the Jordan border (illegally) and hiked through the mountains of Edom in Jordan to Petra. The Jordanian army caught them. There was an international crisis, but luckily, after intervention by the United States diplomats, the teenagers were released unharmed.

Today, there is a peace treaty between Israel and Jordan. There are now continuous tours leaving Israel for Petra. For information about Avdat National Park Tel. (08) 658-6391.

Mizpe Ramon

MIZPE RAMON GEOLOGICAL MUSEUM

The town of Mizpe Ramon was established as an observation point. It overlooks the world's largest crater, the Makhtesh Ramon. It measures 7 kilometers wide, 40 kilometers long, and one half kilometer deep. The greatest influence upon the forma-

Split rock along Mizpe Ramon.
Courtesy of Ministry of Tourism.

The most exciting way of seeing the Negev is on a jeep tour.
Courtesy Israel Ministry of Tourism. Photo by Itamar Greenberg.

tion and configuration of the crater was geologic faulting along its southern flank. Accordingly, magmatic-volcanic rocks are exposed here. There are outcrops of Nubian sandstone in the lower and hard limestone in the upper parts of the crater's slopes. The floor of the crater, covered mainly by Nubian sandstone, also reveals flat-topped basalt formations. The vigorous process of erosion, which swept away the upper strata of the Ramon anticline, penetrated deep into the ground, creating a "window" onto the layers of rock.

The following are points of interest for hikers and 4-wheel drive vehicles in the vicinity of Makhtesh Ramon.

Three sites of particular geological interest are the so-called "Sawmill," where the sandstone crystallized into prism-like shapes; the dikes in Nahal Ardon; and the ammonites wall on the souther side of the crater–a large stone wall studded with the fossils of the large snails known as ammonites.

There are a variety of wild animals roaming the crater region including Nubian ibex, leopards, hyenas, dorcas gazelles, wolves, red foxes, Afghan foxes, caracals, sand foxes. and Syrian hyraxes. Before hiking in or around this geologic paradise, be sure to get information from the Visitor's Center. Hours are Sunday-Thursday & Saturday 8:00-5:00, Friday 8:00-4:00. For further information Tel. (08) 658-8691.

ALPACA FARM

About one kilometer west of the Geologic Museum is the Llama and Alpaca Farm. Alpaca and llamas are related to the camel. For further information Tel. (08) 658-8047. There is a planetarium located at the western edge of the main road in Mizpe Ramon.

MOUNT RAMON

Located along the western side of the crater, Mount Ramon is the highest mountain in the Negev highlands, rising 1,037 meters above sea level. A short dirt road reaches the top of the mountain (easily recognized by the wind turbines). Burial sites dating back to the Bronze Age dot the summit. The observation point offers a panorama of the Negev highands, the crater rim, the Sinai Desert in Egypt, and the mountains of Edom in Jordan. The view is best on winter afternoons. For information about Bio-Ramon Tel. (08) 658-8755.

AROD OBSERVATION POINT

Drive along the dirt road to Ma'aleh Arod. The observation point offers a magnificent view of Mahktesh Ramon. The road has been improved and is passable for all vehicles.

ARDON VALLEY

The Ardon Valley is located in the eastern portion of the crater. Take the dirt road marked in red along Nahal Afor. The road reaches the Eilat-Ashkelon pipeline. Take the road marked in black along the pipeline to a four-way intersection. Follow the dirt road on the right (marked in red) until you come to a fork. The segment marked in red leads to Ein Sharonim, and the one marked in black leads to Giv'at Harut.

EIN SHARONIM

The spring of Ein Sharonim is the only water source in this area. Above it is a Roman fortress.

GIV'AT HARUT

From the parking lot, follow the path to Giv'at Harut, a distinctive conical hill. The red, yellow and blue tones of the sandstone around the hill, together with the black basalt and the white gypsum, create one of the most beautiful sites in the Negev. To the right and left are ancient structures built four thousand years ago.

MOUNT ARDON

This is a six-hour hike up to the top of Mount Ardon. Hikers should be accompanied by an experienced guide.

JEEP TOUR OF THE CRATER

From the Mizpe Ramon gas station, the track follows the rim of the crater to Ma'aleh Mahmal, the ancient camel pass into the crater. The track enters the crater via Ma'aleh Noah. The jeep track reaches Giv'at Harut and continues to Ein Sharonim. Jeep tours should be accompanied by an experienced guide.

Borot Lots

*Take Route 40 north of Mizpe Ramon 5 kilometers to the junction of Route 171. Turn left and take Route 171 about 30 kilometers. Look for signs indicating **Borot Lots**. It's about 3 kilometers from the Israeli-Egyptian border.*

A series of 17 water cisterns were built during the Israelite period, three thousand years ago. Around the cisterns are remains of farm buildings and fields from that same period. Because of the altitude of the site, many plants that grew in the desert during colder periods survived in a little "vegetation island" after the climate grew warmer.

Ancient majestic Atlantic pistachio trees can be found here in large numbers. Figs, almonds, and other trees grow in Nahal Horesha and Nahal Elot. In winter, the area is covered with wildflowers and blossoming almond trees and is a paradise for nature lovers.

Tour #9 - Eilat

Eilat

Eilat is mentioned in the Bible when the Children of Israel "passed by the way of the plain of Eilat" and "camped at Etzion Gaver." After having defeated the local Edomites, King David probably established his furthest southern defense line here, but it was left to his son Solomon to develop the area. Solomon built his navy here and sent it south to bring back gold and spices from the legendary land of Ophir. It was from the same direction that Solomon's most illustrious guest, the Queen of Sheba, passed through on the way to Jerusalem where she went to test the King's great wisdom.

Another navy was built here by King Yehoshophet of Judah though it was lost in a terrible storm. King Uzziah rebuilt the town but during the reign of King Ahaz it fell to Rezin, King of Syria. Thereafter it was taken over by a succession of foreign rulers, its name changing in the process.

The ptolemies of Egypt knew it as Berenice and the Romans as Aila. With the fall of the Roman Empire the area was absorbed into the Byzantine Empire which was itself succeeded in the 7th century by the Arabs. The Arabs were ousted for a short while in the 12th century by the Crusaders. They regained possession of the whole area and held onto it until the rise of the Turks at which time the neighboring port of Aqaba was built and Eilat's importance declined sharply.

It was only in the 20th century that Eilat regained its importance. What was in 1949 a small Turkish police station called Um-Rashrash became Israel's southernmost city and port. Its population has now passed 25,000 inhabitants while its expanding industries include quarrying, mining, fishing, jewelry, film-making and tourism.

SPECIAL WARNINGS
• It is strongly advisable to drink at least 16 glasses (4 liters) of water daily, especially in the summer, because of the low humidity and extremely high temperature in the area. The body becomes dehydrated very rapidly. You will not sweat but will start to feel very tired, have headaches, etc. During the Yom Kippur War, the chaplains in the Israel Defense Forces ordered all soldiers in the battlefields to drink on the holiest day of the year, Yom Kippur, because it was a danger to their health if they did not drink!
• Avoid exaggerated sun bathing, especially between 12:00 and 2:00pm.
• Protect your feet when snorkeling along the coral reef. Sea urchins, those purple-colored thorny balls in the water or in between rock or coral formations, can prick you. It is extremely painful and must be treat immediately by a doctor.

CORAL WORLD
UNDERWATER OBSERVATORY
The Underwater Observatory is one of only four in the world. A hundred-meter-long pier running just above the sea surface connects the dry land to the observation room–a glass-windowed chamber 4.5 meters below the water level. From this vantage point a kaleidoscope of colors flashes by as rainbow-hued tropical fish swim through thickets of sea plants and gem-tinted coral. The visitor also has a choice of either going out on a glass-bottomed boat or under the water in a "Yellow Submarine." The nearest bus line is #15. Hours are Sunday-Thursday & Saturday 8:30-4:30, Friday 8:30-3:00. For further information Tel. (08) 636-4200. For information about the Coral Beach Nature Reserve Tel. (08) 637-6829.

Wind-surfing off the shores of Eilat.
Courtesy Ministry of Tourism. Photo by Albatross

Exploring the coral reef off the shores of Eilat.
Courtesy Ministry of Tourism. Photo by Itamar Greenberg.

UM RASH-RASH

This is Eilat's most important, if not only, historical site. This is where the Israeli flag was first raised over Eilat on March 10, 1949. Eilat was conquered without a shot fired and this was the last military operation of Israel's War of Independence. This site symbolizes the end of that war. None of the soldiers remembered to bring a flag with them, so a soldier by the name of Micha Peri hand drew one by pouring blue ink on a sheet. The building to the left of the statue is the old police station of Um Rash-Rash and is located next to Eilat's biggest shopping mall and is close to the Red Sea.

DOLPHIN REEF

The Dolphin Reef is located along the South Beach. This is a unique opportunity to see dolphins in their natural habitat. There is an observatory, swimming, a dive with dolphins and sea lions. Hours are daily 9:00-5:00. For further information Tel. (08) 637-1846.

ISRAEL PALACE MUSEUM

The Israel Palace Museum is located on North Beach. The visitor can see over one thousand dolls set up in 54 separate dramatic scenes, showing the history of the Jewish people from Adam and Eve to the present. Hours are Saturday-Thursday 9:00-12:00 & 4:00-8:00, Friday 9:00-1:00 (winter); Saturday-Thursday 9:00-12:00 & 6:00-10:00, Friday 9:00-1:00 (summer).

KINGS CITY AMUSEMENT PARK

In this magnificent palace, you'll discover a theme park in the style of the ancient kings offering visitors an amazing trip back in time, including caves, a cruise through King Solomon's Halls, and a wealth of interactive activities with the most up-to-date technologies. Some of the sites at Kings City include: Travel Back in Time–A sensational experience including 3-D and 4-D movies, with moving seats.

Cave of Illusions–An enormous cave containing 65 interactive elements, giant mazes, a room of distortion mirrors, and crazy projections.

Biblical Cave–A 360 meter long cave carved into the rock. An elevator takes visitors 60 meters into the depths of the earth where they can wander freely among the displays that tell Biblical stories through sight and sound. After strolling through the mazes, visitors reach the amazing stalactite and stalagmite cave, with waterfalls.

King Solomon's Waterfalls–A breathtaking cruise through King Solomon's Halls. The trip ends with an enormous heart-stopping water-slide into an artificial lake.

Hours: Sun-Thur 9:00am-1:00am. Closed Fri & Sat. Open Sat. night after Shabbat until 1:00am.

TEXAS RANCH

Just opposite Coral Beach, at the mouth of Nahal Shlomo is a "Wild West" stlye entertainment theme park and film production center. Visitors can enjoy the atmosphere of the "cowboys' street and saloon," ride horses, and watch "Westerns."

OSTRICH FARM

Located just northwest of the Texas Ranch in the Nahal Shlomo Valley is the Ostrich Farm.

BIRD WATCHING

Eilat is located along the migration path between Europe and Africa. There are more than 400 species of birds including eagles, pelicans, and storks. Migration times are twice a year; from September through November the birds head south to Africa, and from March through May they head back north to Europe. In one year, birdwatchers counted an estimated one million birds in migration.

The Birdwatching Center on Hat'marim Boulevard has information and activities relating to birdwatching around Eilat. For further information Tel. (08) 637-4276.

Ein Netafim

*Leaving Eilat, take Route 12 towards **Ein Netafim.***

THE CANYONS

Take Derekh Yotam northwest to a spectacular ravine and spring known as Ein Netafim. The water seeps out of the rock face. Continue on the same road until you reach the impressive sandstone cliffs of Red Canyon. This road continues to the Timna Valley.

NAHAL EIN NETAFIM

This is a full-day hike. Leave Route 90 at the sign pointing to Nahal Roded. After 3 kilometers, turn left at the junction. Follow Nahal Ein Netafim to the foot of Mount Shlomo. A trail marked in blue leads to the top.

LOST GULCH

This is a half-day trip. Turn off Route 90 at Nahal Roded. At the junction to Nahal Netafim, bear right and follow the road marked in blue to the end. Follow the black trail into Lost Gulch.

SHEHORET CANYON

This is a half-day trip. Drive to Amram's Pillars. Turn left on the road marked in green. Continue to Shehoret Canyon.

MOUNT AMIR & ROMAN MINES

This is a two-hour hike. From the Amram's Pillars parking lot, walk back up the road for 600 meters to a trail marked in green, leading toward the right. Just below the summit is a Roman copper mine. Turn right at the mine and follow the red trail back to the parking lot.

EIN NETAFIM & RED CANYON

This is a full day trip. Follow the road to Ein Netafim. A short hike will take you to the spring at the bottom of the cliff. Continue along the Israeli-Egyptian border. Stop at border marker #82, Mount Hizqiyyahu, for a view of Moon Valley.
Continue to the Red Canyon (Nahal Shani). Take the green trail from the parking lot into the canyon. After 2 kilometers, a trail marked in black leads back to the parking lot.

Timna Valley

TIMNA HIKING TRAIL
This is a three-hour hike. The route starts at the park entrance and ends up at Solomon's Pillars. This hike goes through breathtaking granite cliffs and valleys. Small red signs provide explanations of the geological phenomena along the trail.

MOUNT BEREKH
Mount Berekh is the highest point above the Timna Valley, affording a magnificent view of the park, the Arava, the Sinai Desert in Egypt, and the mountains of Edom in Jordan. The trail to Mount Berekh is for experienced hikers only, accompanied by a guide.
The most popular trail is a seven-hour hike that begins at the park entrance. The trail, marked in red, leads to Ma'aleh Milkham and then along the Timna cliffs (Zuqé Timna) to Mount Berekh. The descent from Mount Berekh, marked in black, leads to Solomon's Pillars.

SOLOMON'S PILLARS
The Timna Valley, 19 miles north of Eilat, is a landscape rarity and a vast natural museum of ancient civilization. It comprises the modern Timna copper mines and the remains of the ancient copper and brass mines, first worked 5,000 years ago and later by the Egyptians. The ancient circular stone ovens roasted the copper ore. The air channels were skillfully angled to catch the prevailing winds from the Arava in the north. There were stone channels leading to the collection vessels for the metal. There are also remains of laborers' camps, the watchtower, furnaces, and altars. The Pillars of Solomon are actually a weathered natural formation of Nubian sandstone (a rock formation found throughout the Negev and Sinai Desert). Be sure to see the Mushroom Rock, a granite rock carved by wind and water in the shape of a mushroom. The area around the mines has been developed as a national park, complete with an artificial lake and a network of roads.

Kibbutz Yotvata

HAI BAR NATURE RESERVE
Kibbutz Yotvata is famous for its dairy products. Across the road is a Visitors Center which offers an audio-visual presentation

*From Timna Valley travel east to Route 90. Turn left and proceed north to **Kibbutz Yotvata**.*

Natural arches carved by wind erosion can be found in Timna Park.
Courtesy Ministry of Tourism. Photo by Itamar Greenberg.

Enjoying a camel ride near Eilat.
Courtesy Ministry of Tourism. Photo by Itamar Greenberg.

*The "Mushroom Rock" near Eilat was carved by centuries of
wind and water erosion on the granite rock formation.*
Courtesy Ministry of Tourism, Photo by Itamar Greenberg.,

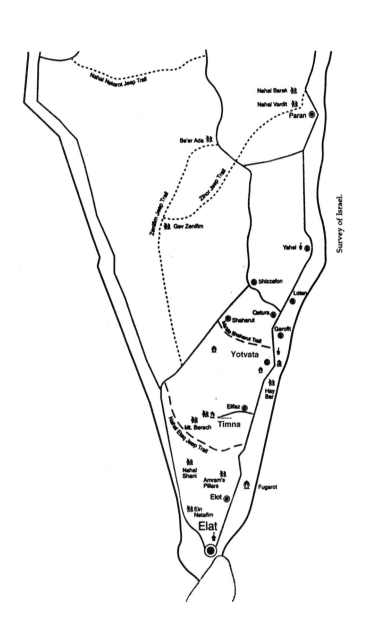

Nahal Nekarot Jeep Trail

Nahal Barak
Nahal Vardit
Paran

Be'er Ada

Zihor Jeep Trail

Zenifim Jeep Trail

Gev Zenifim

Yahel

Shizzafon

Lotan

Qetura
Shaharut
Shaharut Trail
Gerofit

Yotvata

Hay Bar

Elifaz
Mt. Berech
Timna

Nahal Elot Jeep Trail

Nahal Shani
Amram's Pillars
Fugarot

Elot

Ein Netafim

Elat

Survey of Israel.

and literature about the history, archaeology, and nature of the entire region.

The Hai Bar Nature Reserve is very unusual. Its conservationists have imported and bred a variety of animals mentioned in the in the Bible and which had become locally extinct; wild asses, ostriches, and numerous varieties of gazelle. For further information Tel. (08) 637-3057.

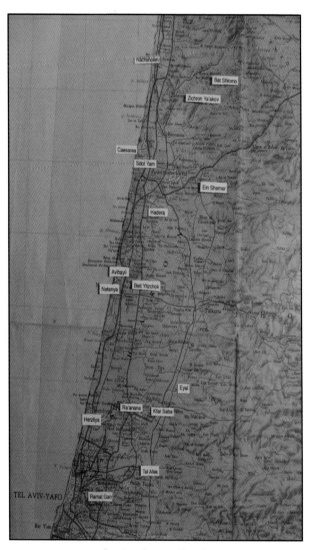

Courtesy Survey of Israel.

Tour #10 - North of Tel Aviv

Herzliya

HERZLIYA MUSEUM OF ART
The Herzliya Museum of Art provides a comprehensive view of all schools of painting and sculpture in this and previous generations. There is a special emphasis on plastic art. The museum is located at 4, Habanim Street. Hours are Sunday, Tuesday, Thursday 4:00-8:00, Monday, Wednesday, Friday-Saturday 10:00-2:00. For further information Tel. (09) 955-1011.

FOUNDERS' MUSEUM
The Founders' Museum reconstructs the story of the settlement from its earliest days up to the establishment of the state. It is located at 8, Ha'nadiv Street.

APOLLONIA (Tel Arsuf)
The Apollonia National Park (Tel Arsuf) is located along the coast just north of Herzliya. There is a magnificent Crusader fortress at the north end of the park. When it was discovered, the locals "ran-off" with some of the beautiful marble and limestone columns and urns and used then in their private gardens and homes. The authorities have since fenced-in the area and have created a national park. For further information Tel. (09) 955-0929.

Ramat Gan

BEIT ABRAHAM KRINIZI
Abraham Krinizi was the first mayor of Ramat Gan. His former home was turned into a museum. There is an exhibition, using audio-visual aids which present the history of Ramat Gan interwoven with the biography of Abraham Krinizi. The museum is located at 64, Krinizi Street. Hours are Sunday-Monday & Wednesday-Thursday 9:00-12:00, Wednesday & Saturday 10:00-1:00. For further information Tel. (03) 673-9050.

HARRY OPPENHEIMER DIAMOND MUSEUM
Israel's diamond industry was started by Belgian industrialists who escaped the Holocaust in Europe during World War II. The exhibit shows how diamonds are formed and mined. See how a diamond is cut. One out of every two polished diamonds in the world is polished in Israel. Sorry, there are no free samples on this tour. The Diamond Museum is located in the Diamond Exchange. The nearest bus line is #51. Hours are Sunday-Thursday 10:00-4:00, Tuesday 10:00-7:00. For further information Tel. (03) 621-4219.

MAN AND THE LIVING WORLD MUSEUM
This museum has exhibits dealing with nature and the effects man has on it. There are constantly changing exhibits. The museum is located in the National Park. Hours are Sunday-Thursday 9:00-2:00, Friday 9:00-1:00, Saturday 10:00-5:00. For further information Tel. (03) 631-5010.

MACCABI SPORTS MUSEUM
Israel's obsession with soccer is very common. The Pierre Gildesgame Maccabi Sports Museum gives the entire history of the sport vis-a-vis the common Israeli. The museum is located in Kfar Maccabiah. Hours are Sunday-Thursday 10:00-3:00. For further information Tel. (03) 574-6565.

MUSEUM OF RUSSIAN ART
The Maria and Michael Zetlin Museum of Russian Art includes about 80 paintings from early 20th century artists such as L. Bakst, A. Benois, and V. Serov. On exhibit are water colors, drawings and theater designs. The Museum of Russian Art is loca-

ted at 18, Hibbat Zion Street.
Hours are Sunday-Thursday 10:00-1:00 & 4:00-7:00, Saturday
10:00-1:00. For further information Tel. (03) 618-8243.

SAFARI PARK
In this 250 acre park African animals roam free. Visitors must
remain in closed vehicles while traversing the five-mile trail.
Some of the animals to be seen include lions, elephants, rhinos,
giraffes, gazelles, impalas, zebras, and flamingos. The nearest
bus lines are #30, 35, 67. Hours are Sunday-Thursday 9:00-
3:00, Friday 9:00-2:00. For further information Tel. (03) 677-
6181.

YECHIEL NAHARI MUSEUM OF FAR EASTERN ART
This is the only museum in Israel which is devoted exclusively
to the arts and crafts of the Far East. There are ceramics, prints
and paintings, bronze vessels, swords, furniture, textiles, carvings in ivory, bamboo, wood, and stone. The collection contains
objects from the 13th to the 20th century. The museum is located at 18, Hibbat Zion Street, in the same building as the
Museum of Russian Art. For further information call (03) 618-
8243.

Ra'anana

THE FOUNDERS ROOM
Ra'anana is a "bedroom" community north of Tel Aviv. The
Founders Room is also known as the Museum of Pioneers at
Yad Le'banim. It depicts the history of the town between 1912
and 1936. The museum is located at 147, Ahuza Street. Hours
are Sunday-Thursday 4:00-7:00, Saturday 11:00-1:00.
Admission is free. For further information Tel. (03) 761-0551.

Kfar Saba

ARCHAEOLOGICAL MUSEUM
There is an audio-visual presentation which describes the
history of ancient Kfar Saba and the artifacts which were found
in the area. There are also photographs, maps, and drawings
on display. Hours are Sunday-Thursday 9:00-2:00. For further
information Tel. (03) 764-9262.

Tel Afek

*Take Route 5 to Route 444 and turn right. Go south to Route 483 and turn right to **Tel Afek**.*

TEL AFEK & YARKON NATIONAL PARK

There are remains of Antipatris which was built by Herod, an impressive Ottoman fortress, an Egyptian governor's mansion from 2000 B.C.E. The Yarkon River site contains a flour mill, a farm, and a lily pond. For further information about the Yarkon National Park and Tel Afek Tel. (03) 934-8463.

Kibbutz Eyal

*Take Route 55 east to Route 444. Turn left and go north to **Kibbutz Eyal**. Just beyond this kibbutz is an exclusive Israeli town called Kochav ya'ir. This is where very wealthy Israeli politicians live including Ehud Barak.*

VINTAGE AUTO MUSEUM

This museum is a must for lovers of vintage cars. The collection consists of beautiful vintage autos mostly from England dating from the 1930s and 1940s. The museum is located in Kibbutz Eyal, which is near Kfar Saba. Admission to the Vintage Auto Museum is free. Hours are only on Saturday from 10:00-1:00. For further information Tel. (03) 749-3628.

Netanya

Nathan Straus made it possible for the poor and young to have pasteurized milk, thereby saving thousands of lives. In 1920, there were 300 Nathan Straus milk stations throughout the United States. Nathan Straus was the brother of Isidor Straus who owned Macy's Department Store in New York City. Isidor and his wife Ida drowned on the maiden voyage of Titanic in 1912. Nathan Straus donated a great deal of his fortune to the Jews living in Israel, when it was under Ottoman rule. In honor of his generosity, they named an entire city in his honor. Nathan's Hebrew name was Natan. They called the city, Netanya.

NETANYA DIAMOND CENTER

Visitors to the Netanya Diamond Center can see a model of a South Africa diamond mine, rows of diamond cutters and polishers, and then visit a gem museum. The Netanya Diamond Center is located at 31, Binyamin Boulevard.

INTERNATIONAL JEWISH SPORTS HALL OF FAME

This museum honors Jewish men and women worldwide who have accomplished extraordinary achievements in sports. The

International Jewish Sports Hall of Fame is located in the Wingate Institute. Hours are Sunday-Thursday 8:00-4:00. For further information Tel. (09) 863-9521.

Beit Yitzchok

MASSUAH HOLOCAUST POST MUSEUM
This museum, located just east of Netanya at Beit Yitzchok, contains a unique collection of stamps and letters sent through the mail during the Holocaust to concentration camp and ghettos.

Avihayil

JEWISH LEGIONS MUSEUM
The Jewish Legions Museum brings to light an exciting chapter describing the activities of the Jewish Legions within the framework of the British army during World War I (1914-1918). These units of Jewish volunteers from the Diaspora and from Palestine, were actively engaged during the war in the implementation of the Zionists goals at the time, to liberate the Land of Israel from Turkish rule.

Continue driving north along the Coastal Highway, Route 2, to Avihayil.

Kibbutz Giv'at Haim

TEREZIN HOUSE
This museum commemorates the memory of the victims who died in the Holocaust at Terezienstadt. There are works of art, historic documents, and a one-man prison cell. Hours are Sunday-Thursday 9:00-1:00, Saturday 12:30-1:30, Holidays 9:00-12:00. For further information Tel. (04) 636-9515.

Take Route 57 east of Netanya to Route 4. Turn left and travel north on Route 4 to Route 581. Turn right and go east about 2 kilometers to Kibbutz Giv'at Haim.

Hadera

KHAN HISTORICAL MUSEUM
Hadera, located midway between Tel Aviv and Haifa, was founded in 1891 by pioneers who braved the malaria-infested swamps. They drained the swamps by introducing the very thirsty eucalyptus trees which absorbed the swamp waters. The Khan Historical Museum, located at 74, Ha'giborim Street, was once an old Turkish Khan or Inn. The museum depicts the story of the early pioneers and exhibits their tools, agricultural imple-

Doubleback to Route 4 and turn right. Go north to Hadera.

ments, and photographs of the period. Hours are Sunday-Thursday 8:30-1:00, Friday 9:00-12:00.

Kibbutz Ein Shemer

Take Route 65, north of Hadera, and go east to **Kibbutz Ein Shemer.**

THE OLD COURTYARD

This museum takes the visitor back in time to a restored early kibbutz with a surrounding wall and a brick stockade. Several types of original agricultural tools and weapons are on display. Hours are Sunday-Thursday 8:00-4:00, Holidays 8:00-1:00. For further information Tel. (04) 637-4327.

Kibbutz Sdot Yam

Return to the Coastal Highway and continue northward to **Kibbutz Sdot Yam.**

BEIT HANNA SENESH

Beit Hanna Senesh is a museum containing a fine collection of Roman statues and tombstones with Greek, Latin, and Hebrew inscriptions. Many of these artifacts were accidently unearthed during the construction of Kibbutz Sdot Yam, located just south of Caesarea. The museum takes its name from Hanna Senesh who was a member of this kibbutz and was parachuted into Hungary, behind German lines, during World War II by the British, in cooperation with the Haganah. She was captured and executed by the Nazis. Hours are Sunday-Friday 9:00-12:00, Saturday 10:00-12:00.

Caesarea

Just to the north of Kibbutz Sdot Yam along the coast is **Caesarea.** *The nearest train station is Binyamina. Take a taxi from there. It's about a ten minute ride.*

Phoenician travelers of the 4th century B.C.E. first established a small settlement and harbor called Strato's Tower on the main trading route between Phoenicia and Egypt. The settlement, along with the rest of the coastal strip, eventually fell into the hands of Caesar Augustus, who granted it to Herod, governor of Judea. Herod turned Strato's Tower into one of the great cities of the eastern Roman Empire.

Construction began in 22 B.C.E., and only 12 years later Strato's Tower was a splendid Roman city with a theater, hippodrome, aqueducts carrying fresh water from the north, and a harbor capable of accommodating 300 ships. Herod named the new city in honor of Caesar Augustus. In 6 C.E., Caesarea, also known as Caesarea Maritima, became the capital of the Roman province of Judea.

In 66 C.E., a riot broke out between Jews and Romans in Caesarea and sparked the six-year Jewish revolt, which ended

Remnants of the Roman aqueduct are located at the Caesarea Beach.

in the destruction of the second Temple in Jerusalem. When the Romans finally squelched the rebellion in 70 C.E. (except for holdouts at Masada), they celebrated by sacrificing 20,000 Jews in Caesarea's amphitheater.

Sixty years later, a second Jewish uprising, the Bar Kochba Revolt, was also brought to a bitter end. This time the Romans were more selective. Ten Jewish sages, among them the famous Rabbi Akiva, were tortured to death in the arena. The detailed description of these martyrs' deaths are recited in the prayers on Tish'a Ba'av and on Yom Kippur.

CAESAREA HARBOR

Get ready to embark on a thrilling adventure through time and places while meeting the diverse people who have made Caesarea the gem that it is today...

The Caesarea Experience–Climb aboard this fascinating expedition that will take you on an enchanted voyage through the thrilling history of Caesarea. As you follow your journey through time, you will encounter the breathtaking diversity of the magnificent cultures that ruled the city at different points throughout history. Take a gigantic leap back in time as you venture through the Herodian Era to the Roman era, the Byzantine Era, the Arab Era and the Crusader Era, all the way to the early days of Zionism in Israel and the settlement project of Baron de Rothschild. You will then meet a broad range of historical figures that helped shape the rich history of Caesarea such as King Herod, Rabbi Akiva, Saint Paul, Saladin, Hannah Senesh, and Baron de Rothschild.

Ascend the Time Tower and see computerized three-dimensional animation displayed on a giant screen. Walk along the Ramparts Road, see the Port of Herod, the Wall and Moat, the Hippodrome, a Roman Aqueduct, the Reef Palace, and the Roman Amphitheater.

Zichron Ya'akov

Travel north along Route 4 to Kibbutz Zichron Ya'akov.

Zichron Ya'akov was founded in 1882 by Rumanian Jews. The early settlers fought unsuccessfully against malaria-infested swamps until Baron Edmund de Rothschild came to their aid with generous donations, establishing an economy gased on vineyards. The town was named in honor of the baron's father, James or Ya'akov.

Caesarea was the major Roman port around the year 70. Many Jews were killed in the Roman Amphitheater including the venerated Rabbi Akiva. Many others were shipped off to Rome as slaves. A modern pier juts out into the Mediterranean Sea in the distance.

Crusader fort at Caesarea was designed with a series of ramparts and a moat.

CARMEL WINERY
Since its early start in wine production, Zichron Ya'akov has come to be known for its Carmel Mizrahi Winery. The winery now produces most of Israel's domestic wine, as well as a large stock for export. The old glass factory in nearby Kibbutz Nachsholim was built by Baron de Rothschild. The factory transformed the white sand on the beach into bottles for the baron's winery. The factory was onced managed by Meir Dizengoff, who later became the first mayor of Tel Aviv. The Carmel Winery is located on Ha'nadiv Street. Tours and wine-tasting are given Sunday-Thursday 8:30-3:00, Friday 8:30-1:00.

AHARONSON HOUSE
This museum commemorates NILI, an early Zionist paramilitary intelligence unit, originally based in Zichron Ya'akov. The Aharonson House is located on Ha'meyasdim Street. Hours are Sunday-Thursday 8:30-1:00, Friday 10:00-1:00.

Bat Shlomo

MOSHAV BAT SHLOMO
This moshav is an almost unchanged example of an early Jewish settlement. Supported by Baron de Rothschild, it was originally founded in 1889 for graduates of an agricultural school established by the Rothschilds in the moshav. You can see the farmyards surrounded by the defense wall.

Kibbutz Nachsholim

OLD GLASS FACTORY
The old glass factory in Kibbutz Nachsholim was built by Baron de Rothschild. The factory transformed the white sand on the beach into bottles for baron's winery in nearby Zichron Ya'akov. The factory was onced managed by Meir Dizengoff, who later became the first mayor of Tel Aviv.

Tour #11 - Haifa

Haifa

Haifa is Israel's third largest city and is the capital of Northern Israel. In Biblical times, Haifa was the site where Elijah the Prophet had his dramatic conflict with the false prophets of Ba'al. In the 14th century B.C.E., the port near Abu Huwam flourished until Hellenistic times. The port was then moved to what is today the Bat-Galim quarter, where it existed as a Roman town. By the 3rd century C.E., Haifa and neighboring Shiqmona, had well established Jewish communities which grew and by the 11th century, Haifa was a thriving Jewish center. In 1100, the town's Jews joined their Moslem neighbors in an unsuccessful attempt to thwart a Crusader attack. Following the capture by the Crusaders the town declined and in the 18th century the local ruler, Dahr El-Omar, demolished and then rebuilt the town with new fortifications. It was not until the Jewish return in the late 19th century that Haifa really began to develop. With the building of the Hedjaz railroad between Damascus and Medina and the construction of the modern port at the beginning of the 20th century, Haifa's importance increased. Haifa became home to Israel's principal port, a major industrial center, as well as to nearly a quarter million inhabitants. It is the home of the Technion, the highly-regarded Israel Institute of Technology. Haifa also boasts of its own university, theater, symphony orchestra, Jewish-Arab cultural center, museums, and other cultural institutions.

Haifa is a city of sea and mountain. It is divided into three distinct levels which are connected by the Carmelit, Israel's only subway. Ha'ir, the lower level, is not only the location of the port but also a major business center. Hadar Ha'Carmel, the middle level, though largely residential, is also the location of many businesses and offices. At the top of the mountain is Har Ha'Carmel which is primarily residential and recreational.

CHAGALL ARTISTS HOUSE
24 Hazionut Boulevard (Hadar section)
The Chagall artists House was established in 1954. It serves as a venue for one-man shows and group exhibitions. There are also lecture programs and chamber music concerts. Hours are Sunday through Thursday 9:00-1:00 and 4:00-7:00 and Saturday 10:00-1:00. Admission is free. For further information call (04) 852-2355. Take BUS #10, 12, 22, 28

CLANDESTINE IMMIGRATION & NAVAL MUSEUM
204 Allenby Road Tel. (04) 853-6249
The museum is devoted to the clandestine immigration and to the history of Israel's navy from the War of Liberation to the Yom Kippur War. The exhibits are housed in an old landing craft converted into an illegal immigrants vessel called "Af Al Pi Chen" (Nevertheless), used to run the blockade during the British Mandate period, prior to Israel's independence. It was successful in bringing 434 immigrants into the country. There are light and sound shows, photographs, battle plans and ship models. Hours are Sunday-Thursday 9:00-4:00 and Friday 9:00-1:00. BUS #3, 5, 26, 43, 103, 113, 114.

NATIONAL MARITIME MUSEUM
198 Allenby Road Tel. (04) 853-6622
BUS #3, 5, 44, 45
The history of seafaring and the development of shipbuilding in the Mediterranean Sea is explained in this museum. The museum contains over seven thousand artifacts

including ancient anchors, Greco-Roman coins, maps of naval battles, with special emphasis on Jewish seafaring.
Hours are Monday, Wednesday & Thursday 10:00-4:00, Tuesday 10:00-8:00, Friday 10:00-1:00 and Saturday 10:00-3:00. Take BUS #114.

DAGON GRAIN SILO & ARCHAEOLOGICAL MUSEUM
Plumer Square   Tel. (04) 866-4221
Grain storage and handling in ancient Israel and the Near East is explained and demonstrated, including working models. Exhibits include wheat grain from 4,000 years ago until today. Admission is free. Hours are Sunday-Thursday 10:30 -11:00. Hours can be arranged by special request.

HAIFA MUSEUM OF ART
26 Shabbetai Levy Street
Tel. (04) 852-3255   BUS #10, 12, 28, 37 CARMELIT to Ha-Nevi'im
The Haifa Museum of Art consists of three separate collections: Museum of Ancient Art - Israel's largest collection of Greco-Roman sculptures, items recovered from Haifa Bay, terra-cottas, rare coins, and finds from Shiqmona (ancient Haifa); Museum of Modern Art - Exhibitions of modern and contemporary Israeli and non-Israeli art; Museum of Music and Ethnology - Exhibitions of musical instruments and ethnographic artifacts.
Hours are Monday, Wednesday & Thursday 10:00-4:00, Tuesday 10:00-8:00, Friday 10:00-1:00 and Saturday 10:00-3:00.

ISRAEL ELECTRIC CORPORATION (IEC) VISITORS CENTER
Shemen Beach   Tel. (04) 864-6176
The Haifa power station has an IEC visitors center, with activities including a guided tour of the display, a film about the IEC and tour

tour of the site. There is a close-up view o the power plant and entry to the contro room. Hours: Sunday-Thursday 8:00-3:00 Reservations are required. BUS #2.

TIKOTIN MUSEUM OF JAPANESE ART
89 Ha'Nassi Avenue   Tel. (04) 838-355 BUS #3, 5, 21, 22, 23, 28, 37
This museum was founded by Felix Tikotin a renowned collector of Japanese art, and Abba Chushi in 1959. The museum house six thousand works of art including paint ings, textiles, ceramics and sketches. Th museum hosts films, lectures, Zen medita tion and Japanese flower arrangements.
Hours are Monday, Wednesday & Thursda 10:00-4:00, Tuesday 10:00-8:00, Frida 10:00-1:00 and Saturday 10:00-3:00. BU #22, 23, 30, 31, 99. CARMELIE: Ha'nevi'ir station.

HAIFA CITY MUSEUM - BEIT HA'AM
11, Ben-Gurion Avenue   Tel. (04) 851-2030 Beit Ha'am was the first house to be built i the German Colony at the end of the 19t century by the Templar families. It was use as a conference hall and a school and wa the center of life in the Colony. The buildin has been restored and renovated and toda serves as the City Museum. The museur has changing displays relating to the City c Haifa. BUS #10, 12, 22, 113.

THE GERMAN COLONY
The German Colony in Haifa was estab lished in 1869 by the Association c Templars, who came from Germany with th aim of training the residents of the Land c Israel, and instructing them in bringing th Messiah. The Templars set up seve colonies around the country and had consic erable influence on modernizing the Ho Land and the City of Haifa, in the field building, agriculture, transport, hotels, con

Million dollar view from the top of Haifa's Mount Carmel. The modern Haifa Government Center (lower left) was built in 2005.

merce and industry. During World War II, the Templars became enemy subjects because of their German origins and were eventually expelled from the country by the British.

In recent years the German Colony in Haifa has been renovated and restored and has become one of the liveliest and most distinctive entertainment areas in the city.

NATIONAL MUSEUM OF SCIENCE, TECHNOLOGY & SPACE
25 Shmeriyahu Levin Street
Tel. (04) 862-8111
This museum is located in the old Technion building in Hadar Ha-Carmel. It is a science activities center, illustrating basic scientific principles as well as technological advances in Israeli industry. The museum features live scientific demonstrations guaranteed to stimulate and entertain children of all ages. Hours are Monday, Wednesday & Thursday 10:00-6:00, Tuesday 10:00-7:30, Friday 10:00-2:00 and Saturday 10:00-6:00. BUS #10, 12, 23, 24, 28, 37, 113, 114, 115 CARMELIT: Ha'nevi'im Street

TECHNION ISRAEL INSTITUTE OF TECHNOLOGY
Kiryat Hatechnion (Neve Sha'anan)
Tel. (04) 832-0664
The Technion is the first and foremost among Israel's institutions of higher education. At the Koler Visitor's Center, displays and a video film tell the story of the Technion and its achievements from its inception in 1912 until today. On Tuesday evenings, there is Israeli folk dancing on the roof of the Student Union Building, overlooking a spectacular view of Haifa Bay. Hours: Sunday-Thursday 8:00-2:00 BUS #17, 19, 31, 142

ZOO, BOTANICAL GARDEN & MUSEUM
Gan Ha-Em (Mother's Park) Carmel Center
Tel. (04) 833-7019

BUS #21, 22, 23, 28, 37
CARMELIT: Gan Ha-Em
Hours are Sunday-Thursday 8:00-4:00, Friday 8:00-1:00, Saturday 9:00-4:00.

SHABBAT TOURS OF HAIFA
Every Saturday at 10:15am a free walking tour leaves from #89, Yefe Nof Street, opposite the Mano Katz Museum. The route of this tour starts at the Louis Promenade, sculpture garden, Baha'i Gardens and down to the Haifa Museum. The tour is about two hours. For further information Tel.(04) 853-5606 or 1-800-30-50-90.

BAHA'I SHRINE & GARDENS
Haifa is a holy city for the Baha'i faith. The gold dome of the Baha'i temple shines from every point in the city. It is surrounded by 19 acres of magnificent Persian terraced gardens, fountains and promenades from the peak of Mount Carmel down to its base. The shrine also houses the mausoleum of one of the founders of the Baha'i faith, El bab. The Baha'i faith is based on brotherhood, love and charity.

Due to the limited capacity and topographical structure, only a certain number of people can visit the gardens at any one time. Visitors should register in advance and confirm their place by phone Tel. (04) 831 3131. Please wear modest attire to the Baha'i Shrine.
Hours are daily for the Bab Shrine 9:00-12:00. Gardens are open 9:00-5:00.

ISRAEL EDIBLE OIL MUSEUM
Shemen Oil Factory Haifa Bay
Tel. (04) 860-4660 BUS #2
Five thousand years of oil production and the development of edible oil technology and processing are on display on the old compound of the Shemen oil factory. Hours are Sunday-Thursday 8:30-4:30.

HAIFA UNIVERSITY - ARCHAEOLOGY MUSEUM
Reuben & Edith Hecht Museum
Crest of Mount Carmel Tel. (04) 825-7773
BUS #22, 24, 30, 36, 37, 141, 143, 192
The Hecht Museum's permanent archaeological exhibition is based on the private collection of the late Dr. Reuben Hecht, which he donated to the University of Haifa. The exhibition concentrates on the subject of "The people of Erezt Israel." Items on the lower floor are displayed in chronological order, beginning with the Chalcolithic period and ending with the Mishnaic and the Talmudic era (Roman and Byzantine periods). The upper floor is devoted to thematic displays, such as coins, seals, weights, and jewelry. A central exhibition consists of finds from the excavations of the Temple Mount in Jerusalem.

Dr. Hecht's private collection of paintings is displayed in the Art Wing. It represents various art movements, with an emphasis on impressionism and the Jewish School of Paris. Works of Monet, Pissaro, Soutine, Struck, and others are exhibited.

The 25-story Eshkol Tower, designed by the Brazilian architect Oscar Niemeyer, is said to straddle a mild geological fault and offers an unparalleled view of northern Israel. Hours are Monday, Wednesday & Thursday 10:00-4:00, Tuesday 10:00-7:00, Friday 10:00-1:00 and Saturday 10:00-2:00. Admission is free.

ANCIENT BOAT MUSEUM
Eshkol Tower in Haifa University
Tel. (04) 824-0450
A unique museum located next to the Hecht Museum in Haifa University. The Ma'agan Michael boat museum serves as a laboratory and workshop for learning about sailing in ancient times.

Hours: Monday, Wednesday, Thursday 10:00-2:00, Tuesday 10:00-3:00

BUS #24, 30, 36, 37, 141

BEIT-HAGEFEN ART GALLERY
2 Hagefen Street Tel. (04) 852-5252
Beit Hagefen, the Arab-Jewish Center, was founded in 1963 to create a social and meeting place for Jews and Arabs. There is a Visitor's Center, Arab Theater, and Children's Cultural Center and library.
Hours are Sunday-Thursday 8:00-7:00, Friday 9:00-1:00, Saturday 10:00-1:00.

ALBADIA–
ARAB BEDOUIN HERITAGE CENTER
1 Aba Hushi Street Tel. (04) 839-1872
(near Haifa University)
This museum is devoted to the lives of the Bedouin. There is Bedouin folklore, the henna ceremony and the wedding ceremony. Hours are by request only.

ELIJAH'S CAVE
Corner of Sderot Ha-Hagannah and Derech Allenby
Tel (04) 852-7430 BUS #3, 5, 43, 44, 45
The Cave of Elijah the Prophet, who lived and preached in the Carmel, is a place of prayer and pilgrimage for Jews, Moslems, and Christians alike. It was here, in this hidden shelter on the western slope, that Elijah taught his disciples, and took refuge from the persecution of King Ahab. In Jewish tradition, the prophet is harbinger of the Messiah, and religious Jews to this day, pray for his return. Admission is free.

HAIFA CABLE CAR
Upper Station - Stella Maris on Mount Carmel crest. Tel. (04) 833-0009.
Lower Station - Bat Galim on the seashore.
While riding the cable-car, one receives explanations about the magnificent landscape and points of interest in the area. The other three cable-car rides in Israel are located at Rosh Hanikra (along the Leban-

Israel's only subway, the Carmelit, is located in Haifa.

ese border), Masada (near the Dead Sea) and at Kibbutz Menara, located just west of Kiryat Shemona. For further information Tel. (04) 833-5970.
Hours are Sunday-Thursday & Saturday 10:00-6:00 (summer until 11:00) and Friday 10:00-2:00.

CARMELIT - HAIFA SUBWAY

This is Israel's only subway. It was cut into the Carmel mountain at an angle and operates like an elevator or funicular. Note the cables between the rails. Each subway train acts as a counter-weight. There is one track at either end. Each train starts at the same time—one at the base and one at the top of the line. In the midway section, the cars side-swipe" (by-pass) each other on two sets of tracks. And then continue their run on one train track. There are only six stations. The entire trip takes about six minutes from sea level up to the Carmel Center.

PANORAMA OBSERVATION POINT

BUS #21, 22, 23
CARMELIT: Carmel Center
All along Rechov Yefe Nof (Panorama Street) there are spectacular views of the city, Haifa Bay, Acre, Rosh Hanikra, and on clear days, the snow capped Mount Hermon.

GAN HA-PESALIM (Sculpture Garden)

Opposite 135 Sderot Ha-Ziyyonut
BUS #22, 23, 25, 26
Over twenty bronze sculptures by Ursala Malbin are set in a garden overlooking Haifa Bay.

MUSIC MUSEUM & AMLI LIBRARY

3 Rechov Arlosoroff Tel. (04) 864-4485
This museum displays folk instruments, ancient and modern, from many countries. The library contains Jewish music and recorded Yiddish folk songs.

STEKLIS MUSEUM
OF PREHISTORY (Gan Ha'Em Museum)

124 Ha-Tishbi Street Tel. (04) 837-1833
CARMELIT: Gan Ha'am station
BUS #3, 5, 22, 23, 28, 37, 99
The Museum of Prehistory, which is located in the Zoo, houses archaeological artifacts from the Carmel and Northern Israel. There are dioramas illustrating prehistoric life in the region.
Hours are Sunday-Thursday & Saturday 9:00-6:00, Friday 9:00-2:00.

MANE-KATZ MUSEUM

89 Rechov Yafe Nof Street
Tel. (04) 838-3482
The world-renowned Jewish-French expressionist artist, Mané-Katz, bequeathed his home, paintings, and other works of art to the City of Haifa. The artist died in Haifa in 1962. Besides his paintings and sculptures, the display also includes his personal collection of Judaica and antique furniture.
Hours are Sunday-Monday & Wednesday-Thursday 10:00-4:00, Tuesday 10:00-6:00, Friday 10:00-1:00 and Saturday 10:00-2:00.
BUS #22, 23, 28, 30, 31, 99, 131, 133
CARMELIT: Gan Ha'am station

JANCO-DADA MUSEUM

Ein Hod (Hof HaCarmel) Tel. (04) 984-2350
This museum is located in the center of the artist village of Ein Hod. There are four exhibition spaces. One of them is the permanent exhibit of works by Marselo Janco.

ISRAEL RAILWAY MUSEUM

1 Hativat Golani Avenue Tel. (04) 856-4293
BUS #17, 42, 93
The idea of building a railway in this country was suggested by Sir Moses Montefiore as early as 1839, after the construction of the first public railway in England. But it was to take 51 years before the first track was laid here. It ran from Jaffa to Jerusalem. It was

ISRAEL RAILWAYS PASSENGER LINES

קוי נוסעים
רכבת ישראל בע״מ

NAHARIYYA נהרייה
AKKO עכו
QIRYAT MOTZKIN קרית מוצקין
QIRYAT HAIM קרית חיים
HUTZOT HAMIFRATZ חוצות המפרץ
LEV HAMIFRATZ לב המפרץ
HAIFA MERKAZ חיפה מרכז
HAIFA BAT GALIM חיפה בת-גלים
HAIFA HOF HACARMEL חיפה חוף הכרמל
ATLIT עתלית
BINYAMINA בנימינה
QESARYYA - PARDES HANNA קיסריה – פרדס חנה
HADERA MAARAV חדרה מערב
NETANYA נתניה
BET YEHOSHUA בית יהושע
HERZLIYYA הרצלייה
T.A. UNIVERSITY ת״א אוניברסיטה
T.A. MERKAZ ת״א מרכז
T.A. HASHALOM ת״א השלום
T.A. HAHAGANA ת״א ההגנה
KEFAR HABAD כפר חב״ד
LOD לוד
BE'ER YA'AQOV באר יעקב
RISHON LEZIYYON - HARISHONIM ראשון לציון-הראשונים
REHOVOT רחובות
YAVNE יבנה
ASHDOD AD-HALOM אשדוד עד הלום
ASHQELON אשקלון

BLUE BERAQ כחול בני ברק
PETAH-TIQWA-SEGULLA פתח-תקוה סגולה
ROSH HA'AYIN Tzafon ראש העין צפון

BEN-GURION AIRPORT נמל התעופה בן-גוריון
RAMLA רמלה
QIRYAT GAT קרית גת

KEFAR SAVA - HOD HASHARON כפר סבא – הוד השרון

THE BIBLICAL ZOO גן החיות התנ״כי
BET SHEMESH בית שמש
JERUSALEM MALHA ירושלים מלחה

BE'ER SHEVA TZAFON/UNIVERSITY באר שבע צפון/אוניברסיטה
BE'ER SHEVA MERKAZ באר שבע מרכז

תחנת נוסעים
PASSENGER STATION
תחנת קשר - תחנה המאפשרת
מעבר נוסעים בין הקוים השונים.
INTERCHANGE STATION
קו בין עירוני נהרייה-חיפה תא-נתב״ג
NAHARIYYA - HAIFA - TEL AVIV
BEN-GURION AIRPORT INTER-CITY SERVICE
קו בין עירוני ת״א-ב״ש
TEL AVIV - BE'ER SHEVA
INTER-CITY SERVICE
פרברית חיפה-קריות
HAIFA - QIRYAT MOTZKIN
SUBURBAN SERVICE
פרברית בנימינה/נתניה/נתב״ג-ת״א-
רחובות/אשדוד/אשקלון
BINYAMINA/NETANYA TEL AVIV -
REHOVOT/ASHDOD/ASHQELON
SUBURBAN SERVICE
קו כפר סבא-ת״א-ירושלים/הראשונים
KEFAR SAVA-TEL AVIV-JERUSALEM/HARISHONIM
SERVICE

built in 1890 and was 87 kilometers long. The distance was covered by the first steam-powered train in the then astounding time of three hours and fifty minutes. The first train steamed into Jerusalem in 1892.

In 1904, the Haifa–Beit She'an section of the famous Hedjaz railway was built. The next year saw the construction of the Dera'a, junction for Damascus and Amman lines. In 1915, the Turkish military railway from Afula to Be'er Sheva and the Sinai desert line were built. In 1919, the British completed the Kantara–Haifa railway line. After taking on the Palestine Mandate, they opened the Petach Tikva line. Rail services also included a daily passenger train between Haifa and Cairo (via Gaza). Traffic on the Jezreel (Hedjaz railway) Valley line ran from Haifa to Dera'a.

The Israel Railway Museum, at the Haifa East station, hosts exhibits illustrating milestones in the development of rail transport in Israel since its early days in 1892, including rail links with neighboring countries. Today's railway system and its various functions are also on display.

The large exhibition building was originally built as the Haifa locomotive shed of the famous Hedjaz railway. The building was renovated in 2000. A special attraction of the museum is the site itself, a railway station in actual daily use. There is a collection of train memorabilia as well as restored locomotives and coaches. Inspect the railway car which served Ethiopian Emperor Haile Selasie during his visit to the Holy Land. The museum is open Sunday, Tuesday and Thursday from 8:30-12:00. Admission is free.

Kosher Dining

Kosher food establishments in Israel must display a valid Certificate of Kashrut. This certificate or *Te'udat Kashrut*, must be renewed every three months. Be sure to look for this certificate and check the date. No responsibility, therefore can be taken for the absolute accuracy of the information in this guide, and travelers are advised to obtain confirmation of kashrut claims. Although every effort has been made to ensure accuracy, changes will occur after this guide has gone to press. Particular attention must be drawn to the fact that kosher food establishments change hands often and suddenly, in some cases going over to a non-kosher owner. All of the restaurants listed below are closed on the Sabbath.

Ben Ezra Fish Castra Center Tel. (04) 859-0071
Broadway Bagel (Dairy) Horev Center Tel. (04) 834-5353
Cafe Bachoresh (Dairy) 36 Michael Street (Kfar Bialik) Tel. (04) 842-4604
Cookie Man (Dairy)
  Note: Not all stores in this chain are kosher.
  Simcha Golan Boulevard (Grand Canion) Tel. (04) 812-0025
El Gaucho 120, Yefei Nof Tel. (04) 837-0997 (Argentinian Steak House)
                              Note: Not all branches are closed on Shabbat.
Hamber 61, Herzl Street Tel. (04) 866-6739
Papagaio Haifa (Meat/South American) Hutzot Hamifratz (Krayot) Tel. (04) 842-2666
Rimonim (Dairy) Shulamit Hotel 15, Kiryat Sefer Tel. (04) 834-2811

Where to Stay

Beit Shalom 110, Hanassi Avenue Tel. (04) 837-7481
Carmel Forest Spa Resort (Ya'arot Ha'carmel) Tel (04) 830-7888
Carmel Youth Hostel 18, Rechov Tzvi Veltzhak Tel. (04) 653-944
Dan Carmel Hotel 85 Ha'nassi Avenue Tel. (04) 830-6306
Dan Panorama Hotel 107, Ha'nassi Avenue Tel. (04) 835-2222
Eden Hotel 8, Shmariahu Levin Street Tel. (04) 866-4816
Haifa Gardens Hotel Tel. (04) 838-9131
Haifa Tower (Migdal) 63, Herzl Street Tel. (04) 867-7111
Holiday Inn 111, Yefe Nof Street Tel. (04) 835-0835
Le Meridian Hotel 10, David Elazar Street Tel. (04) 850-8888
Marom Hotel 51, Ha'palmach Street Tel. (04) 825-4355
Mount Carmel Hotel 103, Derech Hayam Tel. (04) 838-1413
Nof Hotel 101, Ha'nassi Avenue Tel. (04) 835-4311
Shulamit Hotel 15, Kiryat Sefer Street Tel. (04) 834-2811
Zimmer Family Bed & Breakfast Tel. (04) 822-5245

Israeli Folk Dancing

- Mercaz Kehilati Naveh Yosef (Sunday) 7:30pm Meir Amsalem Tel. (054) 441-4120
- Sporton (Sunday) 8:30pm Dede Luski Tel. (050) 530-2233
- Beit Ha'histadrut (Monday) 7:30pm Meir Amsalem
- Mercaz Ohr Chadash (Monday) 8:00pm Oren Ashkenazi Tel. (04) 833-5969
- Beit Sefer Tel Chai (Tuesday) 8:00pm Oren Ashkenazi
- Beit Sefer Romeimah (Wednesday) 8:30pm Oren Ashkenazi
- Sporton (Wednesday) 8:30pm Dede Luski
- Beit Ha'lochem (Thursday) 7:30pm Meir Amsalem

Tour #12 - North of Haifa

Rosh Hanikra

The white cliffs of Rosh Hanikra consist of calcerous (soft chalk) rock running along the Israeli-Lebanese border. The base of the cliffs contain deep sea caves cut by wave erosion. These natural grottos were enlarged when a tunnel, originally designed as a railroad route between Haifa and Beirut, was dug through the cliffs by the British during World War II. This was part of the defense plan to stop the Nazi's "Desert Fox" (Field Marshal Rommel) from advancing into Egypt and then Palestine. That rail line was bricked-up in 1948, during the War of Independence. You can still see those original rails leading into the brick wall! The railroad bridge, which was built by over 100,000 Australian, New Zealand, South African and local laborers, was blown up by the Israeli army at the start of the War of Independence.

This tour starts at the northwest corner of Israel...

In more recent times, the nearby kibbutz blasted additional tunnels through the rock to improve access to the sea caves and topped the cliffs with an observation point and restaurant. There is an artistic 12-minute audio-visual presentation about this site. This theater is located inside the old railroad tunnel leading into Lebanon. Note the original railroad tracks on the floor of the theater.

The only way down to the caves is by cable car. The cable cars run everyday of the year, except during stormy weather. There is a Little Train which runs on rubber tires between Rosh Hanikra and Kibbutz Achziv. This line follows the original railroad route. Visitors can enjoy the option of stopping off at Achziv Beach for a swim, take a short walk, or return by the next Little Train.

The *Al Hag'vool* (On the Border) restaurant has spectacular views, seats 120 people, and is self-service or by set menu. But it is open seven days a week. There is no kashrut certification. For further information about Rosh Hanikra call (04) 985-7108. For information about the Achziv National Park Tel. (04) 982-3263.

WARNING: Do not attempt to go swimming in the grottos. You are right along the Lebanese border, and soldiers (from either side of the border) can mistake you for a terrorist!

STALAGMITE CAVES

There are huge stalagmite caves in the area. For the precise location, get advice at the Achziv Field School (located about one kilometer south of Rosh Hankira, along the Coastal Highway).

Drive south along the Coastal Highway (Route 4) to the junction of Route 899, turn left (east). Continue for about 2 kilometers and turn left.

Rosh Ha'nikra's striking white chalk formation resembles an elephant's foot.

Aerial view from top of Rosh Ha'nikra, looking south toward Nahariya.

Kibbutz Hanita

*At the junction of Routes 899 and 70, turn north onto Route 8990 towards **Kibbutz Hanita.***

KIBBUTZ HANITA MUSEUM

Kibbutz Hanita lies along the Lebanese border. The museum is located in an ancient stone house which was used as a stockade. Towers and stockades were quickly built following the riots of 1936-39. There is an 18-minute audio-visual program. There is a section in the museum devoted to archaeological finds in the egion including a mosaic floor from a Byzantine church of the 6th and 7th centuries. A scale model of that church was assembled as part of the exhibit.

Me'arat Keshet

Doubleback towards Route 899 and turn left or east. Go about five kilometers and turn left onto Route 8993 towards Adamit. Go another 2 to 3 kilometers until you see a hiking trail marker painted red.

NATURAL BRIDGE (Me'arat Keshet)

Take the red path for about 30 minutes until you reach the Keshet Cave (Me'arat Keshet) which was formed after the roof of this cave collapsed. The resulting rock formation is that of a strip of rock connecting two huge rock formations–a natural bridge.

Note: If you follow the black trail, you will end up down in Nahal Namer and a Stalactite cave.

Zomet Hashayara

*Double back on Route 899 and go west to Junction 70. At Route 70 turn left and travel south to Kabri and the **Zomet Hashayara.***

CONVOY JUNCTION (Zomet Hashayara)

This monument honors the 47 Israeli soldiers who were ambushed, trying to break through the blockade at Yehi'am during the War of Independence. Several burned armored vehicles remain as reminders of this tragic event. For further information Tel. (04) 985-6004.

Nahariya

*Double back to Route 70. At the junction take Route 89 west to **Nahariya.***

Nahariya was founded by German Jews in the mid-1930s. It is a popular summer resort, especially for newlyweds. There is a canal running down the middle of the town. Horse carts take visitors through the low-keyed, pleasant small coastal town.

MUSEUM OF GERMAN JEWRY & MUNICIPAL MUSEUM

The Liebermann House today houses the Municipal Building of Nahariya. The fifth floor houses an art exhibit. The sixth floor houses an interesting collection of shells, artifacts, and exhibits

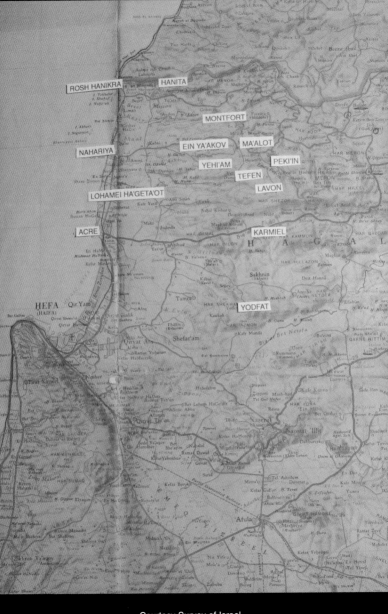

ROSH HANIKRA

HANITA

MONTFORT

NAHARIYA

EIN YA'AKOV

MA'ALOT

YEHI'AM

PEKI'IN

TEFEN

LAVON

LOHAMEI HA'GETA'OT

ACRE

KARMIEL

HEFA
(HAIFA)

YODFAT

Courtesy Survey of Israel.

from the area around Israel's entire north coast, with its fascinating history dating all the way back to the Stone Age.

The seventh floor contains an exhibit about the history of Nahariya and the Museum of German Jewry. There are displays of cultural memorabilia, photographs and writings of Sigmund Freud, Alfred Adler, Erich Fromm, Albert Einstein, and Robert Oppenheimer.

The museums are located in Ha'irya Square at 19 Hagaton Street near the north entrance to the city. Hours are Sunday-Friday 10:00-12:00, Sunday and Wednesday 4:00-6:00. Admission is free. For further information call (04) 982-1516.

Yehi'am

Return to Route 89. Continue east for about 2-3 kilometers. Bear right at the Ga'aton Junction. Take Route 8933 to Yehi'am.

YEHI'AM FORTRESS

This stronghold was used by French and German Crusaders, then by Arab rulers and finally during the War of Independence, by the new Jewish state.

Ein Ya'akov

When going back toward the Ga'aton Junction, make a detour. At Ga'aton turn right and go to Ein Ya'akov along Route 8833. Take the northern road to...

STALACTITE CAVE

Before you go down to Nachal Ga'aton, just past Ein Ya'akov, there is a stalactite cave on the left side of the road. Ask the locals in Ein Ya'akov.

Montfort

Return to Route 89 and continue east towards Ma'alot. Between kilometers 15 and 16 turn left at Mi'ilya, and go toward Hila. Go about 5 kilometers to a parking lot. Walk about 30 minutes along a trail marked in red to Montfort Fortress.

MONTFORT FORTRESS

This fortress was originally built during the Roman period. It was later rebuilt in the 12th century by the Crusaders to protect pilgrims coming to the Holy Land. A German order, The Order of St. Mary of the Teutons, occupied the fortress (later called Starkenberg or "strong mountain") until the Muslim-Mamelukes destroyed it in 1271. The ruins contain a vaulted hall, a church, cistern, and a wine-press.

Ma'alot-Tarshiha

Doubleback to Route 89, turn left and continue east to Ma'alot.

Ma'alot was organized in the 1950s with immigrants coming mostly from Morocco, Romania, and Iran. They moved into houses in the nearby Arab village of Tarshiha which had been abandoned by their Arab residents during the War of Independence. In 1963, Ma'alot and Tarshiha were unified into one municipality. The relations between the Jewish and Christian Arab population are based on co-existence and mutual respect. The breathtaking scenery and clear mountain air impart to the city a distinctive country flavor. It is for this reason that Ma'alot-Tarshiha has been called the "Switzerland of the Galilee."

This beautiful image was shattered on May 15, 1974. A group of visiting Jewish students from Safed were held hostage by Arab terrorists. The Israeli Army stormed the Ntiv Meir School which was where the students were being held. The terrorists opened fire on the students and tossed hand grenades, killing 21 and wounding 70. There are moving monuments in Ma'alot and in Safed to commemorate this tragedy.

Tefen

OPEN MUSEUM - TEFEN INDUSTRIAL PARK

The Open Museum contains an Open Air Park with over one hundred pieces of sculpture designed by Israeli artists. There are also enclosed galleries featuring paintings by Israeli and foreign artists. Look for the antique car collection. There is an audio-visual program about the Tefen Industrial Park as well. Hours are Sunday-Thursday, 9:00-5:00 and Saturday, 10:00-5:00. For further information Tel. (04) 987-2977.

Look for Route 854 which runs south of Ma'alot-Tarshiha. Take this road about 5 kilometers to the Tefen Industrial Park.

Lavon

LAVON SCULPTURE GARDEN

This is a continuation of the Tefen Industrial Park Sculpture Garden. There are works by Ilan Averbach, Shlomo Schwarzberg, Achiam, Amos Kenan, and Ofra Zimbalista. For further information call (04) 987-2022.

Continue driving south along Route 854 towards Karmiel for about 15-20 kilometers. You will come to the Lavon Sculpture Garden.

Karmiel

Karmiel hosts the annual Israeli Folk Dance Festival. Thousands of Israeli folk dancers from around the world gather in July and celebrate this event with several days of non-stop folk dancing. There are seminars, workshops, instruction, and professional performances by dance troupes from around Israel and from around the world. The town closes off all streets dur-

Continue south along Route 854 to Karmiel.

ing the evening hours due to the huge crowds. Special buses transport thousands of visitors from nearby staging areas.

Peki'in

Take Route 85 east of Karmiel and go to the Rama Junction. Turn left onto Route 864. Proceed north to Bukei'a (Peki'in Atica)

PEKI'IN ATICA

Peki'in is known as the spot where Rabbi Shimon bar Yohai and his son Eliezer, fled from a Roman decree prohibiting the study of the Torah. For 13 years the two scholars hid in a small cave in the hillside, sustained by a nearby spring and fertile carob tree. During this period, they composed the *Zohar,* the single most important text of the Kabbalah (Jewish mysticism). Near the cave is a synagogue which existed during the days of Rabbi Shimon bar Yohai. The synagogue is now a museum. Museum hours are Sunday-Thursday, 8:30-12:00 and 2:00-6:00, and Friday, 8:30-2:00.

Peki'in is the only city in Israel with an unbroken chain of Jewish inhabitation from the time of the Second Temple. Parts of an ancient Torah scroll in the synagogue are said to be 1,200 years old.

These ancient sites are located in Peki'in Atica, ancient Peki'in. Continue northward on this road to Peki'in Chadashah (New Peki'in). Note: In recent months there have been disturbances in Peki'in.

Yodfat

Doubleback along Route 864 to Route 85. Turn right on Route 85 and continue west to the junction of Route 784, just west of Karmiel. Take Route 784 south to Route 7955. Turn left and go to Yodfat.

Yodfat was the site of Flavius Josephus' main stronghold against the Roman legions. There are underground caverns prepared for the revolt against Rome, similar to the ones found in the Judean Hills.

Acre (Akko)

Doubleback to Route 784. At the Misgav Junction, turn left onto Route 805. Take Route 805 west to Route 85. Turn left onto Route 85 and continue west until you hit the coast and the City of Akko (Acre).

Acre was a leading Phoenician port in Biblical times. It was part of land allotted to the tribe of Asher. King Solomon gave the town to Hiram, king of Tyre, in return for his help in building the Temple in Jerusalem. Alexander the Great conquered Acre in 332 B.C.E. In 280 B.C.E., it was captured by the Ptolemies. t was later under Roman, Crusader, and Arab rule. Acre declined as a major port with the advent of steamships. Shipping activity was gradually transferred to the larger port at Haifa, across the bay.

MOSQUE OF AHMED JEZZER PASHA

Ahmed Jezzer Pasha was the Ottoman Turkish governor of Acre during the late 1700s. His contributions to Acre included building fountains, a covered market, Turkish baths, and the mosque complex that bears his name.

SUBTERRANEAN CRUSADER CITY

The Crusaders built their fortress atop of what was left of the ancient Roman city. In preparation of the defense of his city, Ahmed Jezzer Pasha ordered the walls heightened, and the Crusader rooms partially filled with sand and dirt, to better support the walls.

TURKISH BATH - MUNICIPAL MUSEUM

The Turkish (Al Basha) baths were built in the 1780s by Ahmed Jezzer Pasha. The first few small rooms hold collections of artifacts from Acre's 2,000-year-history. Next is the folklore exhibit which contains mannequins dressed in Ottoman garb. Next is the actual Turkish bath. It is designed based on the Roman plan.

There are three distinct rooms, each more ornate than the other. The first was the entry and dressing room, the next is the tepidarium, containing warm steam, and the last is the caldarium, containing hot steam. Hours are Sunday-Thursday 9:00-5:00, Friday 9:00-2:00. For further information Tel. (04) 991-0251.

THE CITADEL -
UNDERGROUND PRISONERS MUSEUM

This complex of buildings was used as a prison in Ottoman and British Mandate times, but is now a mental hospital. Part of the prison has been set aside in honor of the Jewish underground fighters imprisoned here by the British. One of the first Jewish prisoners was Zev Jabotinsky. With the help of the Irgun forces, 251 prisoners staged a mass escape in May, 1947. This episode was dramatically portrayed in Leon Uris' book and subsequent movie, *Exodus.*

Among the exhibits are the entrance to the escape tunnel, and displays of material showing the repression of Zionist activity during the British Mandate. Not all prisoners were fortunate enough to escape, however. Eight Irgun members were hanged here. The visitor can view the death chamber, called the Hanging Room, complete with noose.

Some of the earlier inmates in this prison included Bahaullah (1817-92), founder of the Baha'i faith.

The Underground Prisoners Museum is located in the Old City of Acre on Haganah Street and is open daily from 9:00-5:00, except on Saturday and Jewish holidays. For further information call (04) 991-8264.

TOWER OF THE FLIES

The city walls originally encompassed the entire harbor. All that remains of those walls is the ruined Tower of the Flies, the site of the original lighthouse. The original fortifications were toppled by a devastating earthquake in 1837.

KNIGHTS BANQUETING HALLS

This Crusader facility was designed in the Gothic style, complete with stone vaulting. The emblem of the French royal family appears on the columns. The facility also contains a Medieval hospital and tunnel. For further information call (04) 991-0251.

Kibbutz Lohamei Ha'geta'ot

*Drive north of Acre along Route 4, the Coastal Highway. Just north of Acre, look for a shrine dedicated to the Baha'i faith. Continue north to **Kibbutz Lohamei Ha'geta'ot**.*

The Ghetto Fighters House & Holocaust Museum is located in this kibbutz which was founded by concentration camp and Warsaw Ghetto survivors. The heroic Warsaw Ghetto uprising is examined extensively, as are Nazi atrocities in other European countries. The museum has displays, paintings, drawings, sculptures, poetry by Yitzchok Katzenelson, and prints by prisoners and survivors.

Yad La'Yeled is the most recent addition to the museum. It is dedicated to the lives and memories of the one and one half million Jewish children who perished in the Holocaust. Aimed at a young audience between the ages of 8 and 15, the main goal of Yad La'Yeled is to introduce young visitors in a sensitive and age-appropriate way, to the intimate world of the child who experienced the Holocaust. The twelve exhibits which make up the core of the museum reflect the chronological progress of the period, beginning before the war, continuing through the ghettos and extermination camps, and culminating in the release of the survivors. The visit concludes in the hall of the Eternal Flame, where films with testimonies of child survivors still living today can be viewed.

Yad La'Yeled was designed by architect Ram Karmi. The building combines two architectural structures; a central body, the Cone, three stories high, encircled by a descending ramp, and the Lane, connecting them. It does not lead to any apparent end, thus reflecting the uncertainty of life, then and now.

The main exhibition, along the Lane, reveals the life of the children during the Holocaust. The surface of the cone is lit by natural light becoming dimmer as the visitor proceeds downward. This light is a constant reminder of the world outside. It disappears gradually as the visitor reaches the innermost part of the building, the hall of the Eternal Flame.

At the end of the route, the children come to activity workshops in visual arts, drama, music, and writing. These activities help the children to work through the experience of the museum and facilitate their return to the outside world of sunlight, flowers and birds.

Admission to the museum is free. Hours are Sunday-Thursday, 9:00-4:00, Friday, 9:00-1:00, Saturday and holidays, 10:00-5:00. For further information please call (04) 995-8080.

Note: If you are taking public transportation, be sure to take bus #27 (the local or me'asef). The express bus will not stop at the museum but will continue on to Nahariya.

ROMAN AQUEDUCT
The Roman Aqueduct is located just outside the Ghetto Fighters Museum. It was rebuilt by Al-Jazar in 1780 to carry water from the Kabri Springs 15 kilometers to Acre.

*Just outside the Ghetto Fighters House & Holocaust Museum you will see a beautiful **Roman Aqueduct...***

Tour # 13 - The Galilee

Beit She'arim

Beit She'arim became the focus of Jewish national and spiritual life from the second through fourth centuries C.E. Jews fled there after the destruction of the Second Temple and during the Bar Kochba revolt. This was also the seat of the Sanhedrin. Rabbi Yehuda Ha'nasi studied and taught in Beit She'arim while codifying the Mishnah.
Rabbi Yehuda Ha'nasi spent most of his life at Beit She'arim until he fell ill with malaria and moved to Tzipori. A year later he passed away, and was buried in the Beit She'arim catacombs. Jews in all parts of Israel and throughout the Diaspora sought to be buried in these catacombs.
The necropolis consists of a vast labyrinth of vaults carved within the limestone hills. Stone coffins were entombed in the rock niches. Coffins were decorated with Hebrew, Greek, and Aramaic inscriptions, as well as with figures of beasts, birds, geometrical patterns, and flowers. The dead were brought from as far away as Eilat, Antioch, Byblos, Beirut, and Mesopotamia. For information about the Beit She'arim National Park Tel. (04) 983-1643.

*This driving tour starts east of Haifa. Take Route 75 past Kiryat Tiv'on and continue to **Beit She'arim**.*

Kibbutz Ha'zorea

WILFRED ISRAEL MUSEUM

Wilfred Israel collected archaeological stone carvings all his life. He died tragically on a mission to rescue German Jews during World War II. He donated his vast archaeological collection to Kibbutz Ha'zorea. The Wilfred Israel Museum opened in 1951. Hours are Sunday-Thursday 9:00-2:00, Friday 9:00-12:00 and Saturday 10:00-4:00. For further information Tel. (04) 989-9566.

*Continue driving east along Route 75. At the Hashomrim Junction, turn right onto Route 722. Take this road to the Hatishbi Junction. Turn left onto Route 66. Follow this road to **Kibbutz Ha'zorea**.*

Megiddo

MEGIDDO (Armageddon)

In the heap of ruins that make up the Tel Megiddo, archaeologists have unearthed the remains of twenty cities. At the visitors' center, a miniature model of the site gives definition to what the untrained eye could see as just a pile of stones. Among the magnificent finds at Megiddo were stables that sheltered King Solomon's and King Ahab's horses and chariots (built to accommodate five hundred horses), fortifications constructed by King Solomon, a Canaanite shrine, and a grain silo from King Jerob-

*Continue driving south along Route 66 until you reach **Tel Migiddo**.*

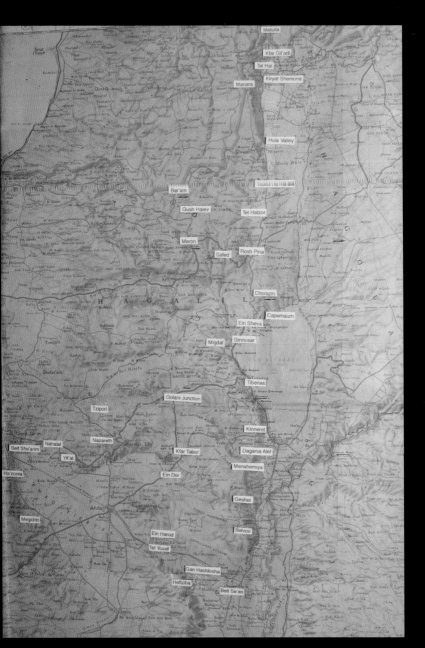

Metulla

Kfar Gil'adi

Tel Hai
Kiryat Shemona
Manara

Hula Valley

Tabgha Ha Tov

Ba'am
Gush Halev
Tel Hatzor

Meron
Rosh Pina
Safed

Chorazin

Capernaum
Ein Sheva
Ginnosar
Migdal

Tiberias

Golani Junction

Tzipori

Kinneret

Nahalal
Nazareth
Beit She'arim
Yif'at
Kfar Tabor
Dagania Alef

Ha'zorea
Menahemiya

Ein Dor

Afula
Gesher

Megiddo
Belvoir

Ein Harod
Tel Yosef

Gan Hashlosha
Heftziba
Beit She'an

Courtesy Survey of Israel.

oam's time. There is an underground water system built by King Ahab almost three thousand years ago to protect the city's water source in times of siege. Steps and lighting have been installed to facilitate exploration of the 390-foot tunnel, along with the almost 200-foot high shaft which once served as the system's well. For information about Tel Megiddo National Park Tel. (03) 776-2186.

Kibbutz Yif'at

KIBBUTZ YIF'AT
The Museum of Pioneer Settlement vividly depicts the early pioneers' settlement of the 1920s and 1930s. There is a Yif'at Fashion House, Orchid Nursery, and picnic area. Hours are Sunday-Friday 8:00-1:00, Saturday 10:00-3:00. For further information Tel. (04) 654-8974.

At the Megiddo Junction turn left onto Route 65 towards Afula. Continue past Afula towards Nazareth, along Route 60. At the Adashim Junction, turn left onto Route 73 and proceed to Kibbutz Yif'at.

Moshav Nahalal

HA'SLICK B'NAHALAL Meshek, 27
There is a secret hiding place of weapons which belonged to the Haganah. It was in a hand-dug tunnel beneath a house on the moshav. It was used from 1943-47 during the British Mandate. It was never discovered by the British. There is a small museum above the secret hideout which describes the family history and the establishment of the State of Israel. Visits are by prior arrangement only. Tel. (04) 641-5660.

Continue driving north along Route 73 until Moshav Nahalal.

Nazareth

Nazareth is the town where Jesus grew up. There are more than 40 churches, convents, monestaries, orphanages, and private parochial schools. The city houses Israel's largest Arab community outside Jerusalem. Half of the Arab population is Christian and the other half is Moslem. In more recent years, the percentage of Arabs in the city has tilted in favor of the Moslems. Just east of Nazareth is the modern Jewish town of Nazareth Ilit.

Continue north along Route 73 to the Nahalal Junction. Turn right onto Route 75 and continue to Nazareth.

BASILICA OF THE ANNUNCIATION
The Basilica of the Annunciation, located on Casa Nova Street, is the site where, according to Christian tradition, the angel Gabriel appeared before Mary informing her that she will bear a

son named Jesus. The church, built in 1966, was built over ea
lier structures dating from 1730 and 1877.

CHURCH OF SAINT JOSEPH
The Church of St. Joseph, 30 meters away, was built on the si
thought to be occupied by Joseph's carpentry workshop.

GREEK CATHOLIC SYNAGOGUE CHURCH
The Greek Catholic Synagogue Church, located on the mai
street in the bazaar, is believed to be the synagogue wher
Jesus attended on the Sabbath.

MARY'S WELL
Mary's Well has its source inside the Greek Orthodox Church (
the Annunciation.

OUR LADY OF FRIGHT CHAPEL
Our Lady of Fright Chapel, located opposite the Galilee Hote
is the spot where Mary watched while the people of Nazaret
attempted to throw Jesus over a cliff.

Tzipori

Proceed west of Nazareth along Route 79 and turn right at the sign for Tzipori.

Tzipori was a major center during the time of Rabbi Yehud
Ha'nasi. He moved the Sanhedrin to Tzipori, making it the car
ital of Israel. Many synagogues were established here; amon
them   were special ones for members of various craft guilds
Today, there are only synagogue ruins, a Roman theatre, an
water reservoir. For information about the Tzipori National Par
Tel. (04) 656-8272.

Kibbutz Ein Harod

Doubleback to Route 60 towards Afula. Turn (left) east onto Route 71 and proceed towards Beit She'an. On the right side of the road are the Gilboa Mountains. On the left side of the road are a series of kibbutzim and moshavim. Be sure to visit Ma'ayon Harod National Park with its natural spring which comes out of a cave at the foot of Mount Gilboa. For further information Tel. (04) 653-2211.

GILBOA REGION MUSEUM
The Mishkan L'Omanut, the Gilboa Region Museum is th
largest museum in the north of Israel. The museum's expansiv
halls are illuminated by natural lighting. The collection include
Jewish liturgical art, paintings, sculpture, graphic art, and phc
tography. Hours are Sunday-Thursday 9:00-4:30, Friday 9:0C
1:30 and Saturday 10:00-4:30. For further information Tel. ((04
648-5701.

BEIT STURMAN MUSEUM
The Beit Sturman Museum on Kibbutz Ein Harod is one the largest archaeological museums in the country. There are exhibits about the fauna and flora of the region. Hours are Sunday-Thursday 8:00-3:00 and Saturday 11:00-3:00. For further information Tel.(04) 653-1605

Kibbutz Tel Yosef

TRUMPELDOR HOUSE
This house honors the memory of Yosef Trumpeldor. He was the first Jewish officer in the Czar's army in Russia. In 1920, he was killed with seven other comrades fighting off Arab invaders at Tel Hai. In memory of these heroes, the town of Kiryat Shemona was named–for the "eight" (*shemona* in Hebrew) who died defending the Jewish settlers. Hours are daily 8:00-1:00. For further information Tel. (04) 653-4714.

*Stay on Route 71 and drive east about one kilometer to **Kibbutz Tel Yosef.***

Kibbutz Heftzi'ba

ANCIENT SYNAGOGUE REMAINS
The Beit Alpha synagogue was discovered by Jewish farmers in Kibbutz Heftzi'ba while digging an irrigation channel in 1928. The sixth century synagogue contains a magnificent floor mosaic. The primitive art figures depict Abraham sacrificing his son, Isaac, a zodiac wheel with the sun god Helios in the center, and a Torah Ark flanked by two menorahs. The mosaics are enclosed in a weatherproof structure (as opposed to similar ancient synagogue floor mosaics found at Hammat Tiberias, which is open and exposed to the elements).

*Continue driving east on Route 71. At the Shlita Junction turn right onto Route 669 and continue to **Kibbutz Heftzi'ba.***

Kibbutz Nir David

WALL AND TOWER MUSEUM
There is a replica of the original Wall and Tower which were built in the early 1900s as part of the security around the kibbutz. There is a similar wall and tower museum along the Lebanese border at Kibbutz Hanita (Tour #1, Stop 3). This historic period is depicted in documents, photographs, and personal interviews. Hours are Sunday-Thursday 8:30-3:30, Friday 8:30-1:00, Saturday 10:00-2:00. For further information Tel. (04) 658-6219.

*While on this road, Route 669, look for **Kibbutz Nir David.***

Gan Hashlosha

*Still on this road, Route 669, look for **Gan Hashlosha**. Be sure to visit the Gan Hashlosha National Park (Sakhne, in Arabic). It is named for three Haganah fighters who were killed when their car drove over a land mine. There are warm springs which are good for swimming (even in the winter). For further information Tel. (04) 658-6219.*

MUSEUM OF REGIONAL & MEDITERRANEAN ARCHAEOLOGY

This museum is located in Gan Hashlosha and contains antiquities from the Beit She'an Valley, ancient synagogues, Greece, Persia, and Egypt. This museum lies upon one of the ancient trades routes from the Mediterranean Basin to the lands of the East. There is a reconstruction of a small Bronze Age Canaanite temple. There is a display demonstrating ancient weaving techniques. There is also an exhibit about rare Etruscan artifacts. The exhibit combines smell, sound, and audio-visual elements. Hours are Sunday-Thursday 9:00-2:00, Saturday and holidays 10:00-2:00. For further information Tel. (04) 658-6352.

Beit She'an

*Continue going east on Route 669. At the junction of Route 6667, take that road directly into **Beit Se'an.***

Beit She'an lies three hundred feet below sea level. It was located on the great caravan route between Damascus and Egypt.

BEIT SHE'AN MUNICIPAL MUSEUM

The Beit She'an Municipal Museum is housed in a 450-year-old former mosque on Rechov Daled. It contains archaeological finds from the Beit She'an area including pottery, coins, mosaic tiled floors, inscriptions, etc. Hours can be arranged in advance. For further information Tel. (04) 658-6221.

TEL BEIT SHE'AN

On a hill called Tel Beit She'an, archaeologists have uncovered 18 layers of ancient civilizations. They unearthed five separate strata of Canaanite and Egyptian cultures, with altars and ruins of the Ramses II period, and early Israelite ceramics dating from the time King Saul's body was hung by the Philistines on the Beit She'an wall. For information about thr Beit She'an National Park Tel. (04) 658-7189.

ROMAN THEATRE

North of town is the best-preserved Roman theatre in Israel. The 8,000-seat amphitheatre, built in the third century C.E., has 15 tiers of white limestone in nearly perfect condition.

TEL ETZTABA

Outside of Beit She'an at Tel Etztaba, are the ruins of an ancient synagogue and a beautiful mosaic floor of a Byzantine church. Tel Etztaba is located just southeast of the junction of Route 71 and 7078.

Belvoir

BELVOIR (Kochav Hayarden)

This beautiful Crusader fortress was built mostly of basalt in the 12th century. Part of the fortress was constructed with stones from an ancient synagogue. There are spectacular views over the entire Jezreel Valley and, on a clear day, the Sea of Galilee. The fortress is 1800 feet above the Jordan River. It was strategically located, overlooking the medieval trade route from Egypt to Damascus. For further information Tel. (04) 658-1766.

From Beit She'an proceed north along Route 90. At the Kochav Hayarden Junction, turn left onto Route 717. Follow signs to **Belvoir.**

Kibbutz Gesher

GESHER BATTLE MUSEUM

This museum is located in an underground bomb shelter which was used as the center of the kibbutz's activities during the War of Independence. Hours are Sunday-Thursday 10:00-4:00, Friday 9:00-1:00, Saturday 10:00-4:00. For further information Tel. (04) 675-3336.

Doubleback to Route 90. Turn left and proceed north to **Kibbutz Gesher.**

Menahemiya

MEDICINE & PIONEERS MUSEUM

The Medicine and Pioneers Museum is located in Menahemiya. There are three sections in the museum: the beginning of the settlement, the first medical center, and the creation of the hydro-electric system. Hours are Sunday-Thursday 8:30-3:30, Friday 8:30-1:00, Saturday 10:00-2:00. For further information Tel. (04) 675-1019.

Continue north along Route 90 to the Ashdot Ya'akov (Ichud) Junction. Turn left toward **Menahemiya.**

Kibbutz Ashdot Ya'akov Me'uhad

BEIT URI & RAMI NEHUSHTAN MUSEUM

The museum is named in honor of the two founders of the kibbutz. There are displays of paintings, sculpture, carpets, and embroideries. Hours are Monday-Thursday 8:00pm-9:30pm, Friday 10:00am-1:00pm. For further information Tel. (04) 675-7737.

Doubleback to Route 90, turn left and go to **Kibbutz Ashdot Ya'akov Me'uhad.**

Kibbutz Dagania Alef

*Return to Route 90, turn left and continue north to **Kibbutz Dagania Alef.***

FIRST KIBBUTZ IN ISRAEL

Dagania Aleph was founded in 1909 and was the first kibbutz in Israel. The Gordon House Museum has various original agricultural implements and tools on display. There is also an exhibit about the region's fauna and flora. Hours are Sunday-Thursday 9:00-3:00, Friday 10:00-1:00, Holidays 9:00-3:00. For further information Tel. (04) 675-0040.

Moshav Kinneret

*Just to the northwest of Kibbutz Dagania Aleph is **Moshav Kinneret.***

KINNERET MUSEUM

The Kinneret Museum is located in Moshav Kinneret. It was founded in 1908. The museum is located in the first hospital of the settlement. There are photographs, documents, and other artifacts about the founding of the moshav. Hours are Sunday-Thursday 9:00-2:00. For further information Tel. (04) 675-1172.

Kfar Tabor

*At the Kinneret Junction, Route 90 & 767, turn left onto Route 767 and go west toward **Kfar Tabor.***

KFAR TABOR SETTLERS MUSEUM

The Settlers Museum authenticates the settlers' way of life via photographs, documents, and an audio-visual program. There is also a Farmyard Museum in a reconstructed original farmer's home. There are craftsmen's workshops, livestock, and an art gallery. The museums are open daily from 8:30-2:00. For further information Tel. (04) 676-5844.

Mount Tabor

*Just west of Kfar Tabor is **Mount Tabor.** There is a road up the mountain.*

MOUNT TABOR

Mount Tabor is a prominent rounded cone 1,843 feet above sea level. In olden days, access to the top was by thousands of steps cut into the steep slope. There is now a narrow road mounting in a series of sharp hairpin bends.

Mount Tabor was of strategic and religious importance in Biblical times. This was the place where Deborah and Barak rallied the northern tribes of Israel for the battle against the Canaanites. In the Jewish revolt of 66 C.E., Josephus held the top of Mount Tabor as a stronghold before he defected to the Romans. He constructed a stone defense wall that can still be seen around the summit.

At the summit of Mount Tabor stands the Basilica of the Trans figuration. According to Christian tradition, this spot marks where Jesus was transfigured in the presence of three of his disciples. There are also remains of the the Crusader-Saracen castle.

Kibbutz Ein Dor

ARCHAEOLOGICAL MUSEUM

The Archaeological Museum in Kibbutz Ein Dor enables the visitor to get a "hands-on" feel for the way of life as it was in ancient times. One can see how olives came off the grove and were pressed and see how wheat was harvested and baked into loaves of bread. Hours are Sunday-Thursday 8:00-3:00, Friday 8:00-2:00, Saturday & holidays 12:00-2:00. For further information Tel. (04) 677-0333.

*Descend Mount Tabor and continue past the Gazit Junction on Route 7276 to **Kibbutz Ein Dor.***

Golani Junction

GOLANI JUNCTION

The Museum of Golani Division Heroism is located at the Golani Junction on a rocky hill overlooking a spectacular pine forest. The monument and museum honor those members of the noted Golani Brigade of the Israeli Defense Forces who fell in combat during the War of Independence and Israel's other wars. During the Yom Kippur War, 126 members of this elite unit lost their lives in the bloody battles on the Golan Heights. Hours are Sunday-Thursday 9:00-4:00, Friday 9:00-1:00, Saturday 9:00-5:00. For further information Tel. (04) 676-7215.

*Take Route 65 about ten kilometers north to the **Golani Junction.***

Tiberias

In the year 18 C.E., Herod Antipas, son of Herod the Great, built a new city in the Hellenistic style over the ruins of Biblical Rakkat, north of the town of Hammat, some 200 meters below sea level. He named it Tiberias in honor of the Emperor Tiberias in Rome.

At first Jews refused to live there, but after the destruction of Jerusalem it became a center of Jewish cultural and spiritual activity. Here the Sanhedrin (Great Jewish Court) met, renowned rabbis, sages and scholars lived, the Jerusalem Talmud and Mishnah (Jewish codes of behavior in daily matters) were completed, and the Massoretic text vocalized. Tiberias won recognition as one of the country's four holy cities.

The others being Jerusalem, Hebron, and Safed.

Under the oppressive Byzantine rule and later under Arab dominion, the Jewish population of Tiberias dwindled, and in the Middle Ages wars and earthquakes led to the utter destruction of the town. It lay waste until Sultan Suleiman the Magnificent gave the city to Don Joseph Nassi and his mother-in-law, Donna Gracia, in the 16th century. They restored the Jewish community, introduced industry, and Tiberias flourished for a hundred years, when it was again devastated. It revived in the 18th century under the rule of bedouin Sheikh el Omar, when it was resettled by a group of Chassidic Jews and since then it has, with some interruptions, thrived and grown into a prosperous town. Today, Tiberias is Israel's most popular northern holiday resort city.

SEA OF GALILEE (Yam Kinneret)

The Sea of Galilee is Israel's largest freshwater lake and is fed by underground springs, but mostly by the Jordan River. Its shape resembles a harp or *kinnor*, hence the name, Kinneret. It lies approximately 200 meters below sea level, making it the lowest freshwater lake on earth and second lowest point in the world after the Dead Sea. It is a bit over 32 miles in circumference and acts as the major source of fresh water for the whole of Israel, supplying fully one third of her annual needs.

OLD CITY WALLS

Tiberias owes much of her picturesque appearance to the remains of the ancient city walls, ramparts, and round towers built of black basalt stone. These walls date from Crusader and later periods, although some were built over earlier walls.

The walls standing today were built during the rule of bedouin Sheikh Dahar el Omar in the mid-1700s. El Omar's son, Chulabi, as

well as the Egyptian Mameluke ruler, Ibrahim Pasha, added to the construction. The earthquake of 1837 badly damaged their work.

The city walls describe the small size of the medieval city, which covered only 37 acres. Small remnants of the walls can be seen at the stop light at Hayarden and Habanim Streets, near the Lev Hagalil Building. The major section of the southern wall winds from the edge of the Sea of Galilee near the Moriah Plaza and Galei Kinneret Hotels. The section has been cleared and rest-ored and a walkway was built along its length. The northwest section of the wall, traditionally called the Crusader Castle or Citadel, is located at Donna Gracia Street. The Donna Gracia complex today houses artists' studios and restaurants.

MUNICIPAL ARCHAEOLOGICAL PARK

During construction of the Jordan River Hotel, workers stumbled on archaeological remains and extensive excavations soon followed. Among the discoveries were the remains of a Crusader church. A long section of the northern wall of Arab or Byzantine Tiberias was also uncovered. Most importantly, a synagogue with one of the most impressive mosaic floors found to date was unearthed. The floor is presently on display at the Israel Museum in Jerusalem.

TOMB OF MAIMONIDES (Rambam)

Rabbi Moses ben Maimon, the Rambam (also known as Maimonides), was born in Cordoba, Spain in 1135. At the age of thirteen, his family was driven out of Spain by the Almohades, fanatical Berber tribesmen from North Africa. Maimonides studied medicine in Cairo, Egypt and published many brilliant medical works. He became the noted theologian, philosopher, and physician. His monumental works, the *Mishna*

Torah and his *Guide to the Perplexed*, were all composed in North Africa. Maimonides, together with his family, spent five months in the Holy Land in 1165. On his death in 1204, he was buried in Tiberias. Maimonides' tomb is a major pilgrimage site. It is located in a small park near the central bus station.

TOMB OF RABBI AKIVA

One of Judaism's fabled heroes, Rabbi Akiva, had a long and eventful life. He was born to a poor Judean family in 50 C.E. When he was a small boy the illiterate Akiva tended the flocks of a wealthy Jerusalemite. His pretty daughter, Rachel, fell in love with the young shepherd and encouraged him to study. Akiva married Rachel only to leave her for many years. During this period he studied and became one of Israel's outstanding scholars and formulators of Jewish thought and ethics.

A great nationalist, Rabbi Akiva identified himself with the revolt of Bar Kochva, and in 135 C.E. the Romans made an example of him and skinned him alive. Special prayers are devoted to Rabbi Akiva and the Ten Martyrs of Judaism on Yom Kippur and Tish'a Ba'Av. His white-domed cave tomb can be seen on the hillside above Tiberias.

LAKESIDE PROMENADE - TAYELET

Seventy-five years ago the buildings of Old Tiberias stood directly on the waters' edge and the lakeshore area was densely populated. This changed dramatically in 1934 when a huge cloudburst caused water, mud, and boulders to rain down on the city. Many people drowned and hundreds more were left injured and homeless.

Following the disaster, the buildings closest to the shore were emptied and the streets were built running perpendicular to the lake to provide better drainage. Along the length of the beach, the waters were pushed back and the *tayelet* or lakeside promenade was built. Today, this is the action spot of Tiberias with its many restaurants, marina, nightclubs, and cafes.

TIBERIAS HOT SPRINGS

Tiberias was already famous in antiquity for its healing springs. The 60 degrees (centigrade) temperature is constant and the springs rise from a pool found some 6,500 feet below ground level.

The ancient Israelites built baths at the site of *Hammei T'verya* and a Roman coin was cast in 100 C.E. depicting the springs with the effigy of Hygeia, goddess of health. The remains of the large and luxurious baths, built two thousand years ago by King Herod, can still be seen. Even more elaborate structures were constructed in medieval times for use by Arab princes vacationing from abroad.

Today, a modern spa has been built on this site which includes a series of pools and private baths, Piloma, mud treatment rooms, a physiotherapy department, laboratories, and clinics.

TOMB OF RABBI BA'AL HA'NESS

Looking down on the Tiberias Hot Springs is the traditional tomb of the second century C.E. Rabbi Ba'al Ha'ness. A student of Rabbi Akiva, his wisdom and knowledge, original wit, and particularly his skill as a teacher, earned him the nickname of *Meir*–the illuminator. Legends tell how he miraculously rescued his sister-in-law from the Romans, subsequently becoming known as the "Miracle Worker" or *Ba'al Ha'ness*. Two synagogues, one Sephardi built in 1873, and the other Ashkenazi built 25 years later, marks the rabbi's tomb. Believers come to his tomb to pray for help in overcoming personal problems. During the Feast of the Second Passover (Pesach Shaynee) of "Mimuna," celebrated by Moroccan Jews, a visit to his tomb is mandatory.

HAMMAT NATIONAL PARK
Ancient Hammat, adjacent to the Tiberias Hot Springs, is named in the Bible as the fortified city given to the tribe of Naftali after the Israelites conquered Canaan. Hammat is noted for the number of ancient synagogues discovered there dating from the third through eighth centuries.

There is a magnificent mosaic floor design in the Hammat National Park. The mosaic is composed of three segments. The bottom segment portrays two lions facing nine Greek inscriptions, which honor the founders of the synagogue. The middle segment portrays the wheel of the zodiac divided into twelve illustrations. The center of the zodiac wheel portrays the pagan sun god, *Helios*.

The upper segment of the mosaic portrays the Holy Ark, flanked by two elaborate menorahs, with two shofars, lulavs, and etrogs. The artistic style of this mosaic floor greatly contrasts that of the synagogue mosaic found at Beit Alpha. The Beit Alpha mosaic is more "primitive" in style.

The people and animals almost appear as cartoon characters. The style of the mosaics in the Hammat ancient synagogue are much more realistic in design–the characters look like "real" people and "real" animals.

The major concern in both of these ancient synagogues is why are pagan symbols incorporated within the mosaic floor designs? There are several theories which seem to resolve this problem. According to some these symbols were accepted in this "Hellenistic" society. Some say that the Greek benefactor presented this synagogue to the community and "threw in" his pagan artisans. So the Jewish community had to accept the building as is–including its pagan artwork. Others simply say that the designers had no religious (pagan) significance at this time in history. They were simply artistic designs. For further information Tel. (04) 672-5287.

Migdal

Migdal was a flourishing metropolis during the Second Temple period. A white-domed shrine marks where the city once stood. Migdal is the birthplace of Mary Magdalene.

*Drive north of Tiberias along Route 90 to the Migdal Junction. Turn left onto Route 807 and proceed to **Migdal**.*

Kibbutz Ginnosar

YIGAL ALLON MUSEUM

A remarkable discovery was made at Kibbutz Ginnosar in 1986. Due to the severe drought that year and the drastic drop in sea level of the Sea of Galilee, a 27-foot wooden fishing boat, about two thousand years old, was uncovered. It was then immersed in a special preserving liquid and put on display in the Yigal Allon Museum. Museum hours are Sunday-Thursday 8:00-5:00, Friday 8:00-1:00, Saturday 8:00-5:00. For further information Tel. (04) 672-1495.

*Return to Route 90 and turn left. Continue north to **Kibbutz Ginnosar**.*

Ein Sheva

EIN SHEVA (Tabgha-Heptapegon)

This site is noteworthy to Christians. It was at this location where Jesus performed the miracle of the loaves and fishes. He fed 5,000 pilgrims with five loaves of bread and two fishes. There is a magnificent Byzantine floor mosaic inside the new Church of the Multiplication depicting this miracle. The mosaic also features exquisite images of birds, plants, and houses. Just east of the Church of the Multiplication is the Heptapegon, also called the Church of the Primacy of St. Peter. This black basalt church was built on the foundations of earlier churches. It was here, on the shores of the Sea of Galilee, that Jesus is believed to have appeared to his disciples after his crucifixion and resurrection. For information about the Kursi National Park Tel. (04) 673-1983.

*Continue driving north along Route 90 to **Ein Sheva**, turn right.*

Capernaum

CAPERNAUM (Kfar Nachum)

When Hadrian expelled the Jews from Jerusalem and the surrounding region after the Bar Kochba revolt in 135 C.E., many Jews resettled in the Galilee. Toward the end of the second century, a new attitude emanated from Rome. Most of the Had-

*At the Kfar Nachum Junction, (Routes 90 and 87) bear right onto Route 87. Proceed to **Capernaum**.*

rianic laws restricting Jews were repealed, and during the late second and third centuries, Jews appear to have flourished and prospered in dozens of small rural Galilean and Golan towns. Being free to do so, they built synagogues.

The most beautiful and best reconstructed of the Galilean synagogues is the one at Capernaum. The common building stone in this part of the Galilee is a hard and durable rough black basalt; all private buildings in Capernaum were constructed with this stone.

The synagogue stands as a kind of town center. It was built with imported shimmering Jerusalem white limestone, highly polished to resemble marble. It must have been an imposing structure—a white jewel in a black setting. The foundation stones, which are still visible at points, were made from the local black basalt.

Other Galilean communities, such as Chorazin, settled for black basalt for their synagogue construction material as well as for their homes. The Capernaum Jewish community was apparently wealthy enough to import the white limestone for their synagogue.

The interior of the three-story synagogue had two rows of stone benches on the first level, probably for the elders, who governed the synagogue. These benches lined the two long walls. The other congregants sat on mats in the center of the floor. Some say that the women were seated in the upstairs gallery.

The Capernaum synagogue was richly decorated both inside and out, but especially on its exterior. The façades, doorways, windows, columns, and capitals were all heavily ornamented with running designs, rosettes, seashells, vines, leaves, garlands, bunches of grapes, scrolls, and wreaths. There were also many Jewish symbols such as a menorah, shofar, and lulav, as well as five- and six-pointed stars (representing the Seal of Solomon and the Star of David).

According to the New Testament, when Jesus walked on water he walked on the Sea of Galilee. He preached to the fishermen from among whom he collected his first followers. In Capernaum, he healed Simon's mother-in-law and the Roman Centurion's servant. This is also the birthplace of Peter. The ruins of a fifth century octagonal church cover the site, believed to be that of Peter's house. Today, a modern church arches over the ruins. The Capernaum synagogue was partly restored by the Franciscans in 1894. For further information Tel. (04) 672 1059.

Return to Route 90 and turn right to...

Detail of the ancient synagogue at Capernaum.

MOUNT OF BEATITUDES

This was the site where Jesus gave his "Sermon on the Mount." A church, built by Italian dictator Mussolini, now stands on the Mount. Its octogonal shape recalls Jesus' eight beatitudes.

Chorazin

Go back to Route 90 and continue north to the Chorazin Junction, turn right.

CHORAZIN (Korazin)

The first thing you will notice in this region is the black basalt rock formations which were caused by volcanic activity many thousands of years ago. The remains of a third or fourth century synagogue made entirely out of basalt rock is located at Chorazin. One of the stones from this ancient synagogue contains a carving of a pagan image, *Medusa*. For further information Tel. (04) 693-4982.

Rosh Pina

Return to Route 90 and proceed north to Rosh Pina.

Rosh Pina was the first Jewish settlement in the Galil. It was founded in 1882 with the assistance of Baron Edward de Rothschild. The original cobblestone streets and some of the original buildings have been restored.

Safed (Z'fat)

At Rosh Pina turn onto Route 89, go west to Safed.

Safed is one of the four Holy Cities, along with Jerusalem Hebron, and Tiberias. Sages say each city represents an element: Jerusalem represents fire, because of the burnt offerings in the Holy Temple; Hebron represents earth, which Abraham purchased for a Jewish burial site; Tiberias represents water because of the Sea of Galilee; and Safed, a walled city perched in the cool upper Galilee hills, represents air.

Safed was founded during the Second Temple period. It was at various times the capital of Galilee. It was a fortified town during the revolt against the Romans. After the destruction of the Second Temple, Safed became a seat of the *Cohanim* (priests) During Mishnaic and Talmudic times, many rabbis and sages (Tana'in and Amora'im) settled here. New moons *(Rashe Chadoshim)* were announced here, marking the beginning of the lunar month. After several centuries without a Jewish presence, while Crusaders and Arabs captured and recaptured Safed, Jews began to return around the beginning of the 13th century.

Following the expulsion from Spain in 1492, many Spanish Jews settled in Safed. One of the ancient synagogues contains a Torah which was brought from Spain during the Inquisition period. After the Turkish conquest, the Sephardic community grew. In the 16th century, Safed became a commercial, religious, and Kabbalah (Jewish mysticism) center. Many rabbis and sages settled in or near Safed during this period, including Rabbi Joseph Caro, author of the *Shulchan Aruch*, Rabbi Yitzchok Luria (the Ari) and others. In 1578, the first printing press in all of the Near East was established by the brothers Ashkenazi. The first Hebrew book was a commentary on the Book of Esther.

Internal war between rival rulers in the 17th century undermined the economic and spiritual life of Safed. This decline continued until the end of the 18th century. At that time, a new wave of settlers arrived. The Baal Shem Tov chassidim arrived in 1778 and the students of the Hagra arrived in 1810. Subsequently, plagues, earthquakes, and wars, reduced the Jewish population. In 1837, the entire city was leveled by a powerful earthquake. At the end of the 19th century, the Jewish presence began to increase, when Jewish settlements (moshavim) were reestablished in Galilee.

During World War I, famine and cholera devested the Jewish Quarter and the town became predominantly Arab. Jews and Arabs coexisted amicably until 1929, when Safed's Arabs participated in bloody anti-Jewish riots sparked by Hajj Amin al-Husseni. In the 1948 War of Independence, Safed was fiercely contested because of its strategic position at the heart of northern Galilee. All 12,000 Arab residents fled as the Israeli forces took over the city in May.

GAN HA'METZUDA

There are remains of a 12th century Crusader fortress that once controlled the main route to Damascus. Be sure to see the Davidka Monument at the summit of the park. The Davidka memorializes a makeshift weapon used in the War of Independence. All it basically did was make a frightening noise–enough to scare away an enemy.

MUSEUM OF PRINTING

Safed was the site of the first Hebrew printing press in Israel. The first book was published in 1577. On display is a copy of the first book printed in Hebrew, printed in 1475 at Reggio de Calabria in Sicily (when it was still under Spanish rule–until 1492).

View a copy of the first newspaper printed in Israel (1863); a copy of the Palestine Post of May 6, 1948, announcing the birth of the State of Israel; a centuries-old Kabbalah printed in Safed; and examples of modern Israeli graphics.

The Museum of Printing is located at Arieh Merzer & Arieh Alwail Streets. Hours are Sunday-Thursday 10:00-12:00 and 4:00-6:00, Friday 10:00-12:00. Admission is free. For further information Tel. (04) 692-0947.

ISRAEL BIBLE MUSEUM

The Israel Bible Museum is located just north of Gan Ha'metzuda. It was previously the home of the Turkish governor of Safed. It displays the work of Phillip Ratner, a modern American artist whose sculptures, lithographs, graphics, and paintings vividly display Biblical scenes and personalities. Hours are Sunday-Saturday (except Friday) 10:00-2:00 For further information Tel. (04) 697-3472.

BEIT HA'ME'IRI MUSEUM

The famous journalist and writer Ihzekei Ha'me'iri (1898-1934) amassed a large collection of paintings, photographs, documents and Judaica during his life. His house is now a museum which depicts the history

Safed is an antique collector's paradise.

Entrance to the Ha'ari Synagogue in Safed. Note the engraved
Stars of David around the windows on the second floor.

MUSEUM OF HUNGARIAN SPEAKING JEWRY

The museum depicts the magnificent past of the Jewish communities of Hungary, Transylvania, Slovakia, Carpathian Russia, Bachka, Banat, and Burgenland. The museum is located on Kikar Ha'atzma'ut. Hours are Sunday-Thursday 9:00-1:00, Friday 9:00-1:00. For further information Tel. (04) 692-5881.

SYNAGOGUE QUARTER

Because Safed lies to the north of Jerusalem, the Arks in these synagogues must face that Holy City and are therefore facing south. When visiting any ancient or contemporary synagogue in Israel please dress modestly and please leave a donation in the charity box or with the caretaker.

CARO SYNAGOGUE

This synagogue, located on Beit Yosef Street, is named in honor of Yosef Caro, the chief rabbi of Safed and author of the *Shulchan Aruch*, which was composed in the 16th century.

Down the hill from the Caro Synagogue, off Abuhav Street in the Spanish Quarter, stand the Abuhav and Alsheih Synagogues.

HA'ARI SYNAGOGUE

Rabbi Isaac Luria, nicknamed the *Ari* (lion), was the great Kabbalist who introduced the *Kabbalat Shabbat*, Friday evening prayer service. His student, Alkabetz, wrote the liturgical hymn, *Le'cha Dodi* in 1580. The four pillars in the center of the synagogue represent the four Holy Cities; Jerusalem, Hebron, Tiberias, and Safed. They also represent the four elements of the world–air, fire, water, and earth. The small hole in the Bimah is from a bullet–a reminder of the fierce fighting which took place in the city during the War of Independence in May, 1948.

BENNEA SYNAGOGUE

This synagogue is dedicated to Rabbi Yossi Bennea or Ha'banai (the builder). He is buried in a small cell next to the hall of prayers. A Torah from the Holy Ark is carried in procession to Meron on Lag Ba'Omer.

CHERNOBYL SYNAGOGUE

The Chernoble Synagogue was founded by Jews from that Ukrainian city. They claim that the nuclear reactor was built over a Jewish cemetery and above their grand rabbi's tomb. The reactor exploded and "melted-down" on the anniversary of the death (yartzheit) of the grand rabbi of Chernobyl.

HOLY CEMETERIES OF SAFED

The oldest of the cemeteries, located on the western outskirts of the Old City, contains the 17th century graves of the most famous Kabbalists. Legend has it that under this hill lies the Biblical prophet Hoshei'ah (in a domed edifice). Hannah and her seven sons, whose martyrdom at the hands of the Greeks is recorded in the Book of Maccabees, are buried here. The exact location of these graves in unknown, but when you suddenly feel fatigued while climbing on this steep hill, you have probably just crossed over the graves.

This cemetery also contains the remains of the children of Safed who were killed in 1974 on a trip to Ma'alot. PLO terrorists took over the school in which these children were sleeping. A large memorial service is held for them each year in May.

SHEM VE'EVER CAVE

This is believed to be the place where Noah's son and great grandson, Shem and Ever, studied and were later buried. The cave is near the top of the bridge, off Ha'Palmach Street.

ETHIOPIAN FOLK ART CENTER
The Ethiopian Folk Art Center, located in the Old City, showcases the talents of Safed's newest immigrants.

FIRST DAIRY IN ISRAEL
The Ha'me'iri Dairy is located between the Old City of Safed and the view of the ancient cemetery and the Meron Mountains. The dairy has existed for over 160 years. There is a guided tour of the facilities which includes a sound and light show of the dairy and cheese production. There is also cheese tasting and dairy meals are available.
The Ha'me'iri Dairy is located at 62nd 12th Street in the Old City of Safed. For further information Tel. (04) 692-1431.

Meron

Mount Meron, at 4,205 feet above sea level, is the highest summit in the Galilee. On the way up is the tomb of Rabbi Shimon bar Yohai. He was ultimately forced to hide in a cave in Peki'in for 13 years. During this period he wrote the *Zohar.* On Lag Ba'Omer (33rd day of the *se'fira,* which starts on the second day of Passover), thousands of people assemble at this tomb to celebrate *Hilula de Rashbi*-the Celebration of Rabbi Shimon bar Yahai.

*Continue traveling west on Route 89 to **Meron.***

The occasion is marked by singing, dancing, lighting bonfires, and feasting. Three-year-old boys are brought here for their first haircuts. This celebration was instituted by the Kabbalists of Safed in the 16th century to commemorate the passing of this prominent Jewish scholar. Among the many great Jewish sages buried in the surrounding hills are Hillel and Shamai. Further up Mount Meron are the remains of one of the oldest Galilean synagogues, dating from the end of the Second Temple period. For further information Tel. (04) 776-2186.

Gush Halav

GUSH HALAV (Jish)
The small village of Gush Halav was an important town during the Great Revolt against the Romans. There are ruins of a synagogue dating from the third to fourth century. The tombs of the sages Shma'ya and Avtalion are located near the entrance to the village.

*Continue driving north on Route 89 to **Gush Halav.***

*One of the most beautiful ancient synagogues in Israel is
located right next to the Lebanese border at Bar'am.*

Bar'am

ANCIENT SYNAGOGUE AT BAR'AM

There are two ancient synagogues at Bar'am. The first was known as Ovadiah's Synagogue, since it was located near the grave of Ovadiah the Prophet. A lintel with the inscription from the synagogue is on display in the Louvre Museum in Paris. The second synagogue remains date from the third century C.E. There are three doorways facing south, toward Jerusalem. The central portal is arched and is decorated with vines and clusters of grapes carved into the stone.

*Route 89 turns west. When you reach Route 899, turn right and continue to **Bar'am**.*

There are several questions about why some synagogues, such as this one in Bar'am seems to be backwards. If all synagogues in Israel must face Jerusalem, then this one seems to be designed the wrong way. The front entrance is facing south. Normally, the Holy Ark would be opposite the front entrance of the synagogue. In this case, the Holy Ark would be facing north! Some of the floor mosaics give an answer to this perplexing question. The Holy Arks in the early days (first through third centuries) were built on wheels. They were kept in a storage room, usually in the back of the synagogue. When it was time to read from the Torah, the Holy Ark would be rolled out and placed along the main entrance of the synagogue, in this case along the southern wall. Everyone in the congregation would rise and turn towards the Holy Ark, now facing south–toward Jerusalem. This synagogue was influential in the change of styles in American synagogue architecture. Before 1897, the first American Jewish architect, Arnold Brunner, designed his synagogues such as Temple Beth El and Shaare Tefila (in New York City) and Mishkan Israel (in New Haven, Connecticut) in the Moorish and Romanesque Revival styles. Following the discovery of the ancient synagogue at Bar'am, Arnold Brunner changed his synagogue designs to the Classical Revival style. He built his Spanish & Portuguese Synagogue (Congregation Shearith Israel in New York City, built in 1897) and his Harry S. Frank Memorial Synagogue, located on the grounds of the Albert Einstein Medical Center (in Philadelphia, built in 1901) in the Classical Revival styles. For further information Tel. (04) 698-9301.

BAR-DAVID MUSEUM (Kibbutz Bar'am)

The Bar-David Museum of Jewish Art and Judaica is located on Kibbutz Bar'am, along the Lebanese border. The museum is housed in a three-story building. One hall is devoted to the permanent collection; one hall is devoted to changing exhibits of paintings, sculpture, photography, etc; and one room is devoted to objects from the region. Hours are Sunday-Thursday 10:00-4:00, Friday 10:00-2:00, Saturday 10:00-4:00. For further information Tel.(04) 698-7505.

TOMB OF QUEEN ESTHER

Along Route 899, near the ancient synagogue at Bar'am, near the 37km road marker, is a narrow path that leads to the grave of Queen Esther. Jews used to assemble on Shushan Purim and read the *Megilla*, the Book of Esther.

Tel Hatzor

Doubleback to Rosh Pina. At Route 90 turn left and drive north about 7 kilometers to Tel Hatzor.

HATZOR ARCHAEOLOGICAL MUSEUM

Hatzor is mentioned in the book of Joshua, which recounts how Joshua slew the King of Hatzor and burnt this leading Canaanite city. Hatzor is in the territory of the tribe of Naftali. King Solomon later converted it into a fortified city.

The archaeological Tel at Hatzor consists of two parts: the acropolis and the lower city. The archaeologists dug through the layers of more than twenty cities built on top of each other. Among the fascinating finds were remains of dwellings from Biblical times, fortresses, Canaanite temples, a wall from Solomon's period, and a spectacular water system built by King Ahab in the 9th century B.C.E.

Hours are Sunday-Thursday 8:00-5:00, Friday 8:00-4:00, Saturday 8:00-5:00. For further information Tel. (04) 693-2111.

Due west of Tel Hatzor is another archaeological site at Khirbet Merot. There is a turnoff to the left of Route 90. Take it for about 4 kilometers.

Khirbet Merot

MEROT

This was an ancient Jewish town with a large synagogue which contained a buried treasure.

Moshav Yesod Ha'ma'ala

Continue north along Route 90 to the Yesod Ha'ma'ala Junction and turn right.

DUBROVIN ESTATE MUSEUM

The Dubrovin family came from Russia over 115 years ago and founded a new settlement, Moshav Yesod Ha'ma'ala. A restored family farmhouse serves as the museum. There are original furniture, pottery and clothing from the founding days. Hours are Sunday-Saturday 9:00-5:00. For further information Tel. (04) 693-7371.

Hula Nature Reserve

HULA NATURE RESERVE
The Hula Valley and Lake Hula are the northernmost, highest and smallest bodies of water in the Jordan Rift. The Jordan River flows into this lake and continues south to the Sea of Galilee. It ultimately ends up in the Dead Sea, a vast endoric basin–without a discharge outlet to the sea. The Hula Valley was once a malaria-infested region. Drainage of the swamps was completed in 1957.
Because this project upset the valley's ecosystem, a nature reserve was set aside in which the area's original flora and fauna were preserved. Among the rich variety of wildlife found here are wild boar, water buffalo, herons, and exotic birds living among the luxuriant flowers, reeds, papyrus, and other swamp vegetation.
The Hula Nature Reserve is open Sunday-Thursday 8:00-4:00 and Friday 8:00-3:00. For further information Tel. (04) 937-7069.

*Continue on the this road and you will come to the **Hula Nature Reserve**.*

Kiryat Shemona

KIRYAT SHEMONA HISTORICAL MUSEUM
The Kiryat Shemona Historical Museum is located at 26, Ha'yarden Street. the building was originally built as a mosque. There are displays from local archaeological finds as well as contemporary historical events of the region. Hours are Sunday-Thursday 8:00-12:00. For further information Tell. (04) 694-0135.

*Go to Route 90, turn right and continue north to **Kiryat Shemona**.*

Manara Cliff

The Manara cliff is the highest cliff in Israel. It loom 800 meters above Kiryat Shemona. The attractions here center around the three stations of the Manara Cable Car, which rises from Kiryat Shemona to a height 740 meters. The first station on the cable car route offers a trip in mini-jeeps along the Manara cliff, a bungee trampoline, and an extreme 1,200-meter-long mountain slide. The middle station offers rock climbing and rapelling, a 200-meter omega, and a climbing wall. At the upper station, there are two options–to hike along the cliff with a local guide or in the summer, visitors can join in the apple picking in the orchards of Kibbutz Manara. The top staion also includes a waterpark with inflatable slides and a swimming pool.
For further information Tel. (04) 690-5830.

Kibbutz Tel Hai

Continue northward along Route 90 to Kibbutz Tel Hai.

TEL HAI MUSEUM

Kibbutz Tel Hai is located three kilometers north of Kiryat Shemona. It was established in 1918 as a military outpost after the British forces withdrew from the area. The town has become a symbol of Israel's early pioneer movement and the struggle for the Hula Valley. A monument to Yosef Trumpeldor stands on the town's outskirts. The original watchtower and stockade settlement, destroyed by Arabs in 1920, has been reconstructed as a small museum displaying simple farming tools. The town of Kiryat Shemona was founded in memory of Yosef Trumpeldor. The name of the town, which means "Town of Eight," refers to Trumpeldor's group of six men and two women who died at nearby Tel Hai defending their settlement from Arab attackers in 1920. The memorial is a statue of a lion at the edge of a cliff. His head thrown back and mouth open, bellowing at the skies. Trumpeldor's grave, beneath the roaring lion, is inscribed with his last words, "It is good to die for our country." Hours are Sunday-Thursday 8:00-4:00, Friday 8:00-1:00, Saturday & Holidays 10:00-5:00. For further information Tel. (04) 695-1333.

MUSEUM OF PHOTOGRAPHY

This museum is located in the Tel Hai Industrial Park. There are changing exhibits by local as well as international photographers. Concerts are also given in this museum. Museum hours are Sunday-Thursday 8:00-4:00, Saturday 10:00-5:00. For further information Tel. (04) 695-0769.

Kfar Gil'adi

In the area, look for Kfar Gil'adi.

BEIT HASHOMER MUSEUM

The Beit Hashomer Museum is located in Kfar Gil'adi. It is dedicated to members of Bar-Giora and the Hashomer associations, the Second Aliya pioneers who were self-defense activists in Russia. Hours are Sunday-Thursday 8:00-12:00 and 2:00-4:00, Friday 8:30-12:00. For further information Tel. (04) 694-1565.

Metulla

THE FARMER'S HOUSE MUSEUM

This museum is located at 8 Ha'rishonim Street. It depicts the history of Metulla which was first settled in 1896. It was far removed from rest of Israel and had no access roads or public transportation. Hours are Sunday-Thursday 4:00-6:00pm, Saturday 5:00-7:00. For further information Tel. (04) 694-0283.

Continue north along Route 90 to Israel's northernmost town, Metulla.

MUSIC BOX OF ZAMI

There is a collection of over 150 musical instrument from around the world. There are string, wind, percussion instruments as well as an extensive display of keyboard instruments. The Music Box of Zami is located in a private home at 5 Mitzpe Emek A'Hula Street. Visits are by private appointment only. For further information Tel. (04) 699-7073.

Fish ponds in the Hula Valley as seen from the Golan Heights.

Tour #14
Golan Heights

Nimrod

Banias

Dan

Ma'ayan Baruch

Mas'ada

Katzrin

B'richat Ha'meshushim

Gamla

Ofir

Ein Gev

Sussita

Ha'on

Sha'ar Ha'golan

Hamat Gader

Courtesy Survey of Israel.

Golan Heights

The Golan Heights differs geologically from the rest of Israel; it is layered with solidified lava flows stemming from several local volcanic cones located in the northern part of the Heights. The most pronounced of these cones are Tell al-Sheikha, about 4,000 feet high, and Tell Abu Nida, which contains a crater with a circumference of about 2.5 miles. There are smaller volcanic cones nearby; Tell Abu Khanzir, Tell Yusuf, and Tell Faras–all located further south. Mount Peres is a volcanic cone. However, Mount Hermon, the tallest mountain in Israel, is not volcanic but sedimentary. For skiing information Tel. (03) 602-5405.

Kibbutz Shaar Ha'golan

*The starting point of the Golan Heights tour is at the southeastern tip of the Sea of Galilee (the Kinneret) at **Kibbutz Shaar Ha'golan**.*

MUSEUM OF YARMUKIAN CULTURE
This museum is located in Kibbutz Shaar Ha'golan. The visitor can explore the daily life as well as the art and culture of Neolithic farmers who lived in the region over five thousand years ago. They lived on the banks of the Yarmuk River, hence the name Museum of Yarmukian Culture. There are over 150 items on display including human figures made of clay, pebbles, basalt pebbles with geometric designs and pendents. Hours are Sunday-Saturday 9:00-12:00. For further information Tel. (04) 667-7386.

Hamat Gader

*Continue eastward along Route 98 to **Hamat Gader**.*

Ancient baths dating from the Roman period are found on the southern Golan Heights at Hamat Gader. These hot baths were built over springs warmed by volcanic activity deep within the earth. During the period of the Mishnah, Rabbi Yehudah Ha'nassi came to bathe in the hot springs.
Hamat Gader has several hot springs, four with mineral waters and one with fresh water. The temperature of the spring water ranges from 40 to 52 degrees, Celsius. In recent years, in order to attract more visitors, alligators from Florida were brought to the pools. Be very careful where you go swimming at Hamat Gader. you don't want to be joined by a hungry alligator!

*Doubleback to Route 92 (located along the eastern shore of the Sea of Galilee) turn right and proceed north to **Ha'on**.*

Ha'on

Be sure to visit the ostrich farm at Ha'on.

Kibbutz Ein Gev

HOUSE OF THE ANCHORS FISHING MUSEUM

Kibbutz Ein Gev was founded in 1937 by German and Czechoslovakian Jewish refugees. Teddy Kolleck, former mayor of Jerusalem, was one of its founders. The kibbutz is located at the foot of the Golan Heights. It bore the brunt of constant Syrian artillery attacks until the Six Day War. The 5,000-seat auditorium hosts the annual classical music festivals. A tour of the kibbutz is given on a mini-train, similar to the ones found at Rosh Ha'nikra.

The House of the Anchors Fishing Museum has displays about the fishing industry on the Sea of Galilee. There are models of fishing nets, anchors, mooring stones and netting needles. There are also demonstrations of fishing techniques in ancient as well as in recent times. Hours are by special appointment only. For further information Tel. (04) 665-8998.

*Continue north along Route 92 to **Kibbutz Ein Gev.***

Sussita

This was originally built as a Roman fortress. There are also archaeological remnants from the fifth and sixth centuries, C.E.

*Due east of Kibbutz Ein Gev there is a bad road. It leads up to **Sussita.***

Ofir Observation Point

MILLION DOLLAR VIEW

The Syrians planned to divert the sources of the Jordan River from the northern Hula Valley to the Yarmuk River south of the Golan and thus cut off Israel from one of its few main water sources. Lebanon and Jordan cooperated in this plan. Israel's quick military response by bombing the construction crews, served its purpose and the Syrians quickly backed-off. This episode was known as the "Battle over the water."

Proceed north along Route 92 to Kursi and the Samakh Junction. Turn right onto Route 789. As you ascend this road, you will see something very special...

Gamla

Gamla was one of the fortified cities in northern Israel that held out in the revolt against the Romans in 66 C.E. The commander of Galilee was Joseph ben Mattathias, later known as Josephus Flavius. In his book, "War of the Jews," he describes some of the events which occurred in Gamla during the siege: "The houses were built on the steep rib and they are joined to-

*Continue driving up the mountainside until you reach the Afik Junction. Turn left onto Route 98. Drive about ten kilometers to Route 808 and turn left. Proceed on Route 808 until you see the sign for **Gamla.***

gether, so that one house fits onto another, and the town looks as if it is suspended in air."

Many refugees fled to the fortified city of Gamla which was the last city to resist the Romans in the region. As you approach the city walls there are signs where the Romans broke through. The Romans were led by Vespasian and his three elite legions, number V, X, and XV, which consisted of six thousand soldiers. In the Roman camp outside the city walls are rooms filled with catapult stones. From the area of Dir Krookh, the Romans shelled Gamla unceasingly. Archaeologists estimate that on average, the Romans succeeded in striking each square foot of Gamla with these catapult stones.

In the city of Gamla today there are remains of a mikveh and one of the oldest synagogues in Israel. It was built before the destruction of the Second Temple in the year 70. A total of 9,000 Jews died in Gamla. Four thousand were killed by the Romans. The remaining five thousand Jews decided not to surrender to the Romans and opted to commit mass suicide by jumping off the northern cliff of the city. Only two women survived. Gamla has been called the "Masada of the Golan."

The peak of Mount Gamla is 540 meters above sea level. *Gamal* in Hebrew means camel, a picturesque description of the shape of the mountain. Be sure to see the highest waterfall in Israel, Gamla Waterfall, measuring 51 meters.

There are many table-like stone structures around Gamla called dolmens. These were ancient burial sites and are about 5,000 years old. There are about two hundred dolmens laid out in a diameter of 500 feet at the Daliyot intersection, just east of Route 808, before the turn-off to Gamla. For further information Tel. (04) 682-2282.

Doubleback to Route 808, turn right and then make another right onto Route 869, which will take you down to the Sea of Galilee (Route 92). At Route 92 turn right and proceed past the Yehudiya Junction (Route 87). Go one half kilometer past the junction and look for a trail on the right side of the road. Take this road (by foot or by a four-wheel drive vehicle) for about three kilometers.

Look for the sign "B'richat Ha'mehushim," and descend to the beautiful waterfalls.

B'richat Ha'meshushim

B'RICHAT HA'MESHUSHIM

B'richat Ha'meshushim is part of the Ya'ar Yehudiya Nature Reserve. There are pools surrounded by hexagonal rock formations which were the result of volcanic lava extrusions. Hexagons form during a certain variation of magma cooling. The fluted columns were formed when mineral-rich molten rock cooled slowly, taking on a crystalline structure. There are hundreds of these fluted basalt pillars surrounding the stream and pools.

There is a similar geologic formation in Wyoming. That formation, known as Devil's Tower National Monument, was also caused by slow-cooling of a lava flow. It looks like a volcanic neck with slender, six-sided fluted basalt columns rising 867 feet. Devil's Tower was the geologic theme in Steven Spielberg's movie, "Close Encounters of a Third Kind." All of the movie's "victims" were drawn or attracted to that mountain. As you dip in the ice-cold water (a wonderful feeling after hiking for over two hours on a hot summer day) at B'richat Ha'meshushim, you'll feel little fish nibbling at you. Don't worry, they are not man-eating fish. For further information Tel. (04) 696-2817.

Katzrin

GOLAN ARCHAEOLOGICAL MUSEUM
Katzrin is known as the "Capital of the Golan." The Golan Archaeological Museum presents the rich prehistoric past of the Golan Heights. Highlights include the heroic story of the Jewish city of Gamla and Jewish, Christian, and Pagan settlement during the Byzantine period. There is an audio-visual presentation. Hours are Sunday-Thursday 8:00-5:00, Friday 8:00-3:00. For further information Tel. (04) 696-9636.

Return to Route 87, take it northeast to the Katzrin Junction, turn left and take Route 9088 to **Katzrin.**

ANCIENT KATZRIN PARK
At nearby Katzrin Park, there is an Open-Air Museum and reconstructed ancient synagogue and village–it recreates Jewish daily life from Talmudic times. The park also includes an outdoor exhibit of modern basalt sculpture in its natural environment.
Be sure to see the restored house dating from Talmudic times and the reconstruction of a dolmen, an ancient burial site, similar to those found nearby in Gamla and also found at Stonehenge, England.
Katzrin is one of 27 ancient Jewish settlements that have been identified in the central Golan. Each of these settlements contained a luxurious synagogue. The Golan Archaeological Museum contains some of the more delicate mosaic floor tiles from these ancient synagogues. Hours are Sunday-Thursday 8:00-5:00, Friday 8:00-3:00, Saturday & Holidays 10:00-4:00. For further information Tel. (04) 696-2412.

Mas'ada Junction

BIRKET RAM (Ram Pool)
This circular body of water is believed to be the source of the

Leave Katzrin on Route 9088 going north. At the Nashut Junction turn right onto Route 91. Take this road to Route 98 and turn left. Take Route 98 to the **Mas'ada Junction.** *Look to the right at the circular lake.*

After hiking in the Golan Heights in the hot sun for two hours, it's so refreshing to dip in the frigid waters of B'richat Ha'meshushim.

Nimrod's Fortress

This magnificent fortress is located at the base of Mount Hermon overlooking the Hula Valley. It was built by the Ayubbi Muslims in the 12th century while preparing to defend themselves against the fifth Crusade. This is the largest complete fortress in the Middle East. Whoever controlled Nimrod's Fortress controlled the principal trade route from Damascus, the Via Maris, to Acre. Inside the fortress are many peep holes. These were designed as 30-foot-deep cisterns or water-storage troughs. For further information Tel. (050) 581-3227.

Route 98 continues up to Mount Hermon, the highest point in Israel, and Israel's only ski resort. At Mas'ada, turn west onto Route 99. When you reach a turnoff for Route 989, take it to Nimrod's Fortress.

Banias Waterfall

Banias is one of the principal sources of the Jordan River. The waters originate on the slopes of Mount Hermon. In ancient times the Canaanites, and later the Greeks, built shrines and temples here. The Greek name "Paneas" was modified in Arabic to Banias since Arabic has no "p" sound. Pan was the god of fertility.

An earthquake collapsed the grotto of the Greeks, but there are still several Hellenistic shrines remaining. Under the Romans, the area was called Caesarea Phillippi, after Phillip, son of Herod, who followed in the ancient paganistic religions. Banias is part of the National Park System. Hours are Sunday-Thursday 8:00-4:00, Friday 8:00-2:00. For firther information Tel. (04) 690-2577.

Doubleback to Route 99 and continue west for about six kilometers. Turn at the sign which reads, "Banias."

Si'on Junction

COVENANT BETWEEN THE PIECES

The place where Abraham made the *Brit bein Habetarim*, "covenant between the pieces," is said to located right at the edge of the Israeli-Syrian border, along Mount Hermon. The exact location is said to be 800 meters from the Ramat Observation Tower. The site of this "covenant" is along Har Dov, at the base of Har Agas. Permission to drive along this road **must** be obtained from the Israeli military in the area.

Continue driving west along Route 99. When you get to the Si'on Junction, try to turn right onto Route 999. It may not be possible to enter this road, since it hugs the Lebanese-Syrian-Israeli border. There have been incidents here over the past few years in this area called Har Dov.

Kibbutz Dan

BEIT USSISHKIN NATURE MUSEUM

The Beit Ussishkin Nature Museum explores the natural history of the Hula Valley, Mount Hermon, Golan Heights, and the Jordan River.There are dioramas and audio-visual presentations. Hours are Sunday-Thursday 8:00-4:30, Friday 8:00-3:00, Saturday 9:30-4:30. For further information Tel. (04) 694-1704.

Continue traveling west along Route 99 to Kibbutz Dan.

TEL DAN NATURE RESERVE

Cold-water springs gush right up from the ground, forming the Dan River. This is one of the three principal sources of the Jordan River. Excavations have revealed Early Bronze through Roman settlements at this site. The site has been called La'ish, Dan, and Antioch. The Temple compound was built by Jeroboam and Ahab as an alternative to Jerusalem. The Nature Reserve is open Sunday-Thursday 8:00-4:00, friday 8:00-3:00.

Kibbutz Ma'ayan Baruch

Continue west along Route 99 past Gan Ha'shloshim, turn right and drive to Kibbutz Ma'ayan Baruch.

MUSEUM OF PREHISTORY

This museum explores the prehistoric period of the Hula Valley. Some of the artifacts on display are stone, flint, bone artifacts, bones of elephants and other animals. Hours are Sunday-Thursday 9:00-12:00. For further information Tel. (04) 695-4611.

Where to Stay

Note: For those people who keep kosher, it is highly recommended to inquire if the bed & breakfast establishments listed below meet their kashrut standards.

ABIRIM
Carmeli Family Bed & Breakfast Tel. (04) 987-0229
Kedar Family Bed & Breakfast Tel. (04) 987-9808
Shamir Family Bed & Breakfast Tel. (04) 987-0859
ACHZIV
Achziv Club Med Tel. (04) 982-1203
Achziv Holiday Village Tel. (04) 982-3602
ACRE
Acre Youth Hostel Tel. (04) 691-1982
Motel Eiris Haifa-Akko Road Tel. (04) 991-8028
Palm Beach Hotel (Club Hotel Sea Shore) Tel. (04) 987-7777
ADAMIT
Nofesh Al Hagova Tel. (04) 985-9139
AFIK
Afikei Nofesh Inn Tel. (04) 675-4150
Orchan Afik Tel. (04) 676-1240
AFIKIM
Afikey Nofesh Tel. (06) 675-4150
ALMAGOR
Gafner Family Bed & Breakfast Tel. (06) 693-7915
Romish Family Bed & Breakfast Tel. (06) 693-8324
KIBBUTZ ALMOG
Almog Holiday Village Tel. (02) 994-5201
KIBBUTZ ALUMIM
Alumim Country Inn Tel. (07) 993-7300
ALUMOT
Melonit Alumot Tel. (06) 677-3494
AMIAD
Erohach Amiad–Bed & Breakfast Tel. (06) 693-3829
AMIRIM
Amirei Ha'galil Tel. (06) 698-9815
Eretz Ha'galil Tel. (06) 698-9170
Dalya & Shlomo Lipshitz–Bed & Breakfast Tel. (06) 698-7569
Nofesh Ne'eman Tel. (06) 698-9620
Rozenblum Family Bed & Breakfast Tel. (06) 698-9820
AMNUN
Romano Family Bed & Breakfast Tel. (06) 693-7839
AMUKA
Kerem Dodim Tel. (06) 692-2277

ARAD
Arad Guest House Tel. (08) 995-5491
Arad Hotel 6, Ha'palmach Street Tel. (08) 995-7040
Blau-Weiss Youth Hostel 4, Ha'atad Street Tel. (08) 995-7150
Holiday on Gilad–Bed & Breakfast Tel. (08) 995-7177
Inbar Hotel 38, Yehudah Street Tel. (08) 997-3303
Margoa Arad Hotel Tel. (08) 995-1222
Melonit in Rotem Tel. (08) 952-2961
Nof Arad Hotel Mo'av Street Tel. (08) 995-7056
Nofesh Banof Tel. (08) 995-9252

ARBEL
Konvitz Family Bed & Breakfast Tel. (06) 679-3355

ASHDOD
Beit Harel Nachal Tzahalim Tel. (08) 854-0885
Miami Hotel 12, Nordau Street Tel. (08) 852-2085
Orly Hotel 22, Nordau Street Tel. (08) 856-5380

ASHKELON
Ashkelon Beach Bed & Breakfast Tel. (08) 672-9134
Dan Gardens Hotel 56, Hatayasim Street Tel. (08) 671-1261
Holiday Inn Yekutiel Adam Street Tel. (08) 674-8888
Samson's Garden Hotel 38, Ha'tamar Street Tel. (08) 673-4666

AVNEI EITAN
Golan Babashan Tel. (06) 676-3852
Ha'mapalim Recreation Site Tel. (06) 676-2151

AVTALYON
Nofesh Moshlam Ba'galil Tel. (06) 678-2392

BAT SHLOMO
Hatzimer Shel Imi Liptel–Bed & Breakfast Tel. (06) 639-7021

BAT YAM
Armon Yam 95, Ben-Gurion Avenue Tel. (03) 552-2424
Bat-Yam Hotel 56 Ben-Gurion Avenue Tel. (03) 506-4373
Mercure Suites 99, Ben-Gurion Avenue Tel. (03) 555-0555
Sarita Hotel 127, Ben-Gurion Avenue Tel. (03) 552-9183
Sun Hotel 136, Ben-Gurion Avenue Tel. (03) 553-2553

BE'ER SHEVA
Arava Hotel 37, Ha'histadrut Street Tel. (08) 627-8792
Aviv Hotel 48, Mordei Ha'geta'ot Street Tel. (08) 627-8059
Be'er Sheva Youth Hostel 79, Ha'atzma'ut St. Tel. (08) 627-7444
Desert Inn Hotel Tuviahu Boulevard Tel. (08) 642-4922
Ha'negev Hotel 26, Ha'atzma'ut Street Tel. (08) 627-7026
Paradise Negev Hotel Henrietta Szold Street Tel. (08) 640-5444

BEIT HILLEL
Beit Ha'etz–Bed & Breakfast Tel. (06) 694-9747
Danny's Farm Tel. (06) 694-9254

Deutsch Family Farm Tel. (06) 694-4896
Pina Ba'emek Holiday Apartments Tel. (06) 699-7953
BEIT MEIR
Ramot Shapira Guest House Tel. (02) 534-4291
BEIT OREN
Kibbutz Hotel Tel. (04) 830-7444
BEIT SHE'AN
Frospar's Home–Bed & Breakfast Tel. (06) 658-8378
BEIT ZAYIT
Ilana's–Bed & Breakfast Tel. (02) 534-6261
BINYAMINA
Bet Groshka Ha'meyasdim Tel. (06) 638-9810
B'NEI BRAK
Wagshal Hotel 13, Meltzer Street Tel. (03) 618-4536
BNEI YEHUDA
Nofesh Ba'tzafon Tel. (06) 676-2478
CAESAREA
Bed & Breakfast Tel. (04) 636-3936
Dan Caesarea Hotel Tel. (04) 626-9111
CHAFETZ CHAIM
Kibbutz Chafetz Chaim Hotel Tel. (08) 859-3888
CHATZEVA
David & Anat Luria Family Bed & Breakfast Tel. (07) 658-1439
DAFNA
Dafna Bed & Breakfast Tel. (06) 694-5011
DEAD SEA
Dead Sea Gardens Tel. (08) 668-9090
Isaac H. Taylor Youth Hostel Tel. (08) 658-4349
DEGANIA BET
Bed & Breakfast Kibbutz Degania Bet Tel. (06) 675-5758
DOR
Nofesh Bak'far Tel. (06) 639-0856
EILAT
Adi Hotel Tel. (08) 637-6151
Ambassador Hotel Coral Beach Tel. (08) 638-2222
Americana Hotel North Beach Tel. (08) 633-3777
Beit Ha'arava Youth Hostel 106, Almogim Street Tel. (08) 637-4687
Beit Zalman Bed & Breakfast Tel. (08) 637-1219
Caesar Resort Hotel North Beach Tel. (08) 630-5555
Club Hotel Eilat Ha'arava Street Tel. (08) 636-1666
Club in Eilat Coral Beach Tel. (08) 638-5555
Crowne Plaza Eilat Hotel North Beach Tel. (08) 636-7777
Dalia Hotel North Beach Tel. (08) 633-4004
Dan Eilat North Beach Tel. (08) 636-2222

EILAT

Dan Panorama North Beach Tel. (08) 638-9999
Edomit Hotel New Tourist Center Tel. (08) 637-9511
Eilat Princess Hotel Tel. (08) 365-5555
Eilat Youth Hostel Tel. (08) 637-0088
Etzion Hotel 1, Ha'tmarim Boulevard Tel. (08) 637-0003
Fawlty Towers Youth Hostel Tel. (08) 637-2371
Galei Eilat Hotel North Shore Tel. (08) 636-7444
Herod's Eilat Hotel Tel. (08) 638-0000
Hilton Eilat - Queen of Sheba North Beach Tel. (08) 630-6666
Holiday Inn Eilat - Patio 3, Shfifon Alley Tel. (08) 636-4364
Holiday Inn Express Tel. (08) 638-0877
Isrotel - King Solomon Palace North Beach Tel. (08) 636-3444
Isrotel - Lagoona North Beach Tel. (08) 636-6666
Isrotel - Riviera Apartment Hotel Tel. (08) 633-3944
Isrotel - Royal Beach Tel. (08) 636-8888
Isrotel - Sport North Beach Tel. (08) 633-3333
La Coquille Hotel Tel. (08) 637-0031
La Meridien Eilat North Beach Tel. (08) 638-3333
Kobi's Home Tel. (08) 637-7520
Magic Palace Hotel North Beach Tel. (08) 636-9999
Magic Sunrise Club (Eilot) Tel. (08) 630-5333
Marina Club (All Suite Hotel) Tel. (08) 633-4191
Mercure Mirage Eilat 3, Ha'tivat Ha'negev St. Tel. (08) 638-2333
Moon Valley Eilat North Beach Tel. (08) 636-6888
Neptune Hotel North Beach Tel. (08) 636-9369
Nova Hotel 6, Ha'tivat Ha'negev Street Tel. (08) 638-2444
Orchid Hotel Coral Beach Tel. (08) 636-0360
Palmira Hotel North Beach Tel. (08) 636-6000
Paradise Club Tel. (08) 636-3636
Paradise Gardens Hotel North Beach Tel. (08) 630-4444
Petra Hotel Derech Ha'arav Tel. (08) 633-5555
Prima Carlton Hotel Corah Beach Tel. (08) 633-3555
Red Rock Hotel North Beach Tel. (08) 637-3171
Red Sea Hotel Ha'tmarim Boulevard Tel. (08) 637-2171
Reef Hotel Coral Beach Tel. (08) 636-4444
Shalom Plaza Eilat 2, Ha'tmarim Boulevard Tel. (08) 636-6777
Sheraton Moriah Eilat North Beach Tel. (08) 636-1111
Spring Youth Hostel Almogim Street Tel. (08) 637-4660
Topaz Hotel Arava Road Tel. (08) 636-2111
Vista Hotel North Beach Tel. (08) 630-3030
The White House Tel. (08) 633-2318

KIBBUTZ EILOT

Eilot Hotel Tel. (07) 635-7967

EIN BOKEK
Caesar Premier Hotel Tel. (08) 668-9666
Carlton Dead Sea Hotel Tel. (08) 658-4311
Crown Plaza Hotel Tel. (08) 658-1919
Ein Bokek Hotel Tel. (08) 659-1666
Golden Tulip Hotel Tel. (08) 668-9999
Grand Nirvana Hotel Tel. (08) 668-9444
Hod Hotel Tel. (08) 668-8222
Le Meridian Dead Sea Resort & Spa Tel. (08) 659-1234
Lot Hotel Tel. (08) 658-4321
Shearyon Moriah Dead Sea Hotel Tel. (08) 659-1592
The Royal Hotel Tel. (08) 668-8555
Tsell Harim Hotel Tel. (08) 658-4121
EIN GEDI
Kibbutz Ein Gedi Guest House Tel. (08) 659-4222
Ein Gedi Youth Hostel Tel. (08) 658-4165
EIN GEV
Ein Gev Holiday Resort Tel. (04) 665-9800
KIBBUTZ EIN TZURIM
Ein Tzurim Inn & Youth Hostel Tel. (08) 858-8318
ELON MOREH
Elon Moreh Bed & Breakfast Tel. (02) 997-3106
KIBBUTZ GADOT
Gadot Country Living Tel. (04) 693-9188
GANEI TAL
Bed & Breakfast Vasertil Family Tel. (07) 684-7256
GEDERA
Neve Bar Guest House Tel. (08) 857-0707
GESHER
Beit Gesher Tel. (02) 624-1015
KIBBUTZ GESHER HA'ZIV
Ziv Ha'galil Country Living Tel. (04) 995-8568
GINOSAR
Nof Ginosar Kibbutz Hotel Tel. (04) 670-0300
Ginosar Inn Tel. (04) 679-8763
GIV'AT SHMUEL
Nof Kinneret Tel. (05) 316-6066
KIBBUTZ GVULOT
Kibbutz Gvulot Guest House Tel. (08) 998-7914
HAD NESS
Bed & Breakfast Kna'an Family Tel. (06) 692-0628
Shimshon's Wife & Husband–Bed & Breakfast Tel.(06) 692-0378
HA'GOSHRIM
Kibbutz Hotel Tel. (04) 681-6000

HAIFA
Beit Shalom 110, Hanassi Avenue Tel. (04) 837-7481
Carmel Forest Spa Resort (Ya'arot Ha'carmel) (04) 830-7888
Carmel Youth Hostel 18, Rechov Tzvi Veltzhak Tel. (04) 653-944
Dan Carmel Hotel 85 Ha'nassi Avenue Tel. (04) 830-6306
Dan Panorama Hotel 107, Ha'nassi Avenue Tel. (04) 835-2222
Eden Hotel 8, Shmariahu Levin Street Tel. (04) 866-4816
Haifa Gardens Hotel Tel. (04) 838-9131
Haifa Tower (Migdal) 63, Herzl Street Tel. (04) 867-7111
Holiday Inn 111, Yefe Nof Street Tel. (04) 835-0835
Le Meridian Hotel 10, David Elazar Street Tel. (04) 850-8888
Marom Hotel 51, Ha'palmach Street Tel. (04) 825-4355
Mount Carmel Hotel 103, Derech Hayam Tel. (04) 838-1413
Nof Hotel 101, Ha'nassi Avenue Tel. (04) 835-4311
Shulamit Hotel 15, Kiryat Sefer Street Tel. (04) 834-2811
Zimmer Family Bed & Breakfast Tel. (04) 822-5245
HA'ON
Ha'on Family Village Tel. (04) 665-6555
HARARIT
Bed & Breakfast Zehava Tel. (06) 678-2790
HAR'EL
Har'el Guest House Tel. (02) 991-8958
HEFTZIBA
Heftziba Bed & Breakfast Tel. (06) 653-4468
HERZLIYA
Dan Accadia Hotel Herzliya-on-the-Sea Tel. (09) 959-7070
Eshel Hotel 3, Ramat-Yam Street Tel. (09) 956-8208
The Daniel Hotel Herzliya-on-the-Sea Tel. (09) 952-8282
The Sharon Hotel Herzliya-on-the-Sea Tel. (09) 952-5777
HEVEL EILOT
Kibbutz Lotan Hostel Tel. (07) 635-6888
HOSEN
Litel's Home Bed & Breakfast Tel. (04) 997-6684
Pninat Ha'tzafon Bed & Breakfast Tel. (04) 997-9233
HULATA
Hulata Guest House Tel. (06) 691-5092
JERUSALEM
American Colony Hotel Nablus Road Tel. (02) 627-9777
Ariel Hotel 31, Hebron Road Tel. (02) 568-9999
Ariela's Place Bed & Breakfast 49, Hebron Road Tel. (02) 673-1872
Barkai Studios 9, Hulda Street Tel. (02) 628-1285
Beit Bernstein Youth Hostel 1, Keren Ha'yesod Street
Beit Shmuel Youth Hostel 6, Shama Street
Boker Tov Yerushalayim Tel. (02) 623-3459

JERUSALEM
Caesar Jerusalem Hotel 208 Jaffa Road Tel. (02) 500-5656
Canter Guest House Tel. (02) 625-8053
Crown Plaza Hotel Givat Ram Tel. (02) 658-8888
Dan Panorama Hotel 39, Keren Ha'yesod Street Tel. (02) 569-5695
David Citadel Hotel 1, King David Street Tel. (02) 621-1111
Eldan Hotel 24, King David Street Tel. (02) 567-9777
Eshel House Bed & Breakfast 11, Lod Street Tel. (02) 623-2604
Felix Holiday Apartment 2/3 Mishmar Ha'gvul Street Tel. (02) 674-3731
Four Season House Bed & Breakfast 4/5 Kubobi Street Tel. (02) 641-0122
Gloria Hotel Jaffa Gate Tel. (02) 628-2431
Rachel Galay Bed & Breakfast 39, Me'ir Nakar Street Tel. (02) 671-4222
Gavriel Holiday Apartment 30, Arnon Street Tel. (02) 623-3258
The Green Corner Bed & Breakfast 4, Hildshimer Street Tel. (02) 567-0070
Ha'davidka Youth Hostel 67, Ha'nevi'im Street
Hai House Bed & Breakfast 35, Tura Street Tel. (02) 624-3836
Hanagid Hotel 7, Shatz Street Tel. (02) 622-1111
Holyland Hotel Bayit Ve'gan Tel. (02) 643-7777
Holyland East Hotel 6, Rashid Street Tel. (02) 627-2888
"House 57" Bed & Breakfast 57, Sinai Desert Street Tel. (02) 581-9944
Inbal (Laromme) Hotel 3, Jabotinsky Street Tel. (02) 675-6666
Isrotel Tower 204, Jaffa Street Tel. (02) 500-7777
Jerusalem Hotel Nablus Road Tel. (02) 628-3282
Jerusalem Gold Hotel 234, Jaffa Road Tel. (02) 501-3333
Jerusalem Panorama Hotel Hill of Getsemane Tel.(02) 627-2277
Jerusalem Regency Hotel 32, Lehi Street Tel. (02) 533-1234
Jerusalem Tower Hotel 23, Hillel Street Tel. (02) 620-9209
King David Hotel 23, King David Street Tel. (02) 620-8888
King Solomon Hotel 32, King David Street Tel (02) 569-5555
Knesset Towers Hotel 4, Wolfson Street Tel. (02) 655-8888
Lev Yerushalayim Hotel 18, King George Street Tel. (02) 530-0333
Levi's House Bed & Breakfast 6, Malcha Street Tel. (02) 679-4605
Menorah Hotel 44, Jaffa Road Tel. (02) 622-3122
Mercure Jerusalem Gate Hotel 43, Yirmiyahu Street Tel. (02) 500-8500
Mevo Yerushalayim Hotel 212, Jaffa Street Tel. (02) 537-6532
Morali Vacation Apartments Tel. (02) 966-157
Mount of Olives Hotel 53, Mount of Olives Road Tel. (02) 628-4877
Mount Scopus Hotel 10, Sheikh Jarrah Tel. (02) 582-8891
Mount Zion Hotel 17, Hebron Road Tel. (02) 568-9555
Natural Home Bed & Breakfast Tel. (02) 641-1288
New Imperial Hotel Jaffa Gate Tel. (02) 627-2000
Novotel Jerusalem 9, St. George Street Tel. (02) 532-0000
Olive Tree Hotel 23, St. George Street Tel. (02) 541-0410
Palatin Hotel 4, Agripas Street Tel. (02) 623-1141

Park Plaza (Sonesta) Hotel 2, Wolfson Street Tel. (02) 658-2222
Petra Hostel 1, David Street (Old City)
Pninat Katamon Bed & Breakfast 7, Abba Hilkia Street Tel. (02) 678-0856
Prima Kings Hotel 60, King George Street Tel. (02) 620-1201
Prima Palace Hotel 6, Pines Street Tel. (02) 538-4111
Reich Hotel 1, Hagai Street Tel. (02) 652-3121
Renaissance Hotel Rupin Bridge at Herzl Boulevard Tel. (02) 659-9999
Seven Arches Hotel Mount of Olives Tel. (02) 626-7777
Shalom Jerusalem Hotel Bayit Ve'gan Tel. (02) 675-2222
Sheraton Jerusalem Plaza Hotel 47, King George Street Tel. (02) 629-8666
Tirat Bat-Sheva Hotel 42, King George Street Tel. (02) 623-2121
YMCA - 3 Arches 26, King David Street Tel. (02) 569-2692
KARMIEL
Kalanit Bed & Breakfast 15, Ne'si'ei Israel Boulevd Tel. (04) 958-0497
KATZRIN
Ha'pagod Bed & Breakfast Tel. (04) 696-2473
Porat Family Bed & Breakfast Tel. (04) 696-1046
Rivlin Family Bed & Breakfast Tel. (04) 696-1831
KFAR BLUM
Kibbutz Hotel Tel. (04) 683-6611
KFAR ETZION
Kfar Etzion Youth Hostel Tel. (02) 993-5133
KFAR GIL'ADI
Kibbutz Hotel Tel. (04) 690-0000
KFAR HA'NASI
The Village Inn Tel. (04) 691-4870
KFAR VITKIN
Kfar Vitkin Youth Hostel Tel. (09) 866-6032
KFAR VRADIM
Beit Arbel Bed & Breakfast Tel. (04) 997-7273
Sharon's Home Bed & Breakfast Tel. (04) 997-6265
KINNERET MOSHAVA
Koren Family Bed & Breakfast Tel. (04) 675-0012
Vasserman Family Bed & Breakfast Tel. (04) 675-0574
KIRYAT ANAVIM
Kibbutz Hotel Tel. (02) 534-8999
KIRYAT SHMONA
Chatuel's Home Bed & Breakfast Tel. (06) 694-4767
Bed & Breakfast Ruchama Tel. (06) 694-1059
KORAZIM
Karei Deshe Youth Hostel Tel. (04) 672-0601
Pnina Ba'galil Bed & Breakfast Tel. (04) 693-1952
Vered Ha'galil Bed & Breakfast Tel. (04) 693-5785
LAVI
Kibbutz Holiday Village Tel. (04) 679-9450

MA'AGAN
Ma'agan Holiday Village Tel. (04) 665-4411
MA'ALE GAMLA
Marom Family Bed & Breakfast Tel. (06) 673-2555
MA'ALEH GILBOA
Margoa Bagilboa Country Inn Tel. (04) 606-7500
MA'ALE HA'CHAMISHA
Kibbutz Holiday Village Tel. (02) 533-1331
MA'AYAN BARUCH
Ma'ayan Baruch Bed & Breakfast Tel. (06) 695-4700
MA'AYAN HAROD
Ma'ayon Harod Youth Hostel Tel. (04) 653-1669
MA'ALOT
Hacienda Mountain Resort (Yeefe Nof) Tel. (04) 957-9000
Rozner Family Bed & Breakfast Tel. (04) 978-8738
MANOT
Mizpe Harim Bed & Breakfast Tel. (04) 980-6246
MENACHANIYA
Rider Family Bed & Breakfast Tel. (06) 675-1916
MEROM GOLAN
Bed & Breakfast Merom Golan Tel. (06) 696-0267
MERON
Adlar Family Bed & Breakfast Tel. (06) 698-9139
Itzkovitz Family Bed & Breakfast Tel. (06) 698-9133
Klein Family Bed & Breakfast Tel. (06) 698-9062
METULLA
Alaska Inn Tel. (04) 699-7111
Arazim Hotel Tel. (04) 699-7143
Frenkel Family Bed & Breakfast Tel. (04) 694-3834
Metulla Bed & Breakfast Tel. (04) 694-1662
Mlonit Beit Sholom Tel. (04) 694-0767
MIGDAL
Mizrachi Family Bed & Breakfast Tel. (06) 679-1629
Trompeldor's Home Tel. (06) 679-1040
MISGAV
Rakefet Hotel Tel. (04) 980-0403
MIZPE RAMON
Isrotel Ramon Inn 1, Ein Aqev Street Tel. (08) 658-8822
Mitzpe Ramon Youth Hostel Tel. (08) 659-5187
Moshav Ha'omanoyot Guest Rooms Tel. (08) 658-7411
KIBBUTZ MORAN
Kibbutz Morah Country Lodging Tel. (04) 698-8910
NACHSHOLIM
Nachsholim Kibbutz Hotel Tel. (04) 639-9533

NAHARIYA
Carlton Hotel Tel. (04) 900-5555
Erna Hotel 29, Jabotinsky Street Tel. (04) 992-0170
Frank Hotel 4, Ha'aliya Street Tel. (04) 992-0278
Kalman Hotel 27, Jabotinsky Hotel Tel. (04) 992-0355
Rosenblatt Hotel 59, Weizman Street Tel. (04) 982-0069
Sol Marine Hotel Ha'alia Street Tel. (04) 995-0555
NEGBA
Negba Guest Rooms Tel. (07) 677-4799
NES AMMIM
Kibbutz Guest House Tel. (04) 995-0099
NETANYA
Blue Bay Hotel Tel. (09) 860-0100
Blue Weiss Hotel 22, Gad Mahness Street Tel. (09) 860-3939
Carmel Netanya Hotel Jabotinsky Street Tel. (09) 860-1111
Galil Hotel 28, Nice Boulevard Tel. (09) 862-4455
Ginot Yam 9, David Ha'melech Street Tel. (09) 834-1007
Grand Yahalom Hotel 15 Gad Mahness Street Tel.(09) 862-4888
Jeremy Hotel Tel. (09) 862-2651
King Koresh Hotel 6, Harav Kook Street Tel. (09) 861-3555
King Solomon Hotel 18, Ha'ma'apalim Street Tel. (09) 833-8444
Margoa Hotel 9, Gad Mahness Street Tel. (09) 862-4434
Metropol Grand 17, Gad Mahness Street Tel. (09) 862-4777
Mizpe-Yam Boutique Hotel 1, Jabotinsky Street Tel. 862-3730
Palace Hotel 33, Gad Mahness Tel. (09) 862-0222
Park Hotel 7, David Ha'melech Street Tel. (09) 862-3344
Le Promenade Apartment Hotel 6, Gad Machnes Street Tel. (09) 862-6450
Residence Hotel 18, Gad Mahness Street Tel. (09) 830-1111
The Seasons 1, Nice Boulevard Tel. (09) 860-1555
NEVE ATIV
Goldshtain Family Bed & Breakfast Tel. (04) 698-1714
Grinfeld Bed & Breakfast Tel. (04) 698-4083
Hermon Resort Tel. (04) 698-4392
Hunters Lodge Holiday Apartments Tel. (04) 698-1686
NEVE ILAN
Kibbutz Resort Hotel Tel. (02) 533-9339
NEVE SHALOM
Jewish-Arab Village Tel. (02) 991-7160
NEVA ZOHAR
Novotel Dead Sea Tel. (08) 955-3333
NIR ETZION
Nir Etzion Kibbutz Hotel Tel. (04) 984-2542
MOSHAV NORDIA
Moshav Nordia Youth Hostel Tel. (09) 862-0089

PEKI'IN
Peki'in Youth Hostel Tel. (04) 957-4111
PETACH TIKVAH
Petach Tikveh Youth Hostel 34, Ya'halom Street Tel. (03) 922-6666
RAMAT GAN
Kfar Maccabiah Hotel Tel. (03) 671-5715
Optima Tower Hotel 1, Krinitzi Street Tel. (03) 675-4444
Sheraton City Tower 14, Zisman Street Tel. (03) 754-4444
RAMAT HA'GOLAN
Moshav Keshet Holiday Village Tel. (04) 696-2505
RAMAT RACHEL
Ramat Rachel Hotel & Spa Tel. (02) 670-2555
RAMAT YOCHANAN
Ramat Yochanan Youth Hostel Tel. (04) 644-2976
RAMOT (Golan)
Barak Family Bed & Breakfast Tel. (06) 673-2525
Chadashi Family Bed & Breakfast Tel. (06) 673-1224
RAMOT NAFTALI
Lasri Family Bed & Breakfast Tel. (06) 694-9618
Tziona Bed & Breakfast Tel. (06) 694-0173
REHOVOT
Margoa Hotel 11, Moskowitz Street Tel. (08) 945-1303
ROSH HANIKRA
Rosh Hanikra Youth Hostel Tel. (04) 682-1330
ROSH PINA
Adva Country Inn Tel. (04) 693-8198
Edana's Home Bed & Breakfast Tel. (04) 698-9591
Habeit Shelano Bed & Breakfast Tel. (04) 693-5665
Mizpe Ha'yamim Tel. (04) 699-4555
Tzameret Bed & Breakfast Tel. (04) 693-7573
SDE BOKER
Beit Hamburg Bed & Breakfast Tel. (07) 653-2079
SAFED
Beit Binyamin Youth Hostel 1, Lohameu Ha'geta'ot Street Tel. (04) 692-1086
Beit Gabay Bed & Breakfast Tel. (04) 692-2828
Berinson House The Old City Tel. (04) 697-2555
Pninat Ha'nofesh Bed & Breakfast Tel. (04) 692-0322
Robinger's Home Bed & Breakfast Tel. (04) 692-0085
Ron Hotel Ha'tivat Yiftah Street Tel. (04) 697-2590
Rozen's Home Bed & Breakfast Tel. (04) 697-1530
Ruckenstein's Hotel Mount Canaan Tel. (04) 692-0060
SHA'AR HA'GOLAN
El Mol Golan Bed & Breakfast Tel. (06) 667-7544
SHE'AR YASHUV
Beit Ha'gefen Bed & Breakfast Tel. (06 694-2291

Fromovitz Family Bed & Breakfast Tel. (06) 694-1045
Kohen Family Bed & Breakfast Tel. (06) 694-0416
SHEFAYIM
Shefayim Kibbutz Hotel Tel. (09) 959-5577
SHARONA
Bar Bakfar Bed & Breakfast Tel. (06) 676-9733
Karaso Country Lodging Tel. (06) 676-0484
SHLOMI
Shlomi Youth Hostel Tel. (04) 980-8975
SHORESH
Kibbutz Holiday Resort Tel. (02) 533-8338
TEL HAI
Tel Hai Youth Hostel Tel. (04) 694-0043
TEL AVIV
Abratel Suites Hotel 3, Ge'ula Street Tel. (03) 516-9966
Adiv Hotel 5, Mendele Street Tel. (03) 522-9141
Alexander Suite Hotel 3, Ha'vakook Street Tel. (03) 545-2222
Ambassador Hotel 56, Promenade Tel. (03) 510-3993
Ami Hotel 152, Ha'yarkon Street Tel. (03) 524-9141
Armon Ha'yarkon Hotel 268, Ha'yarkon Street Tel. (03) 605-5271
Aviv Hotel 88, Ha'yarkon Street Tel. (03) 510-2784
Basel Hotel 156, Ha'yarkon Street Tel. (03) 520-7711
Bell Hotel 12, Allenby Street Tel. (03) 517-7011
Ben Nevet Gitta Bed & Breakfast Tel. (03) 574-2644
Best Western Regency Suites 80, Ha'yarkon Street Tel. (03) 517-3939
Carlton Hotel 10, Eliezer Peri Street Tel. (03) 520-1818
Center Hotel 2, Zamenhof Street Tel. (03) 629-6181
City Hotel 9, Mapu Street Tel. (03) 524-6253
Country Club 300, Namir Road (Glilot) Tel. (03) 699-0666
Crown Plaza Hotel 145, Ha'yarkon Street Tel. (03) 520-1111
Dan Panorama Hotel Charles Clore Park Tel. (03) 519-0190
Dan Hotel 99, Ha'yarkon street Tel. (03) 520-2525
David Intercontinental Hotel 12, Kaufman Street Tel. (03) 795-1111
Deborah Hotel 87, Ben Yehuda Street Tel. (03) 527-8282
Grand Beach Hotel 250, Ha'yarkon Street Tel. (03) 543-3333
Havakook Apartment Hotel 7, Ha'vakook Street Tel. (03) 604-2222
Howard Johnson Hotel 216, Ha'yarkon Street Tel. (03) 524-3277
Shalom Imperial Hotel 66, Ha'yatkon Street Tel. (03) 517-7002
Isrotel Tower 78, Ha'yarkon Street Tel. (03) 511-3636
Lusky Suites Hotel 84, Ha'yarkon Street Tel. (03) 516-3030
Maxim Hotel 86, Ha'yarkon Street Tel. (03) 517-3721
Melody Hotel 220, Ha'yarkon Street Tel. (03) 527-7711
Mercure Marina Hotel 167, Ha'yarkon Street Tel. (03) 521-1777
Metropolitan Hotel
11-15, Trumpeldor Street Tel. (03) 519-2727

TEL AVIV
Miami Hotel 8, Allenby Street Tel. (03) 510-3868
Nes Ziona Hotel 10, Nes Ziona Tel. (03) 510-6084
Olympia Hotel 164, Ha'yarkon Street Tel (03) 524-2184
Ophir Hotel 43, Dizengoff Street Tel. (03) 525-7350
Prima Astor Hotel 105, Ha'yarkon Street Tel. (03) 520-6666
Renaissance Hotel 121, Ha'yarkon Street Tel. (03) 521-5555
Sea.Net Hotel 6, Ness Ziona street Tel. (03) 517-1655
Sheraton Moriah Hotel 155, Ha'yarkon Street Tel. (03) 521-6666
Sheraton Hotel 115, Ha'yarkon Street Tel. (03) 521-1111
Tal Hotel 287, Ha'yarkon Street Tel. (03) 542-5500
Tel Aviv Hilton Independence Park Tel. (03) 520-2222
Top Hotel 35, Ben Yehuda Street Tel. (03) 51700941
Yamit Park Plaza Hotel 79, Ha'yarkon Street Tel. (03) 519-7111
TIBERIAS
Adina's Home Bed & Breakfast Tel. (04) 672-2507
Ariston Hotel 19, Herzl Boulevard
Astoria Hotel 13, Ohel Ya'akov Street Tel. (04) 672-2351
Beit Almog Bed & Breakfast Tel. (04) 672-0303
Berger Bed & Breakfast 25, Neiberg Street Tel. (04) 671-5151
Caesaer Hotel 103, The Promenade Tel. (04) 672-7272
Carmel Jordan River Ha'banim Street Tel. (04) 671-4444
Club Hotel Tiberias Ahad Ha'am Street Tel. (04) 672-8000
Eden Hotel 4, Ohel Ya'akov Street Tel. (04) 679-0070
Four Points Tiberias Hotel Ha'shomer Street Tel. (04) 679-1281
Gai Beach Hotel Derech Ha'merchazot Tel. (04) 670-0700
Galei Kinneret Hotel 1, Eliezer Kaplan Street
Golan Hotel 14, Achad Ha'am Street Tel. (04) 679-1901
Hartman Bed & Breakfast 3, Ahad Ha'am Street Tel. (04) 679-1555
Hawaii Hotel Migdal Tel. (04) 679-0202
Hod Tiberias Hotel Ussishkin Street Tel. (04) 679-2261
Holiday Inn Ha'banim Street Tel. (04) 672-8555
Kinar Hotel (northeast Sea of Galilee) Tel. (04) 673-8888
Kolton Inn 2, Ohel Ya'akov Street Tel. (04) 679-1641
Meital's Home Bed & Breakfast Tel. (04) 672-4660
Mercur Tiberias Hotel Ha'shomer Street Tel. (04) 670-0800
Nofesh Kfar Hittim (Galei Tachton) Tel. (04) 679-5921
Park Tiberias Hotel Tel. (04) 672-4424
Poriah Youth Hostel Tel. (04) 675-0050
Prima Tiberias Hotel El'hadef Street Tel. (04) 679-1166
Restal Hotel Yehuda Ha'levey Street Tel. (04) 679-0555
Ron Beach Hotel Gdud Barak Street Tel. (04) 679-1350
Royal Plaza Hotel Ganei Menorah Boulevard Tel. (04) 670-0000
Shalom Plaza Hotel 13, Zeidel Street Tel. (04) 679-1861

Sheraton Moriah Hotel Ha'banim Street Tel. (04) 679-2233
Terminal Palace Hotel City Center Tel. (04) 671-7176
Tzameret Inn Plus 200 Street Tel. (04) 679-4951
Yosef Meyouhas Youth Hostel 2, Jorelant Street Tel. (04) 672-1775
TIRAT ZVI
Tirat Zvi Bed & Breakfast Tel. (06) 653-8890
VERED HA'GALIL
Vered Ha'galil Bed & Breakfast Tel. (06) 693-5785
YESUD HAMA'ALA
Levy Family Bed & Breakfast Tel. (06) 693-3527
YUVAL
Beit Elisha Bed & Breakfast Tel. (06) 694-1516
Or Ha'yarden Bed & Breakfast Tel. (06) 695-9317
ZICHRON YA'AKOV
Beit Maimon Bed & Breakfast 4, Zahal Street Tel. (04) 639-0212
Carmel Gardens 1, Etzion Street Tel. (04) 630-0111
Eden Inn Aharon Street Tel. (04) 639-3939
Havat Ha'baron Tel. (04) 630-0333
ZIPPORI
Filtzer Family Bed & Breakfast Tel. (06) 646-2647

Amusement, Theme and Water Parks for Kids

ACTION PARK Moshav Lakhish Tel. (08) 681-8818
ASHKELUNA Delilah Beach Tel. (08) 673-9970
Waterpark with high slides.
BEIT HALOMOTAY (Dreamland) Givat Brener Tel. (08) 944-3338
ETZTRUBAL Yaar Chorazim
Mountain bike trail in Chorasim Forest.
FLORENTINE CIRCUS Kfar HaYarok, north of Tel Aviv Tel. (03) 648-3811
A summer circus camp with acrobatics, trapeze, stilt walking, trampoline, juggling, etc.
GO KARTING POLEG Netanya Tel. (09) 885-4477
HAFETZ HAIM WATER PARK Kibbutz Hafetz Haim Tel. (08) 859-3888
Roller-coaster ballerina, airplane carousel, huge sacks glider, baby's car facility, trampoline, huge wave pool, twisted path slide, fast tube slide and tires track.
HUGA WATER PARK Beit She'an Tel. (04) 658-1111
KFAR BLUM AMUSEMENT PARK Kibbutz Kfar Blum Tel. 170-050-6611
Kayaks and assorted climbing bridges.
KIFTZUBA Kibbutz Tzuba Tel. (02) 534-7952
KINGS CITY Eilat Tel. (08) 630-4444
LUNA GAL Hof Golan Tel. (04) 673-2226
Wild outdoor training, canoeing, rafting, etc.
LUNA PARK Tel Aviv Tel. (03) 642-7080
LUNAGRAND Grand Kanyon, Haifa Tel. (04) 822-1000
MANARA CLIFF Northern Israel opposite Kiryat Shemona. For details see page 211.
MEGA KARTING (Grand Kanyon) Petach Tikvah Tel. (03) 921-7786 (Go Karts)
MEYMADION Tel Aviv Tel. (03) 642-2777
MINI GOLF Tel Aviv Tel. (03) 699-0229
Trampolines, simulated rock climbing, plus mini golf.
MINI ISRAEL Kibbutz Nachshon Tel. (08) 920-7458
MOUNT HERMON SKI RESORT Moshav Neve Ativ Tel. (04) 698-1337
Weather permitting.
MY KART 1, Derech Ha'yam, Rechovot Tel. (08) 946-2940 (Go Karts)
NACHSHONIT PARK Kibbutz Nachshonim Tel. (03) 938-6444
PRO KARTING Nachshonim Tel. (08) 946-2940 (Go Karts)
SHEFAYIM WATER PARK Shafayim Tel. (09) 959-5756
SKY PARK Rishon Le'zion Tel. (03) 941-6888
Rock and mountain climbing techniques, rope bridge walking,e tc.
SUPERLAND Rishon Le'zion Tel. (03) 961-9065
Wild and fast rides (roller coasters).
TZAPARI JUNGA JUNGA Yehoshua Park, Tel Aviv Tel. (03) 642-2888

Israeli Folk Dancing

Each listing contains the location, day of the week, time beginners session starts, instructor, and contact telephone number.

ACRE
- Matnas Beit Hayman (Monday) 7:30pm Oren Shmuel Tel. (04) 995-2318
- Country Club Hof Ha'tmarim (Wednesday) 8:15pm Ya'ir Harel Tel. (04) 844-1812

AFEK
- Dining Hall (Nostalgia) (Tuesday) 8:00pm Moshe Oron Tel. (054) 442-4897

ALONIM
- Dining Hall (Wednesday) 7:30pm Ze'ev Nisim Tel. (04) 989-0184
- Nostalgia Session (Saturday in mid-month) 9:00pm Dining Hall

ALON SHVUT
- Women-only session (Sunday) 7:30pm Ruti Ben Daviv Tel. (02) 993-1642

ARAD
- Matnas (Sunday) 8:00pm Hela Himanuel Tel. (052) 344-5034

ARUGOT
- Beit Ha'am (Sunday) 8:00pm Shlomi Ochayon

ASERET
- Ulam Ha'tarbut (Wednesday) 8:00pm Boaz Cohen Tel. (02) 624-4368

ASHDOD
- Matnas Daled (Sunday) 8:00pm Jak Ochayon Tel. (08) 854-0058
- Beit Livron (Monday) 8:00pm Raiym Va'aknin Tel. (052) 270-3651
- Makif Zayin, Kikar Ha'atzma'ut (Wednesday) 8:00pm Jak Ochayon
- Ulam Ha'sport (Thursday) 8:00pm Moti Menachem Tel. (052) 258-1720

BAR'AM
- Dining Hall (Sunday) 8:15pm Eida Kalman Tel. (04) 698-8168

BAT YAM
- Rechov Ha'komemiyut (Sunday) 8:00pm Pnina Aran Tel. (03) 551-0301
- Country Club Bat Yam (Tuesday) 8:00pm Eli Segal Tel. (052) 890-1419
- Tayelet Bat Yam-Chof Ha'selah (Saturday) 8:30pm Pnina Aran

BE'ER SHEVA
- Ulam Sport (Sunday) 8:15pm Yom Tov Ochayon Tel. (050) 539-8800
- Student Center (Ben-Gurion University)
  (Sunday) 8:30pm Netanel Shim'oni Tel. (08) 649-0077
- Ulam Sport (Monday) 8:00pm Rafi Ziv Tel. (052) 338-5885
- Beit Sefer Tichon Makif Ramot (Tuesday) 8:00pm Haiym Va'aknin
- Country Club (Wednesday) 8:00pm Yom Tov Ochayon
- Ulam Sport (Wednesday) 8:00pm Rafi Zif Tel. (052) 338-5885
- Ulam Rabin (Thursday) 8:00pm Eran Biton Tel. (08) 855-1354
- Ulam Sport (Ben-Gurion University) (Saturday) 8:30pm Rafi Zif Tel. (052) 338-5885

BEIT ALFA
- Dining Hall (Sunday) 8:30pm Israel Shabtai Tel. (04) 658-1006

BEIT DAGAN
- Matnas (Monday) 8:00pm Asher Oshri Tel. (03) 658-7488

BEIT NECHEMIYA
- Beit Ha'am (Thursday) 8:00pm Kobi Michaeli Tel. (08) 924-1093

BEIT SHEMESH
- (Monday) 8:30pm Haiym Zemach Tel. (02) 536-1197

BEIT ZERA
- Dining Hall (Monday) 9:00pm Sefi Aviv Tel. (04) 693-3154

CHOF HA'CARMEL
- Ulam Ha'sport (Tuesday) 8:00pm Dede Luski Tel. (050) 530-2233

DIMONA
- Matnas Dimona (Sunday) 9:00pm Yosi Schwatz Tel. (052) 270-0459

EFRAT
- (Wednesday) 8:00pm Ruti Ben Daviv Tel. (02) 993-1642

EILAT
- Matnas Ya'alim (Sunday) 8:30pm Yaki Biton Tel. (08) 633-5794
- Mercaz Pninat Eilat (Monday) 9:30pm Yosi Grada Tel. (08) 637-8305
- Matnas Kolyer (Monday) 9:30pm Yaki Biton
- Mercaz Pninat Eilat (Wednesday) 9:30pm Yosi Grada
- Matnas Ya'alim (Sh'chunah Alef) (Thursday) 9:00pm Yaki Biton
- Mercaz Pninat Eilat (Saturday) 12:00pm Re'uven Avraham Tel. (08) 633-8861
- Beit Rubin (Saturday) 8:00pm Eirit Schwartz Tel. (08) 637-7002
- Sheratin Moriah Hotel (Saturday) 8:30pm Na'nama Zar Tel. (08) 631-9075
Women-only Session
- Mercaz Na'amit (Tuesday) 8:00pm Rinat Rozen Tel. (08) 633-2028

EVRON
- Dining Hall (Monday & Thursday) 7:00pm Haym Millshtein Tel. (04) 992-4223
- Beit Sefer Romeimah (Wednesday) 8:30pm Oren Ashkenazi
- Sporton (Wednesday) 8:30pm Dede Luski
- Beit Ha'lochem (Thursday) 7:30pm Meir Amsalem

GAN SHMUEL
- Dining Hall (Sunday & Wednesday) 8:00pm Yaron Carmel Tel. (052) 465-6080

GAN YAVNE
- Ulam Sport (Monday) 8:00pm Beni Bar Tel. (054) 496-6695

GINOSAR
- Dining Hall (Wednesday) 8:00pm Israel Shabtai Tel. (04) 658-1006

GIVA'ATAYIM
- Country Giva'atayim (Monday & Tuesday) 8:15pm Miri Akuni Tel. (03) 651-2395

GIVAT BRENER
- Ulam Ha'sport (Sunday & Thursday) 8:00pm S. Mordechai Tel. (052) 240-5535

GIVAT HA'SHISHA
- Country Club Sports Hall (Monday & Wednesday) 9:00pm Tel. (052) 260-3415

GIVAT SHMUEL
- Beit Ha'am - Yehuda Ha'levi Street (Tuesday) 8:00pm Yigal Triki Tel. (03) 532-7010

GLIL YAM
• Dining Hall (Monday & Wednesday) 8:00pm Levi Bar Gil Tel. (09) 745-7787
HADERA
Women-only Sessions
• (Monday & Wednesday) 8:30pm Chana Samila Tel. (052) 541-4984
HAIFA
• Mercaz Kehilati Naveh Yosef (Sunday) 7:30pm Meir Amsalem Tel. (054) 441-4120
• Sporton (Sunday) 8:30pm Dede Luski Tel. (050) 530-2233
• Beit Ha'histadrut (Monday) 7:30pm Meir Amsalem
• Mercaz Ohr Chadash (Monday) 8:00pm Oren Ashkenazi Tel. (04) 833-5969
• Beit Sefer Tel Chai (Tuesday) 8:00pm Oren Ashkenazi
HA'OGEN
• Dining Hall (Sunday, Monday, Wednesday, Thursday)
  9:00pm Shimon Shuker Tel. (050) 540-9909
HA'ZOREA
• Dining Hall (Monday) 8:00pm Ze'ev Nissim Tel. (04) 989-0184
HERZLIYA
• 8, Rechov Ha'kuzari (Sunday) 8:00pm Yosi Nakav Tel. (054) 676-2013
• Mercaz Kehilati Nachlat Edah (Sunday) 8:00pm Tuvia Tishler Tel. (03) 699-1135
• Country Club (Jabotinsky St.) (Monday) 8:15pm Erzel Shmueli Tel. (03) 677-2522
• Mercaz Kehilati Nachlat Edah (Tuesday) 8:00pm Eitan Krol tel. (03) 931-0520
• Mo'etzet Ha'poalim (Ben-Gurion St.) (Wednesday) 7:45pm A. Mati Tel. (03) 352-5082
HOD HA'SHARON
• Sporton (Jabotinsky St.) (Tues. & Thursday) 9:00pm Levi Bar Gil Tel. (09) 745-7787
HOLON
• Country Holon (Sunday) 6:00pm Eiyal Levi Tel. (03) 687-6660
• Mo'adon Briza-Golda (Sunday) 8:00pm Israel Shiker Tel. (08) 932-2493
• 54, Ha'histadrut Street (Monday) 8:00pm Raz Magen Tel. (03) 961-2792
• Mo'adon Briza-Golda (Monday) ela Shlomo Tel. (03) 969-3376
• Mo'adon Briza-Golda (Tuesday) 8:00pm Dudu Barzilai Tel. (03) 631-5191
• Country Holon (Tuesday) 8:30pm Victor Gabai Tel. (03) 960-4743
• 20, Rabin Street (Wednesday) 8:00pm Roni Simon Tov Tel. (052) 833-2790
• Country Misrad Ha'rishui (Wednesday) 5:30pm Yigal Triki
• Mo'adon Briza-Golda (Thursday) 8:00pm Shimon Mordechai Tel. (052) 240-5535
JERUSALEM
• Matnas Armon Ha'netziv (Sunday) 8:00pm Mimi Kogan Tel. (052) 370-6395
• 11, Rechov Bezalel (Sunday) 8:00pm Yael Shim'oni Tel. (02) 678-1529
• 137, Sde Herzl Matnas Ziv (Monday) 7:15pm David Zilka Tel. (02) 642-2695
• 243, Jaffa Road (Tuesday) 7:30pm Malka Bachar Tel. (03) 966-8133
• Beit Ha'kerem (Tuesday) 8:45pm David Zilka Tel.(02) 642-2695
• Beit Ha'noar (Tuesday) 6:00pm Boaz Cohen Tel. (02) 624-4368
• Beit Ha'noar (Wednesday) 8:00pm Avner Naeim Tel. (02) 678-2261
• Beit Ha'noar 105, Herzog Street (Thursday) 8:00pm Haim Zemach Tel. (02) 536-1197
• Beit Ha'noar 105, Herzog Street (Saturday) 9:15pm
• Nostalgia Session at Beit Ha'noar (First Monday each month) 9:15pm Avner Naeim

JERUSALEM
Women-only Sessions
- 9, Rechov Aharoni (Sunday) 7:30pm Mali Cohen Tel. (02) 993-2307
- 4, Elazar Ha'gadol Street (Monday) 8:00pm Roni Broza Tel. (02) 642-3419
- Beit Sefer Maimon (Tuesday) 7:00pm Sarit Doron Tel. (02) 641-3342
- Beit Sefer Maimon (Wednesday) 7:30pm Zvia Waill Tel. (02) 999-5556

KABRI
- Dining Hall (Wednesday) 7:30pm Yosi Peretz Tel.(04) 981-5522

KARMIEL
- Matnas Shchunat Rabin (Tuesday) 8:00pm Ve'ev Nisim Tel. (04) 989-0184

KARNEI SHOMRON
- Young Israel (Wednesday) 8:30pm Mazalit Chetzroni Tel. (09) 792-9224

KFAR BILU
- Mo'adon Chaverim (Monday) 8:45pm Arie Wax Tel. (08) 945-1646

KFAR MASARIK
- Dining Hall (Sunday & Wednesday) 7:00pm Avi Amsalam Tel. (04) 988-9871

KFAR SABA
- Heichal Sport Ha'yovel (Sunday & Monday) 8:30pm   Gadi Biton Tel. (03) 532-8993
- Country Club (Monday & Wednesday) 8:30pm Eli Maimon Tel. (052) 458-5691

KIRYAT ARBA
Women-only Sessions
- (Wednesday & Thursday) 8:00pm Ruth Tabechnik Tel. (02) 996-1704

KIRYAT BIALIK
- (Sunday) 7:30pm Itzik Ben Ami Tel. (04) 870-2189
- (Monday) 7:00pm Dede Luski Tel. (050) 530-2233
- Beit Katz (Tuesday) 7:00pm Chanan Dadon Tel. (04) 873-0440

KIRYAT MOTZKIN
- Country Club Galei Gil (Tuesday) 6:00pm Avi Amsalam Tel. (04) 988-9871
- 4, Yigal Alon Street (Thursday & Saturday) 8:15pm Yair Bino Tel. (050) 729-6922

KIRYAT ONO
- Heichal Ha'sport (Monday) 8:00pm Roni Simon Tov Tel. (052) 833-2790

KIRYAT YAM
- Matnas Kiryat Yam (Sunday) 7:30pm Yoav Bashan Tel. (04) 870-5701

MA'AGAN MICHAEL
- Dining Hall (Monday) 8:30pm Yarom Carmel Tel.(052) 465-6080
- Beit Ha'sefer Ha'azuri (Thursday) 5:00pm Mariyon Shemi Tel. (04) 639-4580

MA'ALE ADUMIM
- Ulam Dekel Vilnay (Wednesday) 8:00pm Yarom Ben Simchon Tel. (052) 831-8339
Women-only Session
- (Monday) 8:30pm Michal Zomer Tel. (02) 590-0139

MACHANA'IM
- Dining Hall (Sunday & Thursday) 9:00pm Sefi Aviv Tel. (04) 693-3154

MAZKERET BATYA
- Matnas Sdei Eliyahu, 2 (Monday) 8:30pm Eiyal Ozeri Tel. (03) 534-5571

MEVASERET ZION
- Ulam Ha'matnas Maoz Zion (Tuesday) 7:15pm Yoram Sasson Tel. (054) 569-2156

• Matnas Rechov Ha'rakefet, 2 (Wednesday) 7:45pm David Zilka Tel. (02) 642-2695
MISGAV
• Ulam Sport (Thursday) 8:00pm Yarom Carmel Tel. (052) 465-6080
MISHMAR HA'EMEK
• Dining Hall (Tuesday) 8:30pm Zion Uchayon Tel. (04) 612-7599
MIZRA
• Michlelet Yizrael (Sunday & Tuesday) 8:00pm David Ben Naeim Tel. (04) 652-7847
• Michlelet Yizrael (Thursday) 8:00pm Avi Amsalam Tel. (04) 988-9871
• Nostalgia Session (First Saturday each month) 9:00pm Avi Amsalam
MODI'IN
• Ha'beit Ha'adom (Tuesday) 8:00pm Kobi Michaeli Tel. (08) 924-1093
MORESHET
Women-only Session
• (Monday) 8:30pm Eida Kalman Tel. (04) 698-8168
NACHSHOLIM
• Dining Hall (Sunday & Thursday) 8:00pm Mati Avraham Tel. (052) 352-5082
NAHARIYA
• 68, Wolfson Street (Wednesday) 8:30pm Yair Bino Tel. (050) 729-6922
• Chof Ha'yam Mazach (Wednesday) 7:30pm Chaim Millstein Tel. (04) 992-4223
• Chof Ha'yam Mazach (Saturday) 10:00am Chaim Millstein
NES ZIONA
• Country Club (Sunday) 8:45pm Eli Maimon Tel. (052) 458-5691
NETANYA
• 9, Shmuel Ha'natziv (Sunday) 8:00pm Israel Amrani Tel. (09) 865-3490
• 19, Yehudah Ha'nasi Street (Monday) 8:00pm Eli Segal Tel. (052) 890-1419
• 9, Meyerovitz Street (Tuesday) 8:00pm Yosi Nakav Tel. (054) 676-2013
• Galil Hotel (Wednesday) 8:00pm Yosi Nakav
• Ulam Beit Yisrael (Thursday) 8:00pm Eli Segal
NETIVOT
• Ulam Sport (Saturday) 9:00pm Ofer Alfasi Tel. (052) 888-6900
NEVATIM
• Ulam Ha'sport (Saturday) 8:00pm Netanel Shimo'ni Tel. (08) 649-0077
NEVE MONOSON
• Beit Ha'tarbut (Sunday & Wednesday) 8:00pm Victor Gabai Tel. (03) 960-4743
• Nostalgia Session (First Saturday each month) 8:30 Eiyal Ozeri Tel. (03) 534-5571
OMIT
• Country Club (Sunday) 8:30pm Meir Adi Tel. (03) 936-0908
• Beit Sefer Chativat Beinayim (Tuesday) 8:30pm Meir Adi
PETACH TIKVAH
• Matnas Yosptal (Sunday) 8:15pm Eti Mauda Tel. (03) 908-7454
• 51, Arlozorov Street (Monday) 8:30pm Tzidki Arami Tel. (052) 258-7010
• Sporton (Monday) 8:30pm Victor Gabai Tel. (03) 960-4743
• Sporton (Wednesday) 8:30pm Tzidki Arami
• David Ramaz Street (Wednesday) 8:30pm Eti Mauda Tel. (03) 908-7454
• 51, Arlozorov Street (Thursday) 8:00pm Tzidki Arami

• 10, Shulsinger Street (Thursday) 8:00pm Batya Kronenberg
• Marom Sport Briyoth (Thursday) 8:15pm Eti Mauda
RA'ANANA
• 3, Ya'ir Street (Sunday) 8:00pm Gadi Biton Tel. (03) 532-8993
• Country Club (Sunday) 7:00pm Erzel Shmueli Tel. (03) 677-2522
• Ulam Sport "Aviv" (Monday) 8:00pm Tuvia Tishler Tel. (03) 699-1135
• Mercaz Kehilati (Tuesday) 8:00pm Avi Peretz Tel. (08) 857-0131
• Country Ra'anana (Wednesday) 8:00pm Ayelet Golan Tel. (09) 954-7039
• Heichal Aviv (Wednesday) 8:00pm Yankele Ziv Tel. (08) 970-5519
• Heichal Ha'sport (Thursday) 8:00pm Yom Tov Ochayon Tel. (050) 539-8800
• Nostalgia Session (Second Saturday each month) Heichal Ha'sport
              9:00pm Shimon Mordechai Tel. (052) 240-5535
Women-only Sessions
• 19, Rashi Street (Monday) 8:00pm Roni Grinbaum Tel. (054) 441-1231
• 18, Kazan Street (Wednesday) 8:30pm Roni Grinbaum
RAMAT GAN
• Kfar Ha'maccabiya (Sunday) 8:15pm Didi Dosh Tel. (08) 856-1619
• Rokeach Street (Sunday) 7:00pm Pnina Klayn Tel. (054) 457-5151
• Beit Sefer Bleich (Sunday) 7:30pm Eyal Ozeri Tel. (03) 534-5571
• Kfar Ha'maccabiya (Monday) 8:30pm Mishael Barzilai Tel. (03) 631-5191
• Mo'adon Ha'marganit (Tuesday) 8:00pm Batya Kronenberg Tel. (052) 280-8900
• Beit Sefer Mordei Ha'geta'ot (Tuesday) 8:00pm Yankele Sha'arabani Tel. (03) 648-6089
• Beit Rosen (89, Bialik St.) (Wednesday) 8:00pm Mishael Barzilai
• Kfar Ha'maccabiya (Wednesday) 8:30pm Eiyal Ozeri
• Kfar Ha'maccabiya (Thursday) 8:30pm Pnina Klayn
• Nostalgia Session (Third Saturday each month)
           Kfar Ha'maccabiya America Hall 9:00pm Mishael Barzilai
RAMAT HA'SHARON
• Country Club (Sunday & Thursday) 8:00pm Yardena Lib Tel. (03) 540-6820
• 20, Ezra Street (Monday) 7:30pm Yossi Nakav Tel. (054) 676-2013
• Ulam Sport (Tuesday) 8:15pm Yardena Lib
• Beit Ha'sho'ayvah (Thursday) 8:30pm Yosi Nakav
RAMAT YISHAI
• Ulam Beit Miriam (Thursday) 8:00pm David Ben Naeim Tel. (04) 652-7847
• Nostagia Session (Last Friday of each month)
           Ulam Beit Miriam 9:30pm David Ben Naeim
RAMLE
• Heichal Ha'sport (Wednesday) 8:00pm Shimon Asor Tel. (08) 943-0322
• Ben Zvi Street (Wednesday) 8:00pm Yulanda Velensi Tel. (08) 923-5474
RECHOVOT
• 52, Sirani Street (Monday) 7:30pm Boaz Cohen Tel. (02) 624-4368
• 108 Herzl Street (Monday) 8:00pm Moshe Twili Tel. (08) 940-8015
• ORT Barzilai (Tuesday) 8:00pm Shimon Mordechai Tel. (052) 240-5535
• 108, Herzl Street (Saturday) 8:00pm Moshe Twili

RE'OT
- Ha'mayim Park (Monday) 8:00pm Kobi Michaeli Tel. (08) 924-1093
- Ha'mayim Park (Thursday) 8:00pm Dudu Barzilai Tel. (03) 631-5191

RISHON LE'ZION
- Heichal Ha'sport (Sunday) 8:30pm Shimon Asor Tel. (08) 943-0322
- Country Ha'histadrut (Sunday) 8:30pm Gabi Kuta Tel. (03) 958-5075
- 60, Rothschild Street (Monday) 9:30pm Yehuda Emanuel Tel. (03) 505-6387
- Ulam Sport (Monday) 8:00pm Moti Menachem Tel. (052) 258-1720
- Country Club (Monday) 8:00pm Eitan Tabib Tel. (052) 245-5978
- Heichal Ha'sport (Tuesday) 8:00pm Shimon Asor
- Country Ha'histadrut (Tuesday) 7:00pm Gabi Kuta
- Country Ha'histadrut (Wednesday) 8:15pm Moti Menachem
- Country Club Galei Hadar (Wednesday) 8:00pm Eitan Tabib
- Ulam Yigal Alon (Wednesday) 8:30pm Moshe Twili
- Sderot Bar-Lev, 8 (Thursday) 7:45pm Eitan Tabib
- Heichal Ha'sport Ha'irony (Saturday) 8:00pm Shimon Asor

SAVION
- Mo'adon Savion (Sunday) 8:15pm Yankele Ziv Tel. (08) 970-5519
- Mo'adon Savion (Thursday) 8:15pm Levi Bar Gil Tel. (09) 745-7787

SHA'ALAVIM
Women-only Session
- Dining Hall (Tuesday) 8:00pm Edna Kave Tel. (03) 958-2984

TEL AVIV
- 3, Rechov Kehilat Kiev (Sunday) 7:30pm Miri Akuni Tel. (03) 651-2395
- Beit Dani (Sunday) 8:00pm Mishael Barzilai Tel. (03) 631-5191
- Country Club Azori Chen (Sunday) 7:00pm Sara Gutman Tel. (09) 742-8571
- Country Gimmel (Ramat Aviv) (Sunday) 8:00pm Batya Kronenberg
- Country Dekel (Sunday) 8:00pm Carmela Shlomo Tel. (03) 969-3376
- Countrylee (Monday) 8:00pm Pnina Aran Tel. (03) 551-0301
- Mo'adon Bank L'eumi (Monday) 7:00pm Malka Bachar Tel. (03) 966-8133
- Country Club - 35, Nachalat Yitzchok Street (Monday) 7:30pm Batya Kronenberg
- Country Gimmel (Ramat Aviv) 7:00pm M. Varon
- Heichal Ha'sport Hadar Yosef (Monday) 9:30pm Yankele Ziv Tel. (08) 970-5519
- Bikurei Ha'itim (Monday) 8:00pm Eran Biton Tel. (08) 855-1354
- Country Dekel (Monday) 8:15pm Ofer Alfasi Tel. (052) 888-6900
- 35, Nachalat Yitzchok Street (Tuesday) 7:30 Mishael Barzilai
- Bikurei Ha'itim (Tuesday) 8:00pm Eran Biton
- Beit Dani (Tuesday) 8:00pm Gadi Biton
- Country Club Azori Chen (Tuesday) 7:00pm Sara Gutman
- Lidor - 8, Kehilat Venezia (Thursday) 9:00pm Te'am Lidor
- Lidor - 8, Kehilat Venezia (Tuesday) 8:00pm Te'am Lidor Tel. (03) 649-7065
- Lidor - 8, Kehilat Venezia (Wednesday) 9:00pm Te'am Lidor
- Mo'adon Focus (Wednesday) 8:30pm Ronen Gabai Tel. (052) 272-8309
- 3, Rechov Kehilat Kiev (Wednesday) 7:30pm Miri Akuni
- Country Dekel (Wednesday) 8:00pm Oren Bachar

TEL AVIV
- Tel Aviv University (Thursday) 8:30pm Varda & Gal Tel. (052) 255-8331
- 35, Nachalat Yitzchok Street (Thursday) 7:30 Miri Akuni
- Tel Aviv University - Ulam Ha'sport (Thursday) 8:00pm Gadi Biton
- Country Dekel (Thursday) 7:45pm Yankele Sha'arabani Tel. (03) 648-6089
- Lidor - 8, Kehilat Venezia (Friday) 10:30pm Te'am Lidor
- Lidor - 8, Kehilat Venezia (Saturday) 10:00pm Te'am Lidor
- Mercaz Bikurei Ha'itim (Saturday) 8:30pm Varda & Gal

YAVNE
- Shabazi Street (Monday) 8:30pm Nushi Elias Tel. (054) 687-4381
- Giborei Ha'chayil Street (Tuesday) 8:00pm Moshe Twili Tel. (08) 940-8015
- Shabazi Street (Thursday) 8:30pm Israel Shiker Tel. (08) 932-2493

YERUCHAM
- Ulam Ha'sport (Monday) 9:00pm Yosi Schwartz Tel. (052) 270-0459

ZICHRON YA'AKOV
Women-only Session
- Beit Sefer Yaabetz (Tuesday) 8:00pm Mariyon Shemi Tel. (04) 639-4580

Kosher Dining

Kosher food establishments in Israel must display a valid Certificate of Kashrut. This certificate or *Te'udat Kashrut*, must be renewed every three months. Be sure to look for this certificate and check the date. No responsibility, therefore can be taken for the absolute accuracy of the information in this guide, and travelers are advised to obtain confirmation of kashrut claims. Although every effort has been made to ensure accuracy, changes will occur after this guide has gone to press. Particular attention must be drawn to the fact that kosher food establishments change hands often and suddenly, in some cases going over to a non-kosher owner. All of the restaurants listed below are closed on the Sabbath.

(MOSHAV) AMIRIM
Amirei Ha'galil (Meat) Spa & Resort Tel. (04) 698-9815
Stup's (Dairy) Tel. (04) 698-0946
ASHDOD
Aladin (Meat/Fish) 34 Haavoda Street Tel. (08) 852-2117
ATLIT
Ben Ezra Fish 71, Ha'yayit Tel. (04) 984-2273
BE'ER SHEVA
Ha'shipudia Shel Ezra (Meat) 2, Derech Hebron Tel. (08) 628-7791
La Piazza (Dairy) Government Offices Mall Tel. (08) 665-5007
Shipuday Chompy (Meat) 8/5 Szold Street Tel. (08) 645-0130
Shipuday Ha'tikva (Meat) Only branch which is kosher.
            Government Offices Mall Ha'tikvah Street Tel. (08) 665-5996
Shipudei Sof Ha'derech (Meat) 111 Ha'palmach Street Tel. (08) 628-9155
BEIT GOVRIN
Mizpe Massu'a (Meat) Highway 38 (In British Forest) Tel. (02) 991-2464
            You can see the Mediterranean Sea from this inland restaurant.
BEIT SHEMESH
Not Just Bagels (Dairy) Zol L'mehadrin Center, Nitzanim Street Tel. (02) 991-2077
The Oriental (Chinese/Meat) 1, Ha'oman Tel. (02) 999-9488
B'NEI BRAK
Ben Ezra Fish (Fish/Meat) 13, Ben-Gurion Street Tel. (03) 579-6655
Dag Hayam (Fish) 137, Jabotinsky Street (Dor Gas Station) Tel. (03) 570-8007
CAESAREA
Agenda (Dairy/Sushi Bar) Paz Station (open 24/6) Tel. (04) 626-2092
Minato (Sushi Bar/Japanese Restaurant) Paz Station Tel. (04) 636-0812
EILAT
Brassarie (French/Meat) King Solomon Hotel tel. (08) 636-3439
Buffalo Steak House (Japanese/Meat)
            Hilton Hotel - Queen of Sheba Resort Tel. (08) 630-6666
Denis Kingdom (Fish Hatchery/Restaurant) Shalom Lagoon Tel. (08) 637-9898
Halleluya (Chinese/Moroccan/Meat) Tourist Center Tel. (08) 637-5752
Hummus Yerushalmi (Meat) Solel Boneh Center, Temarim Boulevard Tel. (08) 637-3736
il Pentolino (Italian/Dairy) 112, Ha'temarim Boulevard Tel. (08) 634-3430

Lawrence (Dairy/Fish) Herod's Vitalis Hotel Tel. (08) 638-0115
Metro (Meat) Royal Garden Hotel Tel. (08) 638-6698
Ranch House (Meat) Royal Beach Hotel Tel. (08) 636-8989
Retro (Meat) Le Meridien Hotel Tel. (08) 634-0044
Shauli & Guy (Meat) Lagoon Promenade Tel. (08) 633-3773
Industrial Area Tel. (08) 633-1930
Shipudei Eilat (Meat) 10, Ha'oman Street Tel. (08) 633-2343
Wang's Grill (Chinese/Meat) Royal Beach Hotel Tel. (08) 636-8989
(MOSHAV) EIN VERED
Kalima (Dairy) Tel. (09) 796-4828
EMEK DOTAN
Koresh b'Cafe (Meat) Malibu Center Tel. (08) 970-9159
EMEK HA'CHULA
Parkafe (Dairy) Country Center Tel. (08) 973-9970
(YISHUV) EVEN SAPIR
Almora (Indian/Meat) Tel. (02) 643-1186
GEDERA
Badolina (Dairy) 7 Habiluim Street Tel. (08) 868-0463
Znobar (Meat Grill) 1, Haznov Street Tel. (08) 869-2281
HADERA
Opera (Yemenite/Meat) 61, Ha'nassi Tel. (04) 632-2352
HAIFA
Ben Ezra Fish Castra Center Tel. (04) 859-0071
Broadway Bagel (Dairy) Horev Center Tel. (04) 834-5353
Cafe Bachoresh (Dairy) 36 Michael Street (Kfar Bialik) Tel. (04) 842-4604
Cookie Man (Dairy) Note: Not all stores in this chain are kosher.
Simcha Golan Boulevard (Grand Canion) Tel. (04) 812-0025
El Gaucho 120, Yefei Nof Tel. (04) 837-0997
(Argentinian Steak House) Note: Not all branches are closed on Shabbat.
Hamber 61, Herzl Street Tel. (04) 866-6739
Papagaio Haifa (Meat/South American) Hutzot Hamifratz (Krayot) Tel. (04) 842-2666
Rimonim (Dairy) Shulamit Hotel 15, Kiryat Sefer Tel. (04) 834-2811
HERZLIYA
Bella Venezia (Dairy/Italian) 27 Maskit Street Tel. (09) 950-6502
Ben Ami Cafe (Dairy) 11, Ha'menofim Street Tel. (09) 957-9589
Bistro 56 (French/Meat) Arena Mall Tel. (09) 956-5181
Carmelli's Bagel Bakery (Dairy) 6, Shenkar Street Tel. (09) 951-8555
Lobbystro (Dairy Bar & Sushi) Daniel Hotel 60, Ramot Yam Tel. (09) 952-8282
Me Gusta (Spanish/Meat) 27, Maskit Street Tel. (09) 958-9059
Papagaio Arena (Meat/South American) Arena Mall Tel. (09) 956-4000
Pita Pan (Meat Grill) 17, Sderot Ha'galim Tel. (09) 958-7619
Tarabin (Dairy) 5 Bareket Street Tel. (09) 956-2117
Tzimmes (Meat) 27, Maskit Street Tel. (09) 956-1144
Yapas Bar (Spanish/Japanese/Meat)
Daniel Hotel - Shizen Lifestyle Spa Resort Tel. (09) 952-8221

(MOSHAV) ILANIYA
Makom b'Sejera (Meat/Fish) Tel. (04) 676-0594
JAFFA
l'Alahmbra (Meat) 30, Jerusalem Road Tel. (03) 683-4453
Gueta (Libyan/Meat) 6, Yerushalayim Boulevard Tel. (03) 681-3993
Le Relais Jaffa (French/Meat) 9, Bat Ami Street Tel. (03) 681-0637
Shirat Ha'yam (Meat/Fish) 12, Mifratz Shlomo Tel. (03) 681-3271
JERUSALEM
Ahavat Ha'iam (Fish) Paz Gas Station on Ben-Zvi Avenue [Mehadrin] Tel. (02) 623-6767
Al Dente (Italian/Dairy) 50, Ussishkin Street [Rabbinat Yerushalayim] Tel. (02) 625-1479
Almora (Southern Indian/Meat)
            Yishuv Even Sapir [Rabbinat Mateh Yehuda] Tel. (02) 643-1186
Angelo (Italian/Dairy/Fish)
            9, Horkanos Street [Rabbinat Yerushalayim] Tel. (02) 623-6095
Atcha (Meat) 9 Joel Solomon Street [Rabbinat Yerushalayim] Tel. (02) 623-6603
Bagel Bite (Dairy) 84, Derech Beit Lechem [Rabbinat Yerushalayim] Tel. (02) 671-6890
Beit Ha'ma'ayan (Fish/Dairy)
            14 Ha'ma'ayan Street [Rabbinat Yerushalayim & Mehadrin] Tel. (02) 644-8840
Belinda Coffee Shop (Dairy)
            9, Diskin Street (Wolfson Center) [Mehadrin] Tel. (02) 624-5717
Benny's Dagim (Dairy) 1, Mesilat Yesharim Street [Mehadrin] Tel. (02) 625-2403
Bonkers Bagels (Dairy)
2, Tifereth Israel Street (Old City) [Rabbinat Yerushalayim & Mehadrin] Tel. (02) 627-2590
Brunch Bagel (Dairy) 2, Ezer Yoldot Street (Ge'ula) [Badatz] Tel. (02) 500-4001
Buffalo Steakhouse (Meat)
            54, Emek Refa'im Street [Rabbinat Yerushalayim] Tel. (02) 561-1325
Burger Deli (Meat) 16 Shamgar Street (Rav Shefa Mall) [Badatz] Tel. (02) 500-3070
Cafe Bagina (Garden Cafe) (Dairy)
            74, Beit Lechem Road [Rabbinat Yerushalayim] Tel. (02) 672-0825
Cafe Inbal (Meat) 25-D Ein Kerem [Rabbinat Yerushalayim] Tel. (02) 644-6533
Cafe Neeman (Dairy)
            Malcha Mall [Rabbinat Yerushalayim & Mehadrin] Tel. (02) 679-1515
Caffit (Dairy) 35, Emek Refa'im Street [Rabbinat Yerushalayim] Tel. (02) 563-5284
Canela (Meat) 8 Shlomzion Hamalka Street [Rabbinat Yerushalayim] Tel. (02) 622-229٤
Coolinary (Meat) 31 Emek Refa'im Street [Rabbinat Yerushalayim] Tel. (02) 566-2671
Corus Al Ha'esh (Meat/Fish Grill) 43, Yirmiyahu Street Tel. (02) 538-6061
Corus Dairy (Dairy) Center One [Mehadrin] Tel. (02) 538-3507
Corusin (Chinese/Meat) Jerusalem Mall, Malkha [Mehadrin] Tel. (02) 679-1088
            4 Luntz Street [Mehadrin] Tel. (02) 624-2042
Cup 'O Joe (Dairy) 38 Keren Ha'yesod [Rabbinat Yerushalayim] Tel. (02) 561-0555
Darna (Moroccan/Meat) 3, Horkanus Street [Mehadrin] Tel. (02) 624-5406
1868 (Dairy) 10, King David Street [Rabbinat Yerushalayim] Tel. (02) 622-2313
Eldad Vezehoo (French/Meat)
            31, Jaffa Road [Rabbinat Yerushalayim] Tel. (02) 625-4007

JERUSALEM

El Gaucho Steakhouse 22, Rivlin Street [Rabbinat Yerushalayim] Tel. (02) 624-2227
(Argentinian/Meat) Note: Not all branches are closed on Shabbat.
Eshel Avrohom (Meat)
9, Yirmiyahu Street [Rabbinat Yerushalayim & Mehadrin] Tel. (02) 537-3584
Ethio-Israel (Ethiopian/Meat)
5, Elyashar Street [Rabbinat Yerushalayim] Tel. (077) 622-3994
Eucalyptus (Meat) 7 Horkanus Street [Rabbinat Yerushalayim] Tel. (02) 623-2864
Gabriel (French-Fusion/Meat)
7, Shimon Ben Shetach [Rabbinat Yerushalayim & Mehadrin] Tel. 902) 624-6444
Ginger Noodle Bar (Meat) 103, Herzl Boulevard [Mehadrin] Tel. (077) 211-4440
Goldie (Meat) 5, Yoel Solomon [Rabbinat Yerushalayim & Mehadrin] Tel. (02) 623-3255
Gong (Japanese/Sushi Bar/Meat)
33, Jaffa Road [Badatz & Rabbinat Yerushalayim] Tel. (02) 625-0818
Grill Bar (Meat) 1, Ha'soreg [Rabbinat Yerushalayim & Mehadrin] Tel. (02) 622-3761
Grill on the Terrace (Meat) Inbal Hotel [Rabbinat Yerushalayim] Tel. (02) 675-6688
Ha'Finjan (Meat)
149, Agrippas Street [Rabbinat Yerushalayim & Mehadrin] Tel. (02) 622-2241
Ha'mishpacha (Meat) 12, Yoel Solomon [Rabbinat Yerushalayim] Tel. (02) 623-6886
Hapetilia (Meat)
17, Hauman Street (Lev Talpiot) [Rabbinat Yerushalayim] Tel. (02) 679-8994
Ha'tajeen (Moroccan/Meat)
15, Yad Ha'rutzim Street [Rabbinat Yerushalayim] Tel. (02) 625-4036
Heimisha Essen (Meat)
19, Keren Kayemet Street [Rabbinat Yerushalayim] Tel. (02) 563-9845
Hess (Meat) 9, Heleni Ha'malka [Badatz & Mehadrin] Tel. (02) 625-5115
Holy Bagel (Fish/Dairy) 39, Jaffa Road [Badatz] Tel. (02) 672-0844
Holyland Park Cafe (Dairy) Holyland Hotel [Rabbinat Yerushalayim] Tel. (02) 642-0905
Joy Grill & Beer (Meat)
24, Emek Refa'im Street [Rabbinat Yerushalayim] Tel. (02) 563-0033
Keyara (Meat) 8, Ramban Street [Rabbinat Yerushalayim & Mehadrin] Tel. (02) 566-3271
Kohinoor (Indian/Meat)
Holiday Inn Crowne Plaza [Rabbinat Yerushalayim] Tel. (02) 653-6667
Korea House
23, Joel Solomon Street [Rabbinat Yerushalayim & Mehadrin] Tel. (02) 625-4756
La Boca (Meat)
46, Emek Refa'im Street [Rabbinat Yerushalayim & Mehadrin] Tel. (077) 214-7755
La Carossa
7, Shatz Street (Montefiore Hotel) [Rabbinat Yerushalayim & Mehadrin] Tel. (02) 623-0056
La Guta (French/Oriental/Meat/Fish)
18, Rivlin Street [Rabbinat Yerushalayim] Tel. (02) 623-2322
Little Italy (Italian/Dairy)
38, Keren Ha'yesod Street [Rabbinat Yerushalayim] Tel. (02) 561-7638
Little Jerusalem-Anna Ticho (Dairy/Fish)
9, Ha'rav Kook Street [Rabbinat Yerushalayim] Tel. (02) 624-4186

JERUSALEM
Lugar (Meat) 6, Rabbi Akiva Street [Rabbinat Yerushalayim] Tel. (02) 622-1616
Luigi (Italian/Fish/Dairy)
12, Yoel Solomon Street [Rabbinat Yerushalayim] Tel. (02) 623-2524
Macaroni (Dairy) 28, King George Street [Rabbinat Yerushalayim] Tel. (02) 623-5533
Marvad Ha'ksmamim (Magic Carpet) (Yemenite/Meat)
   16, King George Street [Rabbinat Yerushalayim & Mehadrin] Tel. (02) 625-4470
   42, Emek Refa'im Street Tel. (02) 567-0007
   Malcha Tech Park
Masryk (Fish) 31, Emek Refa'im Street [Rabbinat Yerushalayim] Tel. (02) 563-6418
Menorah Coffee Bar (Dairy)
   87, Ha'yehudim Street (Old City) [Rabbinat Yerushalayim] Tel. (02) 628-9944
Montefiore (Italian/Dairy)
The Windmill (Yemin Moshe) [Rabbinat Yerushalayim] Tel. (02) 623-2928
Muscat (Italian/Dairy) 24, Kanfei Nesharim [Mehadrin] Tel. (02) 652-4414
New Deli (Meat) 33, Hillel Street [Nachlat Yitzchok] Tel. 1 700 700 788
Nina's Bagel Cafe (Dairy) 7, Paran Street [Badatz & Mehadrin] Tel. (02) 581-5434
Norman's Steak 'N Burger (Meat) 27, Emek Refa'im Street [Mehadrin] Tel. (02) 566-6603
Olive Bar & Restaurant (Meat)
   36, Emek Refa'im Street [Rabbinat Yerushalayim] Tel. (02) 561-1102
Olive & Fish (Meat) 2, Jabotinsky Street [Rabbinat Yerushalayim] Tel. (02) 566-5020
Osaka (Japanese/Fish/Sushi)
   7/23, Sapir Center [Rabbinat Yerushalayim & Mehadrin & Badatz]
Pera e Mela (Italian/Dairy) 6 Safra Square [Rabbinat Yerushalayim] Tel. (02) 623-0280
Pninat Hayam (Dairy/Fish)
   7, Hatenufa Street [Rabbinat Yerushalayim] Tel. (02) 673-6746
Primavera (Italian/Dairy/Fish) Sheraton Plaza Hotel [Mehadrin] Tel. (02) 629-8666
Quiche Cafe (Dairy/Vegetarian) 2, Ha'palmach Street Tel. (02) 563-7969
Rachmo Cafeteria (Meat) 16, Yoel Solomon Street Tel. (02) 624-0468
Ragu (Italian/Meat) 41, Derech Beit Lechem Tel. (02) 673-0760
Rimon Cafe (Dairy) 4, Lunz Street [Rabbinat Yerushalayim] Tel. 1 599 501 030
Rimon Meat Restaurant (same as above)
Sbarro Pizza (Dairy) 35, Jaffa Street (new location) Tel. (02) 623-2678
Selina (Dairy/Fish) 24 Emek Refaim [Rabbinat Yerushalayim] Tel. (02) 567-2049
Shakespeare (Dairy/Fish)
   2, Betar Street (Arnona) [Rabbinat Yerushalayim] Tel. (02) 673-2715
Sheyan
   8, Ramban Street (Windmill) [Rabbinat Yerushalayim & Mehadrin] Tel. (02) 561-2007
Sophia (Italian/Dairy) Inbal Hotel [Rabbinate Yerushalaim] Tel. (02) 675-6689
T'mol Shilshom (Dairy & Bookstore)
   5, Yoel Solomon Street [Rabbinate Yerushalayim] Tel. (02) 623-2758
Vaqueiro (South American/Meat)
   54, Ha,nevi'im Street [Rabbinate Yerushalayim] Tel. (02) 624-7432
Village Green (Vegetarian) 33, Jaffa Road [Rabbinate Yerushalayim] Tel. (02) 625-3065

Yo Ja (Japanese/Meat)
25, Emek Refa'im Street [Rabbinate Yerushalayim] Tel. (02) 561-1344
(YISHUV) LAPID
Sangam (Indian/Meat) Tel. (08) 976-2220
KFAR RUTH
Bonnofait (Dairy) Industrial Zone Tel. (08) 976-6992
KFAR SABA
Izmargad (Meat) 30 Tchernikovsky Street Tel. (09) 748-4767
KIRYAT ONO
Don Vito (Italian/Dairy)
      Route 461 (at southern entrance to Tel Ha'shomer base) Tel. (03) 634-5833
KIRYAT SHMONEH
Esh Besh (Meat Grill) 95, Tel Chai Tel. (04) 690-2330
Mon Cheri (Dairy/Fish) Nechamya Mall Tel. (04) 695-9887
MODI'IN
Alberto's Steak House (Meat) Ligat Center Tel. (08) 971-9000
Cafe Angelo (Dairy) Modiin Center Tel. (08) 971-6701
Luciano's (Dairy) Mevo Modi'in Tel. (08) 926-2526
Ristretto (Dairy) Solomon Center 6 Golani Street Tel. (08) 926-8101
(MOSHAV) NECHALIM
Coffee Stop (Dairy) Sonol Station Tel. (03) 933-8792
Te'amim Ba'teva (Meat) Tel. (03) 909-9012
NES ZIONA
Emtza Ha'derech (Eastern European/Meat Grill)
                    1, Ha'harash Street Tel. (08) 940-4022
NETANYA
Canton (Chinese/Meat) Tayelet Hotel 6, Gad Machnes Tel. (09) 832-1883
Lucullus (French/Meat & Fish) 5, Ha'atzma'ut Square Tel. (09) 861-7831
Marrakesh (Moroccan/Meat) 5, David Ha'melech Tel. (09) 833-4797
Pizza Hut (Dairy) 5, Kikar Ha'atzma'ut Tel. (09) 862-5312
Rosmarine (Fish/Dairy) 8, Nitza Boulevard Tel. (09) 832-3322
Time Burger (Meat) 11, Shtemper Tel. (09) 882-2223
MACCABEEM
Beijing (Chinese/Meat) Rananim Center Tel. (08) 926-2212
OR AKIVA
Ben Chamo (Meat Grill) Commercial Center Tel. (04) 610-0463
OR YEHUDA
Etzel Ha'turki (Turkish/Meat) 2, Ha'rishonim Street Tel. (03) 533-1352
PETACH TIKVAH
Alfredo (Dairy) Park Ezorim (Kiryat Aryeh) Tel. (03) 923-0643
Cafe Roma (Dairy/Fish) 16, Moshe Dayan Street Tel. (03) 921-9644
El Guacho (Argentinian Steakhouse) Oark Ezorim Tel. (03) 929-1535
                    Note: Not all branches are closed on Shabbat.
Mangold (Fish/Meat) 39 Ben-Zion Gillis Tel. (03) 913-5553

Qy-Sun (Asian/Meat) 37, Chovevei Zion Street Tel. 1-700-70-30-80
Teriyaki (Japanese/Meat) Park Ezorim Tel. (03) 923-6550
RA'ANANA
Burgers Bar (Meat) 184 Ahuza Street Tel. (09) 774-0505
Cafe Classico (Dairy/Fish) Giron Center (Jabotinsky Street) Tel. (09) 774-4651
Cafe In (Dairy Golan Center Tel. (09) 771-1453
Capitelo (Dairy) Re'nanim Mall Tel. (09) 761-2644
Carrousel (French/Dairy) 2, Rambam Street Tel. (09) 746-0586
Coffee & Friends Bar Cafe (Dairy) 88, Ahuza Street Tel. (09) 741-9003
Cup O' Joe (Dairy) 128, Ahuza Street (inner court) Tel. (09) 740-0056
Flambé (Dairy) 5, Eliezer Yaffe Street Tel. (09) 760-3407
Ha'taboun v'Ha'mangal (Meat Grill) 128, Ahuza Street Tel. (09) 744-2799
The House of Sara & Yefet (Meat) 1 Hanesher Street Tel. (09) 772-8118
La Toscana (Italian/Dairy) 3, Ha'sadna Street Tel. (09) 742-0754
Nixi Cafe (Dairy) 3, Ha'sadna Street Tel. (09) 742-6494 (futuristic interior)
Patisserie Dairy Cafe 88, Borchov Street Tel. (09) 744-2203
Sin Can (Chinese/Meat) 14, Ha'haroshet Street Tel. (09) 741-1058
Tuta Pasta (Dairy) 68, Ahuza Street (Aliav Center) Tel. (09) 744-5655
RAMAT GAN
Apropo Ayalon (Thai/Dairy/Fish) Canyon Ayalon Tel. (03) 619-7478
                    Note: Not all Apropo restaurants are kosher.
Delicative (Meat) Canyon Ayalon Tel. (03) 619-0238
El Gaucho 134, Jabotinsky Street Tel. (03) 751-8937
          (Argentinian Steakhouse) Note: Not all branches are closed on Shabbat.
Gondy Bar (Persian/Meat) 17, Ha'yetzira Street Tel. (03) 612-4007
Katzburg (Meat) Diamond Exchange Building 52, Bezalel Street Tel. (03) 751-7360
Yoko Uno (Japanese/Fish/Sushi Bar) 1, Jabotinsky Street Tel. (03) 752-4666
REHOVOT
Bordeaux (Dairy) 134, Herzl Street Tel. (08) 949-6178
Haim's Inn (Pundak Haim) Mideast Meat Grill
                    2, Abarbanel Street Tel. (08) 941-7077
Kingston Avenue (Meat/Grill) 22 Levin Epstein Street Tel. (08) 946-9980
Margaux (French/Meat) 2, Eisenberg Street Tel. (08) 946-7030
Raphael Center Restaurant (Dairy) Health Club & Spa
                    31, Haganah Street Tel. (08) 949-5555
RISHON LE'ZION
Formajo (Dairy) 7, Barshovski Street Tel. (03) 965-3410
Living Room (Fish/Dairy) 10, Ein Hakore Tel. (03) 956-7916
SAFED
Ha'mifgash (Meat Grill) 75, Yerushalayim Street (on the Midrachav) Tel. (04) 692-0510
Pizza Garden (Dairy) 90, Yerushalayim Street Tel. (04) 697-0902
SAVION
Mazal Dagim (Fish/Pasta) Indoor Seating Commercial Center Tel. (03) 635-9193
Pitango (Dairy/Fish) Outdoor Seating Commercial Center Tel. (03) 635-9193

(MOSHAV) SHECHENYA
The Twins (Lebanese/Meat) Tel. (04) 999-8220
TEL AVIV
Agvania (Dairy) 19, Shenkin Street Tel. (03) 525-6666
Alternative (Fish/Dairy)
    32, Weitzman Street [Rabbanut Tel-Aviv & Mehadrin] Tel. (03) 695-0567
Apropo Alexander (Thai/Fish/Dairy) 3, Chabakuk Street Tel. (03) 544-4442
Ashrav (Persian/Meat) 20, Rothschild Street [Rabbanut Tel-Aviv] Tel. (03) 510-4777
Asia Cafe (Dairy) 4, Weitzman Street Tel. (03) 697-9989
Bari Bar (Health Bar/Dairy) 32, Ha'barzel Street Tel. (03) 644-5049
Berkana (Italian/Dairy) 32, Ha'barzel Street Tel. (03) 644-4411
Bruno (Urban Mediterranean Cuisine/Meat) Azrieli Tower, 3rd Floor Tel. (03) 609-3030
Busi (Meat Grill) 41, Etzel Street (Ha'tikvah section) Tel. (03) 688-1034
Carlton Rooftop BBQ (summer only)
Top of the World - Ha'tikvah Street Tel. (03) 520-1818
Cup O' Joe (Dairy)
    2, Weitzman Street (Europe Tower) [Rabbanut Tel-Aviv] Tel. (03) 693-2005
Dalida (Dairy) 30, Sheinkin Street Tel. (03) 620-1979
Derby Fish & Grill (Meat) 14, Wallenberg Street Tel. (03) 648-0733
Dodo (Meat/Fish) 4, Heichal Ha'talmud Tel. (03) 510-7001
El Gaucho 49, Bograshov Street [Rabbanut Tel-Aviv] Tel. (03) 525-6455
    (Argentinian Steakhouse) Note: Not all branches are closed on Shabbat.
Ha'homa Ha'sinit (Chinese/Meat) 26, Mikveh Yisrael Street Tel. (03) 560-3974
Ha'pina Ha'yeruka (Dairy/Fish) 80, Rokach Boulevard Tel. (03) 642-2741
Hashagrir-Ambassador (Meat)
    82, Hayarkon Street [Rabbanut Tel-Aviv & Mehadrin] Tel. (03) 516-5986
Hungarian Blintzes (Dairy) 35, Yirmiyahu Street [Rabbanut Tel-Aviv] Tel. (03) 605-0674
Kerem Hateimanim (Yemenite/Meat) 6, Frishman Street Tel. (02) 523-4586
Lilith (Fish/Dairy/Vegetarian) 42, Mazeh Street Tel. (03) 629-8772
Muldan (Meat) 98, Ha'yarkon Street [Rabbanut Tel-Aviv & Mehadrin] Tel. (03) 527-8418
Olive Leaf (Meat) Sheraton Hotel Tel. (03) 521-9300
Pacific Bistro & Sushi (Meat)
Crowne Plaza Hotel 145, Ha'yarkon Street Tel. (03) 520-1169
Papagaio Azrieli (South American/Meat)
Azrieli Center [Rabbanut Tel-Aviv] Tel. (03) 609-2000
Parperaot (Dairy/Fish) Yordei Hasira Tel. (03) 544-2774
Petrozelia (Meat Grill) 47, Rothschild Boulevard Tel. (03) 516-2468
Pizza Domino (Dairy) 4, Laskov Street Tel. (03) 695-9103
Providence (Italian/Dairy/Fish) 66, Ha'yarkon Street Tel. (03) 510-5969
Rebecca Dairy Cafe 2, Laskov Street Tel. (03) 696-2099
Shangrila (Thai/Meat) Astor Hotel Ha'yarkon Street Tel. (03) 523-8913
Shaul's Inn (Yemenite/Meat) Upstairs is less expensive. Downstairs is upscale.
                    11, Eliashiv Street Tel. (03) 517-3303
Shipudei Ramat Ha'hayal (Meat Grill) 24, Ha'barzel Street Tel. (03) 649-3625

TEL AVIV
Smoky Deli (Meat) Azrieli Mall Tel. (03) 608-1116
Sushi Bar (Vegetarian) Sheraton Hotel 115, Ha'yarkon St. Tel. (03) 521-1111
Toscana (Thai/Dairy/Fish)
3, Habakuk Street [Rabbanut Tel-Aviv & Mehadrin] Tel. (03) 544-4442
Zion Exclusive (Meat) 28, Pedui'im Street Tel. (03) 517-8714
TIBERIAS
Decks Gourmet Charcoal Grill (Meat) Lido Beach Tel. (04) 672-1538
Pagoda (Chinese/Thai) Lido Beach Tel. (04) 672-5513
YEHUD
Claudine (French/Meat) 2, Mohaliver Street Tel. (03) 632-0692
Cup O' Joe (Dairy) 1, Ravon Street (Ganei Tikva) Tel. (03) 535-5624
Don Vito (Italian/Dairy) Route 461 Tel. (03) 634-5833
YOKNEAM
21st Century Espresso Bar & Restaurant (Dairy) Hadrachim Mall Tel. (04) 959-3519
Ilana Sandwiches (Meat) Hadrachim Mall Tel. (04) 959-0639
ZICHRON YA'AKOV
Bitan Ha'uga (Dairy) Midrachav Tel. (04) 639-9003
Sagazura (Italian Bar/Cafe) 26, Ha'nadiv Street Tel. (04) 629-2923
Tishbi Visitor Center Winery & Restaurant (Dairy)
                (between Binyamina and Zichron Ya'akov) Tel. (04) 628-8195
Tishbi Wine & Coffee 33, Ha'meyasdim Street Tel. (04) 629-0280

Bibliography

Architectural Review *A Great and Golden City* (pp 343-362)
Volume CLXV, Number 988 London June, 1979
Bass, G.J. & Abramson, R.G., *Let's Go Israel & Egypt - 1993*
St. Martin's Press, New York, 1993
Bloch, N. *Israel On A Budget* Israel Tourist Guides Publication, Tel Aviv, 1989
Cohen, M., Ellen, F., Shulman, C., *Jewish Israel* Namlock Ltd., London, 1988
Cohen, S., *Red Sea Diver's Guide* Seapen Books, Israel, 1975
Comay, J., *Israel, An Uncommon Guide* Random House, New York, 1969
de Breffny, B., *The Synagogue* Macmillan Publishing, New York, 1978
Devir, O., *Off the Beaten Track in Israel - A Guide to Beautiful Places*
Modan Publishing, Israel, 1985
Encyclopedia Judaica Keter Publishing, Jerusalem, 1972
Architecture in Israel Magazine Architecture in Israel, Tel Aviv, 1979, 1988, 1990, 1991,
1992, 1994, 1995, 1996, 1998, 1999, 2002, 2002, 2004
Gilon, D. & S., *Bed & Breakfast in Israel–Israel Tourist and Accomodation Guide*
B.B. Gilon Ltd., Gadera, 1993
Goldman, G., *El Al - Star in the Sky* World Transport Press, Miami, 1990
Hofer, H., *Insight Guides Israel* Houghton Mifflin Company, Boston, 1993
Levi, A., *Bazak Israel Guide* Harper & Row, New York, 1972
Levin, Dr. M., *White City: International Style Architecture in Israel* Tel Aviv, 1984
Nahon, Dr. S.U., *Holy Arks and Religious Appurtenances from Italy to Israel*
Dvir, Tel Aviv, 1970
Negev Touring Map Negev Tourism Development Administration–Survey of Israel, 1992
Potok, C., *Wanderings–History of the Jews* Alfred A. Knopf, New York, 1978
Rokdim–Israeli Folk Dance Directory (2007)
Roskin, J., *A Guide to Hiking in Israel* The Jerusalem Post, Israel, 1991
Sacerdoti, A., & Fiorentino, L., *Italy Jewish Travel Guide*
Israelowitz Publishing, New York, 1993
Safdie, M., *Beyond Habitat* M.I.T. Press, Cambridge, 1970
Schiller, E., *The First Photographs of Jerusalem–The Old City*
Ariel Publishing, Jerusalem, 1978
Seelig, M. & J. *Main Street, Jerusalem–The Cardo*
Architectural Record (pp 118-123), New York, May, 1985
Self-Guided Israel Langenschedt Publishers, New York, 1990
Shanks, H., *Judaism In Stone–Archaeology of Ancient Synagogues*
Steimatsky's Agency Limited, Tel Aviv, 1979
Sharp, D., *Twentieth-Century Architecture* Trewin Copplestone Publishing, London, 1972
Sofer, B., *Kids Love Israel/Israel Loves Kids–A Travel Guide for Families*
Kar-Ben Copies, Rockville, 1988
Ullian, R., Frommer's Israel '93-'94 on $45 A Day Prentice Hall Travel, New York, 1992
Vilnay, Z., *Israel Guide (25th Edition)* Daf-Chen Press, Jerusalem, 1985
Wigoder, G., *Jewish Art and Civilization* Chartwell Books, Fribourg, 1972
Your Galilee Touring Map Corazin, Rosh Pina, 1990
Zaharoni, I., *Israel Roots & Routes* MOD Publishing House, Tel Aviv, 1990

Catalog

ISRAEL TRAVEL GUIDE - 5th Edition (2008)
by Oscar Israelowitz 272 pages
ISBN 1-878741-76-4 **$21.95** Paper (plus $5.00 shipping)

GUIDE TO JEWISH NEW YORK CITY
Celebrating 350 Years of Jewish Life in New York
by Oscar Israelowitz 245 pages
ISBN 1-878741-62-4 **$19.95** Paper (plus $5.00 shipping)

UNITED STATES & CANADA JEWISH TRAVEL GUIDE (9th Edition)
by Oscar Israelowitz 400 pages
ISBN 1-878741-73X **$19.95** Paper (plus $5.00 shipping)

GUIDE TO JEWISH EUROPE - Western Europe (10th Edition)
by Oscar Israelowitz 384 pages
ISBN 1-878741-19-5 **$19.95** Paper (plus $5.00 shipping)

ITALY JEWISH TRAVEL GUIDE
by Annie Sacerdoti 242 pages
ISBN 1-878741-42-X **$19.95** Paper (plus $5.00 shipping)

JEWISH HERITAGE TRAIL OF NEW YORK
by Oscar Israelowitz 156 pages
ISBN 1-878741-60-8 **$19.95** Paper (plus $5.00 shipping)

SYNAGOGUES OF THE UNITED STATES **An Architectural & Photographic Survey**
by Oscar Israelowitz 200 pages
ISBN 1-878741-09-8 **$24.95** Paper (plus $5.00 shipping)

SYNAGOGUES OF NEW YORK CITY **History of A Jewish Community**
by Oscar Israelowitz 219 pages
ISBN 1-878741-44-6 **$35.00** Hard Cover ($5.00 shipping)

JEWISH NEW JERSEY in VINTAGE PHOTOGRAPHS
by Oscar Israelowitz 215 pages Landscape Format
ISBN 1-878741-59-4 **$29.95** Hard Cover ($5.00 shipping)

WELCOME BACK TO THE CATSKILLS
by Oscar Israelowitz 215 Pages Landscape Format
ISBN 1-878741-54-3 **$29.95** Hard Cover ($5.00 shipping)

LOWER EAST SIDE TOURBOOK
by Oscar Israelowitz 148 Pages
ISBN 1-878741-68-3 **$9.95** Paper ($5.00 shipping)

WELCOME BACK TO BROOKLYN
by Brian Merlis & Oscar Israelowitz 168 pages
ISBN 1-878741-75-6 **$29.95** Hard Cover (plus $5.00 shipping)

BROOKLYN - THE WAY IT WAS
by Brian Merlis 250 pages Landscape Format
ISBN 1-878741-52-7 **$29.95** Hard Cover ($5.00 shipping)

WELCOME BACK TO BOROUGH PARK
by Oscar Israelowitz 80 pages
ISBN 1-878741-67-5 **$24.95** Paper (plus $5.00 shipping)

BROOKLYN'S PARK SLOPE - A Photo Retrospective
by Brian Merlis & Lee Rosenzweig
165 pages Landscape Format
ISBN 1-878741-47-0 **$29.95** Hard Cover ($5.00 shipping)

BROOKLYN'S BAY RIDGE & FORT HAMILTON
A Photographic Journey 1870 -1970
by Brian Merlis & Lee Rosenzweig
165 pages Landscape Format
ISBN 1-878741-45-4 **$29.95** Hard Cover ($5.00 shipping)

BROOKLYN HEIGHTS & DOWNTOWN Volume I 1860-1922
by Brian Merlis & Lee Rosenzweig 199 pages
ISBN 1-878741-51-9 **$29.95** Hard Cover ($5.00 shipping)

BROOKLYN'S BENSONHURST & BATH BEACH
by Brian Merlis & Lee Rosenzweig 176 Pages
ISBN 1878741-74-5 **$40.00** (plus $5.00 shipping)

SPANNING THE NARROWS
Construction of the Verrazano-Narrows Bridge 1964-2004
by Brian Merlis & Lee Rosenzweig 80 pages
ISBN 1-87874161-6 **$24.95** Hard Cover ($5.00 shipping)

BROOKLYN'S WILLIAMSBURG
by Brian Merlis
246 Pages Landscape Format
ISBN 1878741-66-7 **$39.95** Hard Cover ($5.00 shipping)

SUBWAYS OF NEW YORK in VINTAGE PHOTOGRAPHS
by Oscar Israelowitz & Brian Merlis 245 pages
ISBN 1-878741-63-2 **$34.95** Hard Cover ($5.00 shipping)

BROOKLYN'S FLATBUSH
From Battlefield to Ebbets Field
by Brian Merlis & Lee Rosenzweig 260 pages
ISBN 1878741-70-5 **$40.00** Hard Cover ($5.00 shiiping)

ELLIS ISLAND GUIDE with Lower Manhattan
by Oscar Israelowitz 128 Pages
ISBN 1-878741-72-1 **$9.95** Paper ($5.00 shipping

ISRAELOWITZ PUBLISHING
P.O.Box 228   Brooklyn, NY 11229
Tel. (718) 951-7072
E-mail oscari 477 @aol.com
website: www.israelowitzpublishing.com

Biography

Oscar Israelowitz was born in Brussels, Belgium. He has degrees in architecture and geology and has traveled extensively throughout Europe, the United States, Canada, Africa and Israel. He is an architectural consultant by profession and is registered in the Register of Engineers and Architects in Israel.

Some of his architectural projects include the Synagogue and Holocaust Center of the Bobover chassidim and the Yeshiva Rabbi Chaim Berlin, both in Brooklyn, NY. He has also designed homes and villas for clients in the United States, Haiti and Israel. In recent years, he was involved in salvaging an historic Ark from an abandoned synagogue. That Ark has been restored and is the center point of Temple Chaverim in Plainview, New York.

Mr. Israelowitz is also a professional photographer. His works have been on exhibit at the Whitney Museum of American Art in a show called *Watch the Closing Doors - Mosaics of the New York City Subways* (1973). That exhibit traveled to the Brooklyn Museum and has been incorporated into the permanent exhibition at the New York City Transit Museum. *The Changing Face of New York's Synagogues* was on exhibit at the Yeshiva University Museum in 1976. *Brooklyn: The City of Churches and Synagogues* was on display at Saint Joseph's College Gallery in Brooklyn in 1979 and traveled to the Long Island (now Brooklyn) Historical Society and to the Main Branch of the Brooklyn Public Library at Grand Army Plaza. In all of these exhibitions Mr. Israelowitz served as the guest curator and project coordinator.

Oscar Israelowitz has appeared on several television and radio programs including the *Joe Franklin Show*, NBC's *First Estate - Religion in Review*, the *Ruth Jacobs Jewish Home Show*, French National Television's *Antenne 2*, and the Australian Broadcasting Company's hit show, *Who Do You Think You Are?*

In more recent years, Mr. Israelowitz has been conducting tours of the Lower East Side, Ellis Island, Jewish Harlem, chassidic neighborhoods in Brooklyn, and Jewish Harbor Tours of New York City aboard the NY Water Taxi. These tours have been written-up in *New York Magazine*, the *Washington Post*, the *New York Times*, the *Los Angeles Times*, the *Chicago Tribune*, *Crain's New York Business*, and *TimeOut NY*. He has been conducting private tours for such world-renowned personalities as Leon Uris (author of *Exodus*) and members of the United Nations.

Oscar Israelowitz has been a consulting travel columnist for the Jewish Press of New York. He has written articles about travels throughout the United States, Canada, Europe and Israel. Oscar Israelowitz is a fully-licensed tour guide in New York City.

Index